REAPERS OF THE HARVEST

The Redemptorists in Great Britain and Ireland
1843-1898

REAPERS OF THE HARVEST

The Redemptorists in Great Britain and Ireland 1843-1898

John Sharp

Oscott Series 4
VERITAS PUBLICATIONS

First published 1989 by
Veritas Publications
7/8 Lower Abbey Street
Dublin 1

ISBN 1 85390 068 0

Photographs courtesy of Redemptorist Provincialate, Dublin
The cover illustration is a detail of a poster announcing a mission
in Limerick in 1868, from the Redemptorist archives, Dublin.
Cover design by Philip Melly
Typesetting by Printset & Design Ltd., Dublin
Printed in the Republic of Ireland by Leinster Leader Ltd.

Contents

Illustrations

Abbreviations

The following abbreviations are used throughout:

A. Redemptorist

AGR (Pr.An.)	General Archives, Rome (Provincia Angliae).
ALP	Archives of the London Province.
PC	'Provincial Chronicles, 1843-53'.
CEP	'Chronicles of the English Province',
	Vol. I 1843-53
	Vol. II 1854-1919
ADC	Domestic Archives, Clapham.
CDC	'Chronica Domestica, Clapham',
	Vol. I 1850-68
	Vol. II 1869-92
	Vol. III 1893-1932
ALC	'Apostolici Labores, Clapham',
	Vol. I 1885-1932
ADBE	Domestic Archives, Bishop Eton.
CD/ALBE	'Domestic and Mission Chronicles, Hanley Castle and Bishop Eton',
	Vol. I 1844-55
	Vol. II 1855-57
	Vol. III 1858-61
	Vol. IV 1862-65
	Vol. V 1865-67
CDBE	'Chronica Domestica, Bishop Eton',
	Vol. I 1868-85
	Vol. II 1886-1910
ALBE	'Apostolici Labores, Bishop Eton',
	Vol. I 1868-77
	Vol. II 1877-92
	Vol. III 1892-1901
ADK	Domestic Archives, Kinnoull, Perth.
CDK	'Chronica Domestica, Kinnoull',
	Vol. I 1865-71
	Vol. II 1871-1920

ALK	'Chronica Missionum, Kinnoull', Vol. I 1867-71 Vol. II 1871-82 Vol. III 1883-1900
ADT	Domestic Archives, Teignmouth.
CDT	'Chronica Domestica, Teignmouth, 1875-1900'.
ALT	'Apostolici Labores, Teignmouth, 1875-1900'.
ADP	Archives of the Dublin Province.
ADD	Domestic Archives, Dublin.
ADL	Domestic Archives, Limerick.
CD/ALL	'Chronica Domestica et Apostolici Labores, Limerick', Vol. I 1854-67
CDL	'Chronica Domestica, Limerick', Vol. II 1868-98
ALL	'Apostolici Labores, Limerick', Vol. II 1868-78 Vol. II 1879-1902
ADDk	Domestic Archives, Dundalk
CD/ALDk	'Chronica Domestica et Apostolici Labores, Dundalk', Vol. I 1876-98
ALDk	'Apostolici Labores, Dundalk', Vol. I 1883-98
ADB	Domestic Archives, Clonard, Belfast.
CDB	'Chronica Domestica, Belfast', Vol. I 1896-1930
ALB	'Apostolici Labores, Belfast', Vol. I 1896-1924

B. Sacred Congregation 'de Propaganda Fide' (APF)

Acta	Acta Sacrae Congregationis.
LDB	Lettere e Decreti della Sacra Congregazione e Biglietti di Monsignor Segretario.
CP	Scritture originali riferite nelle Congregazioni Particolari.
SC	Scritture riferite nei Congressi.

C. Diocesan Archives

AAB	Archives of the Archbishop of Birmingham.
AAS	Archives of the Archbishop of Southwark.
AAW	Archives of the Archbishop of Westminster.
LRO, RCLv	Lancashire Record Office, Archives of the Roman Catholic Archdiocese of Liverpool.
SCA	Scottish Catholic Archives.

Preface

To engage in research is to be made aware of the kindness and generosity of others and to be left with debts of gratitude, which this book inadequately recompenses. Thanks must go the Redemptorists, to the Very Reverend Provincial Superiors of the London and Dublin Provinces for their kind permission to work freely in the archives of their Provinces, and to the Very Reverend Fathers Rector of the various Redemptorist houses that I have visited in England, Scotland, Ireland and in Rome. I have always received the most generous of welcomes and unstinting hospitality from the fathers and brothers and have profited much from conversation with them and from the interest they have shown in my work. I intend no disrespect to them all in singling out three of their number for especial thanks: Fr Andreas Sampers, former archivist of the General Archives, and Fr Sam Boland of the Congregation's Historical Institute in Rome have given generously of their time and expertise, as has Fr Patrick O'Donnell, archivist of the Dublin Province.

Work in other archives and libraries has been relieved by the help and kindness of the staff of the Catholic Central Library, Westminster, the British Library, the National Library of Ireland, the Lancashire Record Office and the Cambridge University Library, and of Miss Elizabeth Poyser, Dom Mark Dilsworth, O.S.B., Fr Michael Clifton, Fr Peter Dennison, Monsignor George Bradley, and the staff in the archives of the Sacred Congregation for the Evangelisation of Peoples, Rome.

This book is a slightly revised version of a doctoral thesis presented to the University of London. I am grateful to Dr Eamon Duffy of Magdalene College, Cambridge for his help, advice and encouragement in the work of the original thesis, and to its examiners, Fr Francis Walker, S.J., and Dr Sheridan Gilley for their suggestions for its improvement. The book's remaining inadequacies and defects are solely mine. I am conscious that the transition from thesis to book is neither easy nor necessarily felicitous and that certain problems remain. One of these concerns the translation into English of foreign-language quotations. It will be obvious from the context or from the notes which are my translations; it is unfortunate that the inclusion of the original quotations would have made the notes too bulky.

Without the encouragement of His Grace the Archbishop of Birmingham, the Most Reverend Maurice Couve de Murville, it is doubtful that the book would have found its way into print. I am grateful to the Oscott Foundation and to the Irish and English Redemptorist Provincialates for their financial assistance with its publication. Thanks are also due to Fiona Biggs of Veritas

Reapers of the Harvest

Publications for her initial encouragement and to Máire Ní Chearbhaill for her endless patience, enthusiasm and painstaking work as my literary editor.

Finally, in acknowledging my primary debt, I should like to dedicate this work to my mother and to the memory of my father; it is an unworthy, though sincere, offering of filial love and gratitude.

Doncaster, England
May 1989   John Sharp

1

Introduction
and
early development,
1843-1855

In an article in the *Dublin Review* on Hurrell Froude's *Remains* in May 1839, Dr Nicholas Wiseman, Rector of the English College in Rome, ruminated on his two visits to England in 1835 and 1839 and wrote of the need for a group of clergy

> devoted to the task of going from town to town, relieving the overworked local clergy of part of their labours, by giving well-prepared and systematic courses of instruction and arousing the slumbering energies of congregations in which stronger excitement is required than the voice of ordinary admonition.[1]

This need for a missionary institute was reiterated the following year in a petition he made to Pope Gregory XVI. In this Wiseman outlined the purpose of such an institute: to visit places where the Catholic religion was entirely unknown and to instil the truths of the faith into the hearts of the faithful; to give missions in places where Catholics lived in order to arouse them to greater zeal and fervour, such missions being as yet unknown in England; further, its priests would be energetic expositors of the Word of God, preaching courses of sermons and giving spiritual exercises in ecclesiastical colleges and convents and to the clergy.

With the exception of Bishop Walsh, Vicar Apostolic of the Midland District, the Vicars Apostolic were unfavourable to Wiseman's plans and did not share his sanguine views of the revival of Catholicism in England in the ways he suggested. His vision of a revitalised, aggressive Catholicism creating an irresistible tide of conversions was, however, shared by some members of those missionary institutes which he had seen as the disseminators of vital, Ultramontane Catholicism. Fr Luigi Gentili, of the Institute of Charity, had come to England in 1835 and in the same month as Wiseman's review article preached a mission to the little congregation attached to Spettisbury, near Grace Dieu in Leicestershire. It was a small affair, but it was, nonetheless, the first public mission in England and the start of Gentili's apostolic labours.[2] The Passionists too were known to be eager to come to England, although it was 1842 before the first of them set foot in the land, and 1844 before parochial missions were undertaken. The next few years were to witness the tentative beginnings of that apostolic work whose necessity Wiseman had urged in 1839 and the arrival of religious orders to carry it out.[3] Among them was the Congregation of the Most Holy Redeemer.

The Congregation had been founded in the Kingdom of Naples by Alphonsus Liguori (1696-1787) in 1732 as a group of religious in simple, though perpetual, vows, to which was added an oath of perseverance to death, committed to the preaching of the Gospel to the poor, especially the most abandoned souls in rural areas. To this end, Alphonsus laid great stress on the need for his missioners to model their lives upon Christ as their exemplar, requiring them to be, in a popular paraphrase of his ideals, 'apostles abroad and Carthusians at home'. In common with most religious orders, the first years of the Congregation were hesitant, and it was only after its canonical establishment in 1749 that its fortunes began to improve. Thereafter, provision could be made for houses to be established outside the kingdom, whereby the Institute's dependence on the whims of the Neapolitan government for survival and growth was decreased. Although the government was sympathetic to the work of the missioners, who managed to extend a measure of social control over some of the country's wilder and more savage inhabitants, regalist opposition to property-owning religious orders had denied the Congregation any legal recognition in the kingdom, and had caused the royal *exequatur*, necessary to confirm the papal brief of 1749, to be withheld. Drawn into the politics of eighteenth-century church-state relations, royal approbation of the Institute was given only after a revised rule, or *Regolamento*, had been signed by Alphonsus. The *Regolamento* was acceptable to the government because it made the Congregation dependent upon the King rather than upon the Pope, and restricted its freedom of independent development and activity. The immediate response of the papacy was to declare a division of the Institute; the Neapolitan houses were no longer regarded as communities of the Congregation.

This division lasted from 1780 to 1793 and had the effect of freeing the Congregation from the bonds of Neapolitan regalism and of strengthening it outside the Kingdom of Naples. With its centre now in Rome, it was not long before the Congregation attracted its first non-Italian members, who then established it north of the Alps in eastern and central Europe. Even after 1793, when the Congregation was reunited, the upheavals caused by the French armies meant that although theoretically and canonically dependent upon the Neapolitan mother house at Nocera dei Pagani, where the Rector Major lived, the rest of the Congregation developed separately. Especially was this true of the virtually-independent transalpine houses, which came in time to form a *de facto* province, never formally constituted, presided over by a Vicar General. This arrangement was regularised by the decree *Presbyterorum Saecularium* of July 1841, by which Gregory XVI divided the Congregation into six Provinces — the Roman, Neapolitan, Sicilian, Austrian, Belgian, and Gallo-Helvetic. The position of the Transalpine Vicar General was confirmed, and he was endowed with all the powers of the Rector Major, except those concerning the establishment of new foundations, the erection or division of provinces, the dismissal of subjects or dispensation from vows, and the convoking of provincial chapters.

The Transalpine Vicariate had been presided over since 1820 by Joseph Passerat, under whose generalship the Congregation north of the Alps had experienced a steady rise in the number of vocations and houses and its expansion into western Europe. With a reputation for austerity, poverty and apostolic zeal, the Redemptorists were peculiarly well placed to benefit from the renewal of interest in religion which followed in the wake of the Romantic Revival and from the resurgence of Ultramontane ideas which they epitomised. Although it was 1826 before they were able to preach their first mission outside Italy — at Hagenau in the diocese of Strasbourg — within ten years the popularity of Redemptorist missions had firmly established them in western and central Europe. In particular, the 1830s witnessed the emergence to importance within the Transalpine Vicariate of the Belgian houses, the first of which was founded in Tournai in 1833. Belgium was one of the few countries where the Redemptorists had full liberty to develop their Institute on a canonical basis, and several houses were founded, including a novitiate and house of studies. Full of confidence, the Belgian Redemptorists were keen to spread the work of the Congregation and enlarge the area of Alphonsian influence. Within its first hundred years, the Belgian Province established eighty-eight houses in Holland, England, Ireland, Canada, North and South America. St Alphonsus himself had spoken of his desire to see England return to the Catholic faith and his subjects wished to share in the restoration of the kingdom to the ancient faith. Geographical propinquity, the renewed interest in England on the part of the Roman authorities after Catholic Emancipation (1829) and the beckoning hand of Providence all conspired to make a natural field of Redemptorist expansion a country, where

> there are more souls destitute of spiritual aid than in the whole of Italy; so that it may be said with truth, that in the designs of Providence, St Alphonsus founded the Congregation of Missionary Priests for the whole world, but more especially for this country, since here are found *en masse* in large towns and cities what he saw scattered abroad in the whole of the kingdom of Italy in small villages and hamlets.[4]

Providence came in the unlikely form of Bishop Baines, Vicar Apostolic of the Western District. Visiting Liège in 1837, he met Frederick de Held, Superior of the Belgian Redemptorists, with whom he was much impressed. His admiration aroused, Baines was keen to introduce the Congregation into his district, and invited de Held to make a foundation in Wales, 'which was at this time extremely destitute of spiritual aid'.[5] Owing to the want of subjects, de Held was not able to accede to the bishop's request. Undeterred, Baines appealed again the following year, and de Held went as far as to visit him at Prior Park. Given his stormy relations with Gentili and the Rosminians, Baines's eagerness to introduce the Redemptorists is somewhat surprising. His views were certainly opposed to those of Wiseman — even to the extent, for example, of condemning in his Lenten Pastoral of 1840 such things as devotion to the Sacred Heart and Immaculate Conception, the use of scapulars, medals and other objects of piety favoured by the Rosminian missionaries, and declaring that the conversion of England was 'as morally impossible as the return of the negro's skin to its antediluvian whiteness'.[6] Nor can he have been left in much doubt by the Redemptorists themselves of their doctrinal and devotional sympathies, which were floridly Italianate after the founder, and of their missionary ambitions, which were their *raison d'être*.

Events rested in a state of indecision until 1842 when de Held, accompanied by Fr Auguste Lempfried, journeyed to Scotland at the invitation of Bishop Scott, Vicar Apostolic of the Western District, who offered to establish the Congregation in that country. Scott, however, required individual mission-priests, not a missionary order, and insisted that they undertake the cure of souls. This was unacceptable to the Redemptorists, who, while they might undertake a regular mission on a temporary basis and use it as a base from which to perform their apostolic work, were unwilling to be bound by the canonical restrictions which the cure of souls entailed and which were contrary to their Rule. When Scott's northern episcopal neighbour heard of the Redemptorists' refusal, he sounded forth against them:

> Why don't they send the Redemptorists to me? ... But
> never will one of them offer himself to this remote and
> unhonoured mission. It is not the advancement of religion
> or the good of souls that these men seek, but that they
> may live at ease, and make a noise in the world with tales,
> true or false, of the good they do — I have heard nothing
> from Rome on the subject. If I did, I would be tempted
> to let them know pretty firmly my mind.[7]

De Held, meanwhile, had journeyed south and again visited
Baines, who offered him the mission of Falmouth in Cornwall
on favourable terms. Thus, after five years of negotiations,
in June 1843, Fr Lempfried, together with Fr Louis de
Buggenoms and Br Felician Dubucquoi, arrived in England
to make the first Redemptorist foundation.

They were wholly unprepared for their task. Of the three
men, only de Buggenoms spoke any English. They were
shocked by the material and spiritual neglect of the mission,
which served a Catholic population in the surrounding villages
and hamlets to a distance of thirty miles. Only seven or eight
people attended Mass, which was celebrated once a week, the
chapel being otherwise closed. Work was taken in hand to
beautify the chapel and to improve liturgical standards.[8] The
arrival of foreign religious had stirred local curiosity, and it
was hoped that converts would rapidly be made. Sermons
were begun on Sundays and holy days, morning and evening,
and it was found that the two hundred places in the chapel
were easily filled. The fathers, however, mistook curiosity for
sympathetic interest, and their confident expectations received
a sharp blow on the first Sunday that Benediction of the
Blessed Sacrament was given. Despite careful explanation of
the doctrine of the Real Presence beforehand, the citizens of
Falmouth were scandalised; one was heard to remark that
'now we have seen with our own eyes that these papists
worship the sun'.[9] The initial optimism of the small
community gave way to a mood of increasing depression as
their courage faltered and they considered the difficulty of their
task, the fragile circumstances of the foundation, and their own

6

spiritual isolation; shorn of community support in a hostile, Protestant land, 'it was as if the air that I breathed was full of evil spirits'.[10] Signs of the mental instability and dictatorial inflexibility, which were to ensure Lempfried's recall to Belgium within two years, exacerbated the difficulties.

Internal pressures were not the only threat to the precarious fortunes of the community. At the end of July 1843, de Held wrote to the Rector Major, Camillo Ripoli, informing him of the establishment of 'a small group (piccola Colonia) of missionaries in England ... in the town of Falmouth', and of the urgent appeal of the Vicar Apostolic of another district for some Redemptorists, 'but it is necessary to wait until the Lord sends us subjects who speak the English language'.[11] Rather than express pleasure, as de Held had imagined, Ripoli berated the Provincial's presumption and unilateral action in making a foundation without his express permission and in defiance of the papal decree of 1841.[12] In voicing his apprehension that such foundations would weaken the character of the Congregation by cutting off the fathers and brothers from the regular life of a full community, where regular observance of the Rule could be maintained, Ripoli expressed a genuine fear. On the other hand, his caution would have precluded any experimentation and adaptation not strictly allowed by the Rule. It is difficult not to see in the Rector Major's position a reflection of the prejudice and continuing strife between the bold, pioneering transalpine Redemptorists and their more timid, temporising Neapolitan brethren. Ripoli's reluctance to appreciate the dynamism of his Belgian subjects was further compounded by the personal animosity that existed between him and the Belgian Provincial.[13] The latter's reaction to Ripoli's letter was typical; he pleaded the great need of English Catholics, assured Ripoli that a full, regular foundation was hoped for soon (very unlikely given the want of English-speaking subjects) and that full observance of the Rule and Constitutions was insisted upon, and then he ignored the Rector Major.[14] Ripoli was powerless to insist on a withdrawal from England, and no more was heard from him.

At Falmouth itself, the strain of deteriorating personal

relations was increased by financial difficulties caused by Lempfried's decision to enlarge the chapel by adding a gallery and porch. The Superior also attracted unwelcome publicity from *The Times* over his encouragement of some converts to tear up their old (Protestant) bibles, prayer and hymn books. Such things apart, the situation was not wholly bleak. The community was cheered by a visit from the Counts de Montalembert and de Merode, and their labours were bearing some fruit. The enlargement of the chapel was necessitated by the increasing numbers frequenting it on a regular basis. The Catholics of the locality were becoming more fervent and assiduous in their religious duties and many Protestants, including the children of mixed marriages, were being attracted to the Church, so that by Easter 1844 there were seventy-six communicants. Indeed, the number of Catholics was to rise from ten in 1843 to 170 in 1845. Two benefactors presented themselves, and the community was joined by another lay brother. When de Held made his canonical visitation in June 1844, he was sufficiently satisfied with the situation to allow another foundation to be made by Lempfried and the newly-arrived lay brother, Stephen Senegres.

Left as Superior of Falmouth, de Buggenoms realised that there would be no lasting results without the establishment of schools. A boys' school was a failure and closed within two years, but de Buggenoms did succeed in persuading the Sisters of Notre Dame to make an English foundation and establish a girls' school at nearby Penryn, thereby introducing their Institute into Britain. The Sisters were so successful that within a short time 150 girls attended the school and were catechised (together with some of their mothers) on Sunday afternoons. Local Protestant opposition, and even threats, however, reduced their number to twenty, all of whom were received into the Church.

Hostility of this kind was not experienced at the new foundation at Hanley Castle, Blackmore Park, near Worcester. The foundation had been made at the invitation of John Vincent Gandolphi and with the permission of Bishop Walsh, Vicar Apostolic of the Central District.[15] The Redemptorists proved themselves excellent mission priests and quickly established their popularity among Catholics and non-Catholics alike. Fr Lans, the Superior after Lempfried's return to Belgium in 1845, was particularly well liked, and he established good relations with the local parson. Visiting the sick and poor, ministering to itinerant Irish in search of work, offering Mass at Hanley and the stations of Red Marley and Upton-on-Severn, and giving instruction to those who were interested provided the staple work of the mission. In 1849, for example, there were thirty-two baptisms (of which twenty-one were of converts), two marriages, thirteen funerals, the confirmation of sixty-four people, and 2,300 communions were received. At the Midnight Mass of that year, nine people were conditionally baptised, as a result of which three more Protestants sought instruction.[16] There seems to have been little opposition to the large number of conversions — 470 by 1851 — save from the Baptist minister, and Hanley was seen 'as a second Thonon, gathering converts like St Francis de Sales'.[17] But however good this work, the fact remained that the mission-stations fully employed the energies of the Redemptorist priests and prevented them from doing that apostolic work that was their special concern. They offered little scope for expansion beyond the cure of souls and of those living in the vicinity. Nor did they provide much opportunity for attracting vocations, vital if the Congregation were to flourish in England. What was needed was a regular foundation which would enable the Redemptorists to concentrate their forces and energies and direct them to the preaching of missions and retreats, rather than be tied to the restrictions of parochial work.

A move was made towards this end at the close of 1847 when de Held resigned as Belgian Provincial and Passerat conceived the idea of sending him to England to make a foundation in which there would be a full community and the Rule and Constitutions would be fully and canonically observed. Accordingly, de Held was made Visitor of England and Superior of Hanley Castle. He never reached Blackmore Park. Passing through London, he was persuaded to consider

9

acquiring property there. He went to see Wiseman, Pro-Vicar Apostolic of the London District, who was known to favour the religious orders and who was sympathetic to the project. The property in question was in Clapham, South London, and had formerly belonged to Lord Teignmouth, a member of the Clapham Sect, a fact on which the Provincial Chronicler was later to make great play.[18] There were only thirty or forty Catholics living in Clapham, which was still served by St George's, Southwark. The fathers took charge of the district 'in titulo caritatis' and began work immediately, visiting from house to house in order to discover lapsed Catholics. Many were found who had received no spiritual ministrations for years and whose children were unbaptised.[19] The influx of Irish immigrants swelled the number of Catholics in the area and the decision was taken to build a public church, dedicated to Our Lady Immaculate of Victories.[20] When built, it was immediately popular and attracted people from far afield, as well as the inhabitants of Clapham and its environs. Besides a regular round of confessions, Masses, sermons and instructions, there was a Confraternity of the Immaculate Heart of Mary, the Society of St Vincent de Paul, a Catholic lending library and extra-liturgical devotions such as Benediction, Litany and Rosary, the Way of the Cross, devotions to the Infant Jesus, for a Happy Death, the *Quarant' Ore* and May devotions.[21] In short, a regime was established which reflected normal continental conditions but which stood in marked contrast to the prevailing practices of English Catholicism.

The presence of the Redemptorists in what had hitherto been a stronghold of Evangelicalism occasioned much Protestant disquiet, especially as the building programme coincided with the furore associated with Papal Aggression. Wiseman was heckled at the church's opening, demonstrations on Clapham Common resulted in the burning of the pope's effigy, there were threats of violence, rumours of dead infants buried in the nuns' garden, and assorted other troubles. In addition, a neighbour objected to the ringing of the bells, which were silenced until 1869.[22] Few of the protestors would have disagreed with one author's complaint that 'if ever there was a body of men assembled with the avowed object of disturbing our blessed Redeemer Jesus Christ, and placing in his stead the Virgin Mary, it is the self-styled REDEMPTORISTS'.[23]

One reason for the London foundation was to gain greater prominence for the Congregation in England, to advertise its presence as a means of attracting vocations.[24] It certainly paid off in the short-term; 1850 was an 'annus mirabilis' for vocations, and augured well for the future.[25] Of the seven novices in that year (Furniss, Bradshaw, Vaughan, Plunkett, Stevens, Coffin and Bridgett), all of whom were to play a prominent part in the life of the Congregation, three (Stevens, Coffin and Bridgett) were converts from Anglicanism. It is interesting that they should have chosen to become Redemptorists, at that date relatively unimportant, certainly in comparison with the Oratorians. Bridgett decided against the Oratorians, precisely because they were nearly all converts, 'straining to be ultra-Catholic ... I wished to be thoroughly Catholic, but among those to whom it came easily and harmoniously'.[26] This idea that the Alphonsian spiritual tradition provided an authentic and vital example of Catholicism, in which apostolic verve was engendered, was echoed by Coffin, himself an Oratorian, who found among the Redemptorists 'what I never tasted of elsewhere, much less in our own Congregation'.[27] The influence of the 'Oxford converts' within the Congregation was to be disproportionate to their numbers and was to have a profoundly disturbing effect upon the Province in the last quarter of the century, but in the context of the London foundation, the increase in vocations proved its worth.

Another result of the Clapham house was the abandonment of the mission at Falmouth, the subjects there being transferred to London. Writing some years later, de Buggenoms believed that this was the right thing to have done; the work of the mission, extending as it did to a distance of thirty miles out of Falmouth, had so increased that it was necessary to establish residential stations, for which the Redemptorists had neither the money nor the personnel. Moreover, the work was nothing

that a secular priest could not perform, whereas the Clapham
foundation offered a regular base for apostolic work.[28] The
work of the Falmouth mission did, however, suffer as a result
of the Redemptorist withdrawal. When de Buggenoms visited
it in 1858, he found that many of those whom the fathers had
converted had relapsed into heresy and indifference and that,
of those who persevered, the majority had been educated by
the Notre Dame Sisters who had themselves moved to
Clapham with the Redemptorists to take care of the poor girls
of the district.[29]

Nor was everyone pleased at the Clapham foundation. De
Held had been made Superior of Hanley Castle at the request
of Fr Lans, who wished to be freed of the responsibility
so that he could begin mission work. He was upset and
complained to the Provincial that foundations in large cities
would inevitably result in a diminution of apostolic work in
rural areas, so favoured by the Rule. The Provincial replied
that the better communications afforded by a city like London
would facilitate the undertaking of missions and retreats in
the future, and that 'if the Congregation is to work for the
conversion either of the upper or of the lower class (soit de
la haute soit de la basse classe), it will not have many mission
stations in the countryside where the religious movement is
nil'.[30] Indeed, after five years in England, it was only with
the Clapham foundation that the beginning was made of the
Redemptorists' apostolic labours as envisaged by their
founder. A quasi-mission was preached in December 1848 at
St George's Cathedral, Southwark and de Held gave
a retreat to the Sacred Heart Nuns at Roehampton. The
European revolutions of that year, and the suppression of the
Austrian houses, resulted in a large increase in the number
of Redemptorists working in England, although the existing
foundations could not accommodate them all. As a result, the
chaplaincy to nuns at Llanherne in Cornwall and at Rotherwas
was undertaken, as was the mission of Great Marlowe in
Buckinghamshire.[31] The German Chapel in London was also
undertaken by the Redemptorists. Situated in what de Held
later described as 'the most pestilential place in London', the

attached house was uninhabitable on account of a nearby open sewer.[32] De Held hoped initially to move it to a better site and establish a community 'sine cura animarum'.[33] Although this was heroic work, responsibility for the chapel further diffused personnel, so that although by the middle of 1849 there were fourteen Redemptorist priests in England, few of them were as yet free to undertake mission and retreat work.

The European situation had improved sufficiently by late 1850 for a meeting of the transalpine superiors of the Congregation at Bischenberg, near Strasbourg, to decide to abandon all missionary stations and chaplaincy work and for regular communities to be established according to the spirit of the Rule. In explaining to Bishop Wareing of Northampton the abandonment of Great Marlowe, de Held wrote that the time had come

> when it was necessary for us in accordance with the rule and spirit of our Institute to retain only such missions as held out to us the hope of being able within a reasonable time to found a full community, and at the same time were so situated to give facility for the accomplishment of the great object of our order, that is, to give missions and retreats wherever our services might be required.[34]

With this object in mind, only the Clapham foundation was retained, the house was raised to the status of a 'collegium', with de Held as its first Rector, and the decision was taken to make a second, regular foundation as soon as possible. Writing some years after the events, the Provincial Chronicler indulged in poetic licence in describing how, just as a bird coming to an unknown land does not build its nest in the first tree it comes to, but flies around until it finds the best place to shelter from the night of tempest, so the Congregation was to go from home to home until, by divine Providence, it found a place where, according to the mind of St Alphonsus and its apostolic labours, it could establish itself for its work.[35] If that is how it appeared in retrospect, the truth had been otherwise. Far from the deliberate, considered progress, the

Redemptorists had staggered from experiment to experiment, maintaining a precarious presence in a country where their future was far from assured. Once again, Fr Lans questioned the wisdom of the Bischenberg decision and de Held's mode of implementing it. He was joined in his protest by Fr Prost, who viewed the purchase of a house in Bishop Eton, near Liverpool, with disgust and thought the money would have been more profitably used in the mission fund.[36] The house itself had formerly been the residence of Bishop Brown, Vicar Apostolic of the Lancashire District, and of his coadjutor, Bishop Sharples, who were pleased to have the Redemptorists in the diocese.

The misgivings of de Held's subjects could easily be overcome with a lecture on obedience. More seriously, some of the bishops began to express disfavour. Bishop Ullathorne, Vicar Apostolic of the Western District, had already deprecated the Redemptorists' abandonment of the Falmouth mission in 1848. His critical opinion of them was conveyed to Fr Walworth in an interview he had with Ullathorne in 1849, and whenever the bishop visited Hanley Castle (having been translated to the Central District), 'he always found fault very roughly and unreasonably. His complaints were always of a general nature, which would apply equally to any religious order that was steadfastly disposed to adhere to its own vocation'.[37] His irritation with the Congregation was increased by the Bischenberg decision, and in this he was joined by the other bishops in whose dioceses the Redemptorists were working. De Held complained that a false and damaging impression was being communicated by the bishops' agents to the Roman authorities.[38] Instead of mollifying them, however, de Held antagonised the bishops even more by his manner and actions. He created a *cause célèbre* by accepting into the novitiate an ecclesiastical student from Oscott who had left the college without the knowledge or permission of the president or of the bishop to whom he was indebted for six months' lodging. Ullathorne was furious and demanded the student's return. What made him particularly angry was that the student had been advised on his secret course of action by a Redemptorist

14

priest who had been at Oscott to conduct a clergy retreat and who, when challenged with having betrayed the confidence placed in him by the bishop, replied that the student had been right to equivocate and that it was dangerous for young foreigners (as the student was) to be out of religious houses.[39] Rather than seek to pacify Ullathorne, de Held merely informed him that in no other country were seminarians required to seek episcopal permission before joining a religious order, and then added insult to injury by quoting the relevant papal decrees on the subject.[40] This insensitive and maladroit action caused Ullathorne to withdraw his confidence in the Congregation. Ten years after this incident, it was 'understood by our Fathers that the bishop, Dr Ullathorne, did not look on us with too favourable an eye',[41] and not until 1872 did Ullathorne invite a Redemptorist to give the clergy retreat again at Oscott.[42]

The loss of the support of so influential a bishop was potentially very dangerous, since it made other bishops a little cautious with regard to the Congregation. De Held believed that it was Ullathorne who turned the Cardinal against him.[43] In fact, Wiseman was already upset by the Redemptorists' refusal to undertake a mission in Wandsworth and by their declared intention to withdraw from the work of the German Chapel.[44] In a letter to Faber of 27 October 1852, Wiseman poured out his complaints against the inactivity of those male religious orders in London, whose foundations he had encouraged in the hope that they would work among the poor.[45] Of the Redemptorists, he wrote that they

> came to London as a missionary Order, and I cheerfully approved of and encouraged their coming. When they were settled down, I spoke to them of my cherished plan of missions to and among the poor. I was told that this was not the purpose of their Institute *in towns* and that 'another order would be required for what I wanted'. The plea of 'rule' is one which I have all along determined to respect; and I have no more to say. They have become, as far as London is concerned, a parochial body, taking excellent care of Clapham (having five or six priests and

abundant means for it), and they have given two or three missions with varied success in chapels, but no more than they have done in Birmingham and Manchester. They have exercised no local influence; and, though lately they have offered to work among the poor (being no longer in the diocese), something seems to have paralysed their efforts.

Like the Jesuits, Oratorians, Passionists and Marists, the Redemptorists were said to plead their Rule to excuse their inactivity, 'so that souls are perishing around them, but they are prevented by their Rules, given by saints, from helping to save them — at least in any but a particular and definite way'. Had those saints seen the need in London at that time, the Cardinal doubted that they would have held back:

> For example, the Redemptorists tell me, 'These missions among the poor are not according to our Rule'; that is, probably, have not been foreseen or ordered by it. Certainly not. St Alphonsus was a country bishop and, therefore, 'pauperum praesertim et ruricolarum misertus', he instituted his congregation. Suppose he had been placed where there were cities filled with dens of infamy as deep as any robbers' caves in the Abruzzian fastnesses, and vice as inaccessible to common means of grace as a castello on a peak of the Apennines is to human foot, would he have said, 'These not being *ruricolae*, my disciples must not try to save them'?

Wiseman's rhetoric conveys a disappointment compounded by de Held's tactlessness. It may also be true that the Cardinal 'sometimes asked from religious orders more than they could conscientiously concede'.[46] The Redemptorists did not wish to become mere diocesan missioners, on the pattern of Wiseman's Oblates of St Charles, but the excuse of Rule was a hollow one in view of their withdrawal from the countryside. Beneath the conflict of interests was genuine misunderstanding, and for that de Held must be held partly responsible.

The worsening relations between the Congregation and the bishops were gloomily monitored on the Continent by the

Vicar General, who wrote at the end of December that a temporary withdrawal from England might prove necessary:

> England at the present time is certainly not a land where the Congregation can develop. The bishops are determined to thwart its progress by any means in their power, and every success it might achieve, however small, would only reawaken their jealousy.[47]

De Held replied that the situation was not as bad as Smetana feared. In October, the Belgian Provincial, Dechamps, had written to Wiseman in order to placate the bishops and also to express his regret at the conflict between Wiseman and his suffragans and the Congregation. Reviewing the contentious issues, Dechamps pointed out that the mission stations had not all been abandoned at the same time, nor in a manner to leave the respective dioceses in need; they had proved impossible to continue because they were unable to maintain regular communities. Begging Wiseman to look kindly on the Institute in England, which was poor and did not constitute 'such a flourishing state', the Provincial wrote of the determination of the Congregation's authorities that the fathers in England should work 'in perfect union with the episcopate by the submission which is due to it'.[48]

Of greater sway with the bishops than such pious assurances was the removal to Belgium of de Held, whose continued presence endangered the struggling Institute in England. Nor was his removal altogether unwelcome among the fathers in England. His stiff government and the exacting nature of his asceticism, combining with a want of human sympathy and adaptability in meeting and appreciating an opposing view, had created a party hostile to him among his subjects in England. De Buggenoms held him wholly culpable for the bad relations with the Cardinal and other bishops, although he believed that 'he had only the temporal welfare of the Congregation in mind'.[49] Yet this did not mitigate some distressing flaws of character:

> Fr de Held was a noble man ... but he had no idea how to govern others. He expected everything to go the right way; if it went awry, he did not know what to do.[50]

On the other hand, whatever the failings of his rigid exterior and inflexible manner, the Institute in England owed him a great debt. Not only was he its founder, but also, as Fr Coffin later remarked, its preserver as a congregation of missionaries and not an association of small communities administering parishes, a fate which befell the greater number of religious orders in England.[51]

The troubles which revolved around de Held did not blight altogether the work and progress of the Congregation in England. The year 1850 witnessed, in addition to an increase in the number of vocations, the real beginning of the expansion of the Redemptorists' labours. The conducting of retreats for other religious, clergy and clerical students, and the occasional small mission in large, London churches such as St James's, Spanish Place, St Patrick's, Soho or the French Chapel, was supplemented by the first large-scale exercise. This was a twenty-day mission in St Wilfred's, Manchester, and was followed by missions at Formby in Lancashire and at St Oswald's, Old Swan, Liverpool. All of these missions were a great success, with large numbers of penitents crowding the confessionals. At St Wilfred's, there was a solemn procession of the Blessed Sacrament, 'a thing altogether new in these heretical regions'.[52] At Formby, it was recorded that 'an infinite number of sinners were converted to God. I saw a wonderful thing in these exercises: young men and women (adolescentulos et adolescentulas) from twenty to forty years of age who had never received Holy Communion (numquam ad Sacrum Communionem accesserant)'.[53] Wherever they went, the missioners exerted great efforts to establish devotion to our Lady by means of the rosary and scapular. A mission in the Pro-Cathedral of St Nicholas, Copperas Hill, Liverpool in the following year was the occasion for a general dedication to the Virgin and for the renewal of baptismal vows, both of which ceremonies were comparative novelties in England. Opportunity was also taken to speak to the Italian merchant seamen, who were in port, and to hear their confessions.[54]

Parish missions were still rare in 1851. It was their novelty value which drew large crowds, though not necessarily those for whom the mission was intended:

> All of our first missions were given in large towns. There was no difficulty, of course, in filling the church. On the contrary, it was the crowd itself that embarrassed us most. The parishioners who ought to be present were crowded out to make way for outsiders who had no special claims on the parish. If these were truly devout persons, they did not belong to the class of neglected souls. If they were merely devotees, they could not, as a class, be expected to profit much by the mission. In fine, the general result was that too few of those who came could receive that benefit which a successful mission brings with it, namely, the gradual accumulation upon the heart of divine truth conveyed to it through solid reasoning.

An attempt to overcome this perennial problem for all missioners was made at St Nicholas's. When the clergy said that they wished to reach those who were mainly indifferent with regard to religious matters, it was decided to go out into the streets, alleys and courts in order to announce the mission and invite the people to attend:

> A sodality of young men preceded us in their uniform, carrying a large banner. We found a small square or court with an opening from the street, into which we entered and planted our banner. We were soon surrounded by an interested audience, to whom I preached a skeleton of the morning's sermon in church, with such a modification as circumstances made necessary. Of course, we had no altar, no Mass, no tall, black mission cross with its nine yards of drapery drawn over the arms ... but an empty egg-box ... served for a pulpit. My audience was all that could be wished in numbers and respectful attitude, not only looking up to me, but down at me from tiers of windows on every side.[55]

From the outset, the fathers' work was characterised by an uncompromising spirit and met with a degree of success that gave renewed confidence to the missioners. In turn, that confidence bred the eager wish to spread the work of the Institute over a large geographical area, and so reach those people whom the Rule had especially in mind. Although only just beginning their work in England, the fathers cast an eye over the Irish Sea. The establishment of a house in Liverpool made this inevitable. Bishop Eton soon became, as intended, the main missionary house and the residence of the Superior of the Missions, Fr Prost. Following the warm reception given to Fr Petcherine by attentive crowds of poor people in Omagh, Co. Tyrone, where he was giving a retreat to some nuns, and Cappagh, Co. Limerick, the Redemptorists gave their first Irish mission in October 1851 at St John's Cathedral, Limerick. It was the largest mission to date, involving five fathers, and was a huge success, with over five thousand people attending the planting of the mission cross at its close. It was followed by an equally successful mission at Omagh, where twelve thousand people kept ten priests busy in the confessionals from five o'clock in the morning until late at night during the whole course of the mission.[56] Overwhelmed by this enthusiastic response, the fathers recognised immediately that Ireland provided a vast and proper outlet for their missionary endeavours.[57] In addition, it provided the key to their work in Great Britain and Ireland as a whole, and its unifying theme; as was later remarked, 'it was principally for [the poor Irish Catholics] that the Congregation was able to develop its work in Great Britain'.[58] Henceforth, the fortunes of the Institute were inextricably linked with the general drive in the Catholic Church, both in Ireland and in the cities and towns of Britain, to reclaim and recall the Irish masses to the practice of their faith, as defined and approved by the institutional Church; a drive which invaded every department of the Church's life and utilised all its energies.

In Ireland, the inadequacies of the pre-famine Church had been highlighted by the proselytising activity of such Protestant bodies as the Connaught Mission Society. Although the charges and effects of 'souperism' were exaggerated, the Catholic authorities were sufficiently challenged before 1850 to serve some of the Church's long-neglected people. Archbishop Paul Cullen's arrival from Rome transformed these tentative movements into a full-scale programme of reform and renewal in line with what was happening in the rest of the Universal Church. His drive towards the re-evangelisation of the masses involved, if it did not inaugurate, a 'devotional revolution', and encouraged the deliberate cultivation of an uncompromising, exclusive spirit of religious triumphalism, included in which was the restoration of a Catholic sense of pride and cultural self-identity against the predominant Protestant culture. Within this regenerative process, the role of parish missions was widely recognised, and their success noted, in recapturing many for the faith, in fostering piety and devotion, and in introducing the people to new forms of spirituality from the Continent, which, it was hoped, would consolidate their re-integration into the fold.[59]

The Redemptorists fitted well into this larger programme, and it is not surprising that Cullen should have taken an early interest in the possibility of a Redemptorist foundation in the country.[60] The future importance of Ireland to the Congregation, which he foresaw, and the inconvenience of returning to Bishop Eton between the Irish missions, determined Fr Prost to make an early establishment there. He thought of Dublin, but Cullen suggested Limerick as an alternative; he hoped that the presence of the Redemptorists would bring about a renascence of religious observance among the relaxed Franciscans and Dominicans who were already in the town and that the Redemptorists would best aid his scheme of reform in the west of Ireland, where his efforts were most opposed.[61] Bishop Ryan of Limerick was favourable to the suggestion, and by early October 1852 a suitable property had been found in Bank Place. The Redemptorists moved into it in the following year, and Prost established an 'hospitium' there. This was done, however, without the permission of the Visitor, de Held, who caused his final upset by protesting 'against the tendency of Father Prost to make a hospice of the Limerick house, which was only designed to receive our Fathers in the interval of several days which separates the missions in Ireland from one another'.[62] He changed his mind, however, after the canonical visitation in October of that year, and Fr de Buggenoms was made Superior. A room was opened in the house as a public chapel, so that sermons could be preached and confessions heard. To the consternation of the local clergy, it proved immediately popular.[63] In 1854, a move was made to the west of the city, where a temporary church was constructed. This served until a newly-built church and monastery were solemnly dedicated in 1862.[64] Early publicity was provided by a woman, whom the locals dubbed a Banshee, who went around encouraging people to go to the Redemptorists. Her success was supplemented by the willingness of the fathers to hear general confessions, which resulted in a stream of pentitents to Mount St Alphonsus; some of them came thirty or forty miles, and gave the impression of 'a continual mission'.[65] The frequent absence of so many of the fathers on missions did not encourage regular penitents, but 'always large numbers came from town and country *occasionally*, to make a *long*, general, or more exact than usual confession'.[66] In the first ten years of their work in Limerick, the Redemptorists received 192 Protestants into the Church, 'certainly a large number for Ireland'.[67]

The Irish missions represented a vast field of activity, and the Limerick house offered a future potential, which made it 'one of the most important [missionary] stations in the whole of the Congregation'.[68] It was the assured prospects for the future, after much earlier uncertainty, that led the General Chapter of 1855 to agree to the separation of the Redemptorists in England and Ireland from the Belgian Province and the formation, with their Dutch brethren, of an Anglo-Dutch Province. The previous year, a move had been made towards this by the raising of Bishop Eton to a 'collegium', with Fr Lans as Rector, and the temporary establishment of an Anglo-Dutch Vice-Province within the Belgian Province. The new Province comprised the houses of Amsterdam, Wittem (house of studies), Bois-le-Duc (novitiate), Clapham, Bishop Eton and Limerick. Fr Swinkels was named as Provincial, with Fr Lans as Superior of the English Vice-Province.

2

Expansion and consolidation, 1855-1882

The introduction of the Congregation into Ireland, and the immediate success of the fathers' labours, represented a new orientation and created an imbalance between mission work in Ireland and in Britain.[1] Some of the fathers were sufficiently seduced by Ireland to feel that, in comparison, nothing good was to be done in England.[2] Here, an apathetic people, a hostile clergy and a general lack of faith were pinpointed as inhibiting factors, which precluded the kind of enthusiasm displayed by the Irish.[3] By contrast, several factors confirmed the Redemptorists' attraction to Ireland, exciting their anticipation; de Buggenoms felt that they were not qualified to work in the midst of Protestants, 'whilst we are, as it were, made on purpose for a country like Ireland, where both the clergy and the people are in extreme need of our example and services':

> It is very consoling ... to find oneself in a centre of missionary labours so perfectly in harmony with the 2nd great object of our holy vocation regarding the sanctification of our neighbour, for it is only since we have been established in Ireland that I have felt at home as a Redemptorist. Our two other Houses at Clapham and Bishop Eton appear to me more than ever two artificial foundations, which have cost and will continue to cost large expenses, yielding little or nothing comparatively to what the same would have yielded in Ireland.[4]

In the first place, there were the social conditions which called for general concern but which were also capable of spiritual exploitation and stimulated the Redemptorists' desire to work among 'the most abandoned souls'. Fr Prost was struck by

23

the appalling poverty in food, clothing and shelter among the mass of the population, the endemic injustice of landlordism and the continuing penalties against Catholics, while noting that a lessening of active religious persecution had led to a decline of religious fervour. Alcoholism was widespread, drink being a substitute for food and a means of escape from the harsh realities of life; Prost did not believe that Fr Mathew's abstinence campaigns had produced any lasting effects, because they had lacked the necessary spiritual foundation of a deepening of the religious sense through prayer and the frequentation of the sacraments. Worse still, in the face of social and political injustice, was the desperate and violent attraction of, and sympathy for, the secret societies of Ribbonmen, Hibernians and (after 1859) Fenians.[5] Believing that they could cut through the political currents into which many of the Irish secular clergy were often drawn, the Redemptorists sought to appeal to a natural, simple faith of the people, albeit wanting as yet in religious instruction, and to present the Catholic faith as a redeeming and uplifting experience that was both socially and politically ameliorative. So, during the *Amende Honorable* at a mission in Wexford in 1853, Prost asked his hearers 'why they did not come in their miseries to Him who can alone deliver them from their miseries? Why did they put their trust in men, in meetings, in parliament, rather than in Him who was there to listen to them?'.[6] Such a spiritual diagnosis meant that the fathers always attempted to avoid political controversy, although it is interesting that the most popular Redemptorist in Ireland was reprimanded by his superiors for his politically-liberal views, and condemned as 'exclusivement Irlandais'.[7] His acquittal of the charge of Bible-burning in Kingstown (now Dún Laoghaire), Co. Dublin in 1855 made him 'the idol of Ireland' and 'such a favourite in this country that if he could bilocate himself he would be wanted everywhere, and everywhere cheered'.[8]

The second attraction of the Irish mission was the enthusiasm with which they were greeted in all parts of the country. Wherever they went, the Redemptorists attracted huge crowds, with the result that the churches were often packed to suffocation.[9] At Randalstown, Co. Antrim in 1853, for example, ten thousand people attended the ceremony of the erecting of the mission cross out of a supposed population of five thousand;[10] Cork Cathedral, which could hold seven thousand, was filled to overflowing during a mission in April/May 1854, with people perched on ladders and scaffolding at open windows to hear the mission sermons of Fr Bernard;[11] at Carndonagh, Co. Donegal in 1858, the missioner was forced to preach from a platform in the churchyard because the vast crowd could not be squeezed into the church.[12] Many of these poor people had no shoes, but would stand barefoot all day on the stone floors, even in the depths of winter, and then kept night vigil in the churches, or nearby, so as not to lose their places in the queue for confession.[13] At St Finbarr's, Cork in October 1854, thirty confessors were kept busy from five o'clock in the morning until eleven o'clock at night for over three weeks. At this same mission, twenty thousand people received Holy Communion, 'the altar rail being crowded [daily] from early morning until midday'.[14] Many would have waited for up to three days without food to make their communion. Large numbers attended the sacraments for the first time, or after a lapse of many years, publicly proclaiming the length of their absence and the great sins they had committed, while it was not uncommon to come across people of fifty, sixty or even seventy years who had never received the sacraments, not even baptism or marriage, but were eager to do so. Loud sobbing and crying out during the sermons and public acts was a common feature; at Cork Cathedral this was so great that Fr Bernard had to ask for quiet, and elsewhere a bell was rung to stop the people's noise.[15]

Wails of lamentation often accompanied the closing sermon and departure of the fathers, which were turned into public demonstrations of thanksgiving to the missioners. At Wexford, in 1853, Fr Prost recalled that all the shops were closed, as for a holiday, the windows lining the fathers' route were crowded with people, waving handkerchiefs and throwing flowers, and children from the orphanage were ranged along the road waving banners. The crowds followed the missioners' carriage for several miles out of the town, and when they begged the people to go home, eighty carriages still followed for some distance.[16] At Gorey, Co. Wexford, the missioners' departure was made 'amidst the lamentations of hundreds', who accompanied them for miles outside the town.[17] At Cork, the horses were unhitched from the missioners' carriage, and it was dragged by the people to the railway station, and at Clonmel in 1863, not only was this scene re-enacted, but the people also insisted upon a final oration, and knelt on the platform for the fathers' blessing.[18] Such was the people's faith in the power of the missioners that it was thought that they could cure sickness, and people jostled to touch the fringe of their habits. Although poor, the people purchased vast quantities of pious books and objects from the hawkers who followed the missioners; it was not unknown for between one and three hundred pounds' worth of merchandise to be bought. Rarely, it was said, were sinners found in any of the parishes who did not attend the mission and receive the sacraments; secret societies were disbanded, as at Letterkenny, Co. Donegal in 1852, and Strabane, Co. Tyrone in 1853; other evils, ranging from mixed schools and marriages to the opening of public houses on Sundays and holy days, were also attended to.[19] It had to be admitted that more women than men attended the mission exercises, and that there were many young men, 'who, ensnared by drunkenness or occasions of other sins, obstinately refused to make their peace with God'.[20] But this was mainly in the large towns, where there were also 'a few of the better class who, if they do not avail themselves of the graces of the mission, do nothing to retard [its] progress'.[21]

The exhilarating effect all this had on the Redemptorists can be seen in an extant letter from one of the missioners at Cork Cathedral in 1854:

> I know now a little what an Irish mission is. What a good people. I heard so many in the confessional, all in rags, men and women, and although in sin, I found in them a wonderful faith. I could help them all. Great was the

excitement of our departure; in the streets, at the station, and farther even in some places where the train had to pass, there was an immense crowd crying aloud and weeping ... They did feel a difference between the Fathers and their own priests. They touched many times my soutane, as if I would have been a saint ... It is wonderful how Fr Bernard knows how to move and catch the hearts of the Irish ... At Limerick Junction, the Director of the Locomotive entered our carriage, fell on his knees and said that he had attended the mission and would henceforth say his beads all the time he was directing the locomotive.[22]

There were, however, dangers inherent in the very success of the missions. They created a demand for more, a demand which could not always be met.[23] In the effort to meet it, there was an undue stretching of resources and a temptation to take shortcuts; the result was hurried missions. As early as 1853, de Held urged the fathers not to be anxious to take on too much work, to establish themselves slowly but surely, and he laid down certain guidelines for the conduct of missions.[24] Nevertheless, his warnings went unheeded and too much work was undertaken. One missioner recalled the common practice of starting a mission, to be joined later by those who were concluding the previous one.[25] Among the complaints against Fr Petcherine was that he heard too many confessions in one day (140), not allowing the penitents sufficient time to make a general confession.[26] Worse still, the short duration of some missions left many unconfessed. It was this unease at the continuous work of the missions that prompted Fr Prost to return to the Continent in 1855.[27]

The problem of too many, hurried missions was not confined to the Redemptorists' work in Ireland, but it was there that abuses arising from it were grave, and murmurs against their Irish missions reached Rome: 'Is it not the fact that the missions are too hurried in Ireland? ... I believe that the superior instructions which the Lazarists give, is the reason why Archbishop Cullen prefers their missions to ours. Add to this that the Lazarists stay a month if necessary in the same place'.[28] The Limerick fathers were told to undertake fewer missions, to make the duration of each mission proportional to the size of the parish, and never of less than three weeks.[29] In addition, the necessity of making them more instructive was insisted upon to prevent them becoming 'mere occasions of exhortation and feeling and noise'.[30] To this end, great care was taken in December 1859 over the mission in Dundalk, 'as the mission was intended to be a model for towns of similar magnitude and importance'.[31] Although the Roman authorities were appeased by the success of this mission and the assurances of reform, it was still not uncommon for three or four young priests to give a fifteen-day mission to over four thousand people, and 'for indigestion to be the order of the day'.[32] In spite of a further strong letter to the Rector of Limerick,[33] the problem remained and served merely to highlight the immensity of available work and the previous neglect of the people by ecclesiastical authority.

Whatever the problems for the Redemptorists, the Irish laity were in no doubt as to the value of 'these indefatigable missioners — who, with so much zeal, fervour and perseverance, preach the Gospel among the poor, and bring the hearts of the rich also to an appreciation of their duties to their fellow man and to God'.[34] Frequent adulatory newspaper reports testify not only to the novelty of parish missions, and the high value placed on them, but also to the recognised worth of the missioners themselves. Indeed, so commonplace were these reports that the Limerick Chronicler finished his report of a mission in Queenstown (now Cóbh), Co. Cork in 1855 by opining that 'the newspaper will take care to praise the Fathers'.[35] To an outsider, the Redemptorists stood out as

> the most laborious and ascetic Order of the Church. It is a rule of the order to avoid controversy and proselytism, their crusade being solely directed against immorality and infidelity. To estimate the value of their Apostolic Labours too highly would be impossible; wherever they have reared their missionary cross in Ireland, thousands have been brought into permanent connexion with the

sacraments, among whom, perhaps, the local clergy would have long laboured in vain.[36]

Reviewing their first ten years in Ireland, the *Freeman's Journal* related 'the deep sympathy and ardent affection for the Redemptorist Fathers', which had been everywhere created. Their extensive labours, it continued, had made them known to a great body of the Irish people,

> and the Irish Catholic heart has not failed to appreciate their laborious and single-minded toils, their simple, apostolic eloquence, and the wonderful fruits of their zeal and charity in combating everywhere those evils which spring from the ignorance of the poor or the indifferentism of the rich.[37]

The importance of these early years in Ireland was not just that the Redemptorists were able to expand their work (and numbers) in a conducive atmosphere, but that in Ireland, especially under Fr Bernard Hafkenscheid (Superior of the Missions, 1853-5), they perfected the mission technique among the Irish for both Britain and Ireland. Although there was a danger that the Redemptorists might give the impression that 'we were merely in England for the sake of Ireland',[38] work in both countries was of a piece. By evangelising the Irish in their own country, it was hoped that they would facilitate the spread of the faith in the countries to which they emigrated, so that

> the light of faith and grace, concealed in their hearts, immediately began to bring light to those heretical regions sunk in the shadow of death, so that it could be said that the immigration of the Irish was both the twilight and the dawning of a new day (crepusculum que aurora novi diei) for the Catholic Church'.[39]

Like the Church in Ireland, the Church in England and Scotland during the 1850s and 1860s was involved in a subtle plan to convert the residual Catholicism of a folk-religion type of many immigrants into strong, firm habits of participation in the complex of religious acts and observances which had characterised Catholicism since the Counter-Reformation. Among the generation of pre-famine Irish immigrants, this meant introducing them for the first time to the full range of Counter-Reformation spirituality and ecclesiological demands. The revival of the Irish Church before 1850 had hardly touched the west of the country. Here, Mass attendance was low; the survival of pagan rituals and folk beliefs conspired with the low educational standards among the populace, including the clergy, to produce a low level of participation in the cycle of parish rituals and a general ignorance of orthodox Catholic doctrine. Even in the eastern counties, from where the majority of immigrants to Britain came and where Mass attendance was higher, the same problems obtained to a lesser degree.

The great wave of Irish immigration from 1840 onwards confirmed the demographic change of Catholicism in Britain from a predominantly rural to a predominantly urban phenomenon. It stretched the resources of the Church beyond its capacity to cope; there were simply not enough priests, churches or schools to accommodate the influx. In their new and bewildering environment, many Irish Catholics, even if they had the opportunity of attending Mass, joined the 'leakage' from the faith bemoaned by Catholic writers. On the other hand, since many of these immigrants from rural Ireland were not 'practising' Catholics, in the ecclesially-accepted sense, it was less a question of stemming the 'leakage' than of converting an innate sense of Catholic identity into an acceptable level of membership-commitment. Fr Coffin was vastly underestimating both the complexity of the situation and the difficulty of the Church's task when he wrote that in England, living in the midst of Protestants, the faithful Irish Catholics neglected to come to church, but 'once our missioners, by their domiciliary visits, have attached them to the Church, their hearts are moulded like wax, and the missioner can do with them as he pleases'.[40] This certainly did not tally with the experience of a Marist priest in East London in the 1850s, who deplored the woeful ignorance among the first generation of Irish immigrants of 'the most essential truths of our Religion', and observed that almost none of them had received their first communion.[41] This, of course, is what we should expect, and the problem to which the Irish Church revival was addressing itself. In addition, it underlies the Catholic Church's missionary endeavour throughout the second half of the nineteenth century, in which the Redemptorists were involved.

The task was greatly facilitated by the agglomeration of the Irish, the maintenance of group solidarity in their marriages, by their close historical identification with the Church and the indigenous opposition to the Irish on religious, social, economic and national grounds.[42] The Church sought to capitalise on these assets by striving to create and consolidate strong, urban Catholic communities; self-contained, almost self-segregated communities in which the values of sobriety and solid good behaviour prevailed, and which stood in marked contrast to the prevailing 'pagan' or 'Protestant' culture, where religious indifference was seen to reign supreme. It was, of course, impossible to abstract Catholics from their social milieu, with all its dangers and potential destroyers of religious sensibility. Efforts were made, however, to combat it through the undertaking of a programme of church building, the creation of a system of Catholic schools and the sponsoring of a whole gamut of social, recreational and educational societies, often mirroring existing working-class organisations, in order to mould and to hold the faithful together. Equally important, the Church sought to remould Irish popular culture to its own interests by the application and inculcation of an ideology which defined Catholics over against their Protestant neighbours, and so helped to consolidate the Catholic community. This ideology was an idealisation of selective elements of proletarian culture as a near approximation to Catholic holiness; holiness was to be sought in the daily lives of Catholics, not in abstraction from their lives. The ideal of Holy Poverty was one manifestation of this concept, which gave shape and form to the practical work of building up the life of the Church and compacting the Catholic community. So, too, was the creation of the myth, reflected in Coffin's remark, that the Irish had maintained the

Faith intact for centuries through their loyalty to the Church. The creation of what has been called 'integral Catholicism' was itself an outgrowth of the Ultramontane ideal,[43] characterised by a highly dogmatic, anti-rationalist theology, a warmly emotional, clerically-directed and clerically-controlled pietistical devotion, and a preference for life in the Catholic ghetto, where the Faith could be preserved from contamination. Yet it served also to attach its adherents firmly to the Church.

As the spiritual sons of one of its major prophets, the Redemptorists were committed to the Ultramontane ideal. They were well placed to benefit from the growing prestige of St Alphonsus, as the Ultramontane programme of reconstruction and renewal gained ever greater support, until it came to characterise and define Catholicism in the pontificate of Pius IX. Just as the 1850s saw the triumph of Alphonsus's theology and spiritual ideas, so the Redemptorists rode high on the tide of his popularity, reaping its benefits and contributing to its consolidation. Moreover, during this decade, they gained the kudos of epitomising in their apostolic work all that the bishops were striving to achieve in the Church as a whole. In turn, their welcome contribution reflected the aims and ideals of the wider movement of Ultramontane Catholic revivalism to the extent that a Redemptorist could say of England that 'S. Alphonsus is like a Saviour for this country. I believe that in no other country, perhaps, is our Congregation called to do more good'.[44] In a real sense, missions built parish communities; they were intended to attract together large numbers of lapsed, nominal or desultory Catholics, provide them with an unforgettable demonstration of Catholic holiness, suitably adapted to their circumstances, with which they were to be made to identify as the first step in their full participation in it.

These are themes to which we shall return later; their introduction here is intended to suggest both how and why the Redemptorists and their apostolic labours coalesced with the wider ecclesiastical scene. This integration contributed to their prosperity and ensured their continued importance. The general well-being of the Institute can, in part, be measured by the progress of the novitiate. The need for a novitiate in England was recognised as early as 1850, and had lain behind negotiations to take over the Oratorian house of St Wilfrid's in Staffordshire.[45] It was then intended that Bishop Eton should house a novitiate,[46] and a further attempt was made on the eve of the creation of the Anglo-Dutch Province, when the offer of the Earl of Shrewsbury to take over a house in Cheadle was seriously considered.[47] An English novitiate was finally opened at Bishop Eton in 1860, although the clerical students continued to study on the Continent. This arrangement did ensure that they received the best available teaching and, in stressing the international character of the Congregation, helped to avoid that insularity and isolation which was later to be a source of difficulty for members of the English Province.

The establishment of a novitiate did lead to an increase in British, and particularly Irish, aspirants to the Congregation, thereby reducing the dependence on foreign Redemptorists. The number of subjects in Great Britain and Ireland was never very high; it was not much above sixty professed priests during the whole of the century, and that figure was not reached until the 1880s. Between 1860 and 1900, 218 clerical novices were clothed, of whom one died and seventy-seven left before profession. Six more left during the studentate and one became a lay brother. A further twenty-five departed after ordination, or were expelled, and the remaining 108 persevered. During the same period, 102 lay novices were clothed, of whom only thirty-four persevered.[48] Writing at the end of 1875, Coffin lamented that 'we have few vocations; the Jesuits and communities without vows, the Oratorians and Oblates of S. Charles, are in fashion', and he believed that this was due to 'the true state of the world in general, which does not dispose souls to give up their liberty in the religious life; and in England in particular, where the youth is accustomed to baths each morning, to physical exercises, and to so many of life's comforts'.[49] The controversy surrounding Petcherine's retreat at Oscott in 1850 illustrates the difficulty of recruiting from the ecclesiastical colleges.[50] The shortage of secular priests explains the opposition of bishops and the presidents of the colleges to attempts by the religious orders to recruit students or to draw them away from the dioceses. John Gibson, a young priest who taught rhetoric at Ushaw, joined the Redemptorists in 1851 to the indignation of the president, Dr Newsham. When he returned to the college some years later to give a retreat, as a result of which a student joined the Congregation, the president was again displeased.[51] As late as 1886, Bishop Riddell of Northampton informed a would-be Redemptorist that he should give up the idea of a religious vocation because the diocese was short of priests.[52]

In spite of official opposition, vocations were gained from colleges, usually as a result of retreats, and from the diocesan clergy, usually as a result of the missions.[53] The missions were also responsible for drawing laymen to the Congregation; their effect upon the religiously-minded can be seen from the letter of a young man to Fr Leo, who had attended a Redemptorist mission in Kilmessan, Co. Meath as a boy and now felt that he had a vocation to the order.[54] This also illustrates the power of individual Redemptorist priests and underlines the importance of personal contact for the gaining of vocations, although this was recognised as a somewhat haphazard means of recruitment.[55] The continued difficulty of obtaining a substantial number of English vocations constituted a major problem for the Institute, as it gave a strong Irish flavour to the Province and led to agitation among the Irish fathers that their preponderance be reflected in its government. Animosity between the English and Irish priests became a prominent feature of the Province, reflecting national antipathy and also, perhaps, certain social tensions. The English priests were, almost without exception, from the professional classes and regarded themselves as natural governors, while the Irish were from a wider social mix and resented the hauteur of some of their English confrères.[56] Paul Reyners, the novice master at St Trond in 1852, found his English novices 'fastidious and difficult by nature'.[57] Nevertheless, he admitted that he liked '1000-times better the English than the Irish vocations', although he gave no reason beyond a 'you know the reason'.[58] Not everyone agreed; Reyners admitted that Fr Bernard thought otherwise, and Fr Van der Aa complained a few years later that of the English priests, one did not like preaching, another did not like missions, and a third did not take to confessions, which was somewhat strange for Redemptorists.[59]

Whatever the difficulties of the novitiate, the Redemptorist authorities in Rome regarded the Congregation's progress in the three countries with satisfaction.[60] In 1863, the English Vice-Provincial, R.A. Coffin, who had succeeded Fr Lans in 1859, was told to prepare for the establishment of a Province. This came two years later; as expected, Coffin was named as Provincial, a position he held for the next seventeen years until his elevation to the see of Southwark in 1882.[61] His long period of government was of great consequence for the Congregation, not only for the continuity and stability that he was able to introduce, but also in terms of its ethos and the good relations with the English, Irish and Scottish episcopal hierarchies with which it was marked. Ambitious, intelligent and immensely able, Coffin ruled his subjects in a manner that mirrored that of the Rector Major who had appointed him, Nicholas Mauron.[62] Formerly Provincial of the French Redemptorists, Mauron had been unexpectedly elected Rector Major by the General Chapter of 1855, at the early age of thirty-seven. A deeply interior man, he leaned towards a literal interpretation of the Rule and Constitutions, for which he had great veneration, and of the law of the Church. His period of government was one of stabilisation and consolidation for the Congregation: he settled the vexed question of poverty, re-unified the Congregation (1869), and obtained the declaration of St Alphonsus's doctorate (1871). The prestige of the Congregation increased greatly during his term of office, both in Roman circles and abroad. Like Pius IX, with whom he was on terms of friendship, Mauron mixed personal magnetism with an authoritarian style of ruling. He preferred to govern the Congregation through trusted satraps rather than through general chapters, only one of which was called during his time; that was in 1893, six years after the

Frederick de Held (1799-1881). Belgian Provincial at the time the Redemptorists came to Britain in 1843. He later became first Rector of the Clapham foundation.

Nicholas Mauron (1818-1893). He was elected Rector Major of the Redemptorist Congregation in 1855 at the age of thirty-seven, and died in office.

onset of the illness which had left him a virtual invalid and finally resulted in his death, before the chapter met, in 1894. An indication of his ecclesiastical sympathies is given by his invitation to the Infallibilists at the First Vatican Council to make the principal house of the Congregation, S. Alfonso's, their headquarters in Rome. The tone of his rule can be measured by the remarks of Richard Simpson. Writing to Paul Hecker, founder of the Paulists, who had been expelled from the Redemptorists in 1858, Simpson claimed that Vladimir Petcherine had been 'driven forth of the Redemptorists by their political illiberality ... squeezed out of the narrow affair into wh[ich] yr old Congregation is fast degenerating under its new General. We lament the spirit of Held and his heroic days'.[63]

In Coffin, Mauron found a man after his own heart, through whom he could direct the affairs of the Congregation in Britain and Ireland. In spite of severe illness, which prevented him from performing many of his duties, he was re-appointed by the Rector Major at each of six triennials. For his part, Coffin wrote copiously to Rome on matters ranging from signs of episcopal favour, or the health of confrères and visitation reports, to such trivia as the hiring of domestic servants. He thereby displayed a dependence upon, and respect for, central authority, which Mauron found gratifying, but which bordered at times on servility: 'The least desire of Your Paternity has always been for me like a formal order, and long ago I made the firm resolution to place myself without question in obedience to your desires (le ferme propos de me tenir prêt à obéir à ces desirs sans aucun raisonnement)'.[64] More telling, perhaps, he could anticipate a visit to Rome, 'my true and real home on Earth', by opining that 'to be with his Paternity is to be allowed to look on the face of God's Vicar'.[65] In turn, Mauron expressed for his subordinate 'a great esteem and entire confidence which, for your part, you have always justified.'[66]

Coffin's personal qualities, his efficiency and industry, may not wholly explain the Rector Major's confidence. He was a great friend and confidant of Manning, in whose elevation to

Westminster he is supposed to have been instrumental, and was to become the confessor of the majority of the English Hierarchy and of some of the Irish bishops.[67] He also played a prominent part in opposing Newman's plans to establish an Oratory in Oxford, and the sending of Catholics to Oxford and Cambridge.[68] His good relations with, and the confidence he elicited from, the bishops was beneficial to the Congregation; Bishop Grant of Southwark, for example, commended the visit to Rome in 1862 of

> the distinguished and zealous Superior of these Redemptorists ... and I am happy to be able to offer you through him my sincere regards and to assure the Sacred Congregation of the pious, edifying and regular life of the Institute to which he belongs.[69]

The personal stature of Coffin among the bishops affirmed the advantage of having an Englishman as head of the Congregation in Britain, thus removing any suggestion of 'continentalism', which some of the bishops might have regarded with suspicion. At the same time, Coffin was a convert, committed to the ideals of the 'second spring', who had a sympathy for other converts.[70] This did not blind him to the needs of 'cradle' Catholics, particularly priests, who sought him out as a confessor and spiritual director, and who valued his retreats, described as 'the main work of Fr Coffin outside the Congregation'.[71] In short, he was peculiarly placed to be sensitive to the needs and demands of all sections of Catholic opinion. It was this quality that was highlighted in his obituary, where it was admitted that 'although his name was at no time conspicuously before the world, his influence had been widely and deeply felt, and few ecclesiastics in England were held in greater esteem or affection'.[72]

Coffin was more than a public figure-head, for he had a decisive influence on the life and work of the Congregation. He had an almost passionate belief in a strict, though flexible, application of the Rule and Constitutions, especially regarding the conduct of the missions. Under his guidance, both a priests' *Manuale* (1866) and a *Directory of the Missions* (1877) were produced, providing all the necessary liturgical forms for public and private use, and laying down guidelines for missions, thereby ensuring 'uniformity, regularity and the true spirit of the Congregation in our method of giving Missions'.[73] These two publications helped not only to shape the new Province but also to preserve strict uniformity with Roman norms. Coffin kept a firm control on every aspect of the Province's life through the system of visitation and by means of regular circular letters, designed to rectify faults, expose any infringement of the Constitutions and check anything likely to compromise or weaken the Congregation's spirit and apostolic labours. Constant exhortations and instructions issued from his pen; few things escaped his notice, and he aimed to maintain high standards on the missions and in the monasteries. He thus presided over a consolidation of the work and reputation of the Redemptorists, together with a geographical and numerical growth of the Congregation in Britain and Ireland.

At the time of the Province's inauguration, Mauron informed Coffin that it was the wish of the Roman Provincial, Edward Douglas, to see a house of the order established in his native Scotland, for which he would provide the money. The natural location was the west of Scotland, where the majority of Catholics were to be found. This was ruled out by the presence of the Jesuits and Passionists, and by the virtual schism between the Irish and Scottish secular priests in the District, which, given the number of Irish Redemptorists, Coffin feared would be a source of trouble to the Congregation.[74] Stirling furnished 'unmistakable signs of anti-Catholic spirit', and Edinburgh was, likewise, unsuitable.[75] Directed to Perth, successful negotiations with the Earl of Kinnoull resulted in the purchase of land overlooking the town. A temporary hospice was established at Dundee in June 1867, and a year later work began on the church and community house, the first purpose-built monastery in Scotland since the Reformation.[76] The new house soon resulted in an increase of the Redemptorists' activities in the northern kingdom, where there had previously been only fourteen missions, and in the north of England. Kinnoull became 'our purely Missionary House ... the real Mission House of the Province', performing more missions and renewals than any other house in the Province.[77] The new foundation also allowed the establishment of the second novitiate, which first took place there in 1870.[78] In addition, the house was used extensively by the Scottish bishops for clergy retreats. For its part, the Catholic press rejoiced at 'the blessings to be reaped by the Catholic Church in Scotland from the establishment of so well-organised a house, and from the labours of the zealous Fathers, who give themselves up entirely to their holy work'.[79]

A further requirement of the Province to make it a fully autonomous unit was a house of studies for the post-novitiate clerical students. An attempt to establish a studentate at Bishop Eton in 1863, in the wake of preparation for the new Province, had to be abandoned; the Redemptorists in England did not have the personnel to staff it, and the students continued to be sent to Wittem or to Tetcheren in France. It was found, however, that the health of many of the younger students suffered badly on the Continent. The Irish students were particularly affected: 'The continental system, with a strange language, an imagination peculiar to themselves, the difference in food, make it more than they can bear — consumption for some and insanity for others will be the result'.[80] A return to Bishop Eton in 1872 did not prove any more salubrious, and Coffin began to look for a house in the milder climate of the south coast, which would serve as both a house of studies and convalescent home. In 1875, Bishop William Vaughan of Plymouth, brother of the Rector of Kinnoull, wrote to Coffin, inviting the Redemptorists to the diocese.[81] He promised a warm welcome from the local clergy, and, since there were no other religious in the diocese, 'a clean stage'.[82] In return, the bishop expected the Redemptorists to help him 'by means of little missions, exercises to religious and other fruits for the good of his flock'.[83] Accordingly, a house was rented from the bishop, on a five-year lease, at Teignmouth in Devon.[84] It was to prove an ideal place, although the local population were not altogether welcoming. Teignmouth comprised 'mostly heretics, who do not molest the fathers, but do not afford much opportunity of making known the Catholic faith', so that 'prayer, rather than preaching, must be the instrument employed for their spiritual good'.[85] Fear that the Redemptorists would undertake aggressive proselytism seems to have been the cause of initial unfriendliness. Relations improved 'when it was found that [the fathers] needed bread and meat and beer like other people, and, as they paid their bills every month, their custom was sought'.[86]

Little external work was done by the new house, although there was a public chapel and the spiritual guidance of some local Benedictine nuns was taken over. In the twenty-five years of its existence, a steadily-increasing stream of students pursued their academic training at Teignmouth; 144 in all, rising from six in 1870 to forty-five by 1900.[87] Until 1891, when it was transferred to Bishop Eton, the humanities course was taught at Teignmouth; at that date, the house was so full that two or three students were sharing a bedroom.[88] The studentate represented a major asset for the Province, in which Coffin took much pride and satisfaction. He was also able to control the students' training and to exercise a keener and more direct influence over them than had been possible when they studied abroad. The good effects of the studentate continued to be felt until the end of the century; as the Rector Major remarked in 1890, 'the studentate of the English Province has gained greatly over several years, as much by the number of young men as by their good spirit and the level of their studies'.[89]

In giving his permission for the Teignmouth foundation, Mauron had insisted that it should not impede a new establishment in Ireland.[90] This was considered a priority on the part of the Roman authorities. On the one hand, there was the fear that the influence of the fathers in that country was 'a little on the wane'.[91] On the other hand, it seemed incredible that only one house had been founded in Ireland, where the majority of novices were recruited and where much work was still being performed.[92] A second Irish foundation had been suggested in 1857, when a Mr Trevelyan, with the approval of Cardinal Cullen, offered to establish the Redemptorists at Kingstown.[93] His offer was refused on the grounds that there was an insufficient number of subjects, but the intimation was made that the next Redemptorist foundation would be in Kingstown.[94] Coffin seems, however, to have forgotten this promise, and showed a marked disinclination to found another house in Ireland; when there were enough subjects to make another foundation, he pursued an offer of the Bishop of Beverley.[95] The clamour of the Irish fathers, however, was sufficient to persuade the Roman authorities to insist on a new Irish house.[96]

It was hoped that it could be in the north-east of the country in order to aid the mission work there. Belfast proved impossible since the bishop attached certain unacceptable conditions to his offer. Dublin was passed over because of the superabundance of religious there already and fears that the Redemptorists might find themselves as little more than confessors to the 'dévots'.[97] The Archbishop of Armagh expressed an interest in having the fathers in his diocese, and a site was inspected in the see-city.[98] Three years later, in 1876, a temporary hospice was established in Dundalk, where the archbishop assured the Redemptorists that the secular clergy would welcome their arrival to supplement the Dominicans and Marists who were already there. McGettigan was over-optimistic, and the Redemptorists had to endure much opposition from the local clergy.[99] This opposition was not reflected by the laity, who welcomed the increase of mission work in the north of Ireland which the new house afforded to the fathers.[100] The presence of the Primate, six bishops, many clergy and hundreds of lay people at the solemn opening of St Joseph's monastery in 1881 testified to 'the esteem in which the Redemptorist Fathers are held by all sections of the Catholics in Ulster'.[101]

A notable conclusion to Coffin's provincialate, and a testimony to the strength, vitality and outward-looking nature of the Province, was provided by the response to a request made as early as 1862 for the Redemptorists to make a foundation in Australia. In February 1882, six Redemptorists

Robert Aston Coffin (1819-1885), first Provincial of the English Province, a position he held for seventeen years until his elevation to the See of Southwark in 1882.

44

left England to make a foundation at Singleton, in the diocese of Ballarat, thereby opening a new chapter in the life of the Congregation.[102]

Within two months, Coffin received news that he had been appointed Bishop of Southwark by Leo XIII, 'an act of special pontifical consideration'.[103] Coffin's name did not appear on the original *terna* of either the bishops or the cathedral chapter. His name was suggested only after an anonymous letter, written in French, purporting to come from several members of the Southwark diocesan clergy, had been received by Propaganda. This letter asked for 'a man who has had experience beyond the diocese, who knows of the progress made elsewhere, and the great needs of the diverse areas [of the diocese]; a practical man who, with zeal and energy, will put new blood into our clergy'. In suggesting that Coffin satisfied the requirements, the letter explained that 'he is already almost a bishop as the chief counsellor of all our bishops, and the intimate friend of the majority of them, especially of His Eminence, Cardinal Manning. He also has the confidence of a good section of the clergy'.[104] Although one newspaper regarded the appointment as designed to have 'a proselytising influence', it is more likely that Manning lay behind the promoting of his candidature.[105]

Coffin's influence continued to be felt by his Redemptorist confrères until his death, three years later. Indeed, he wanted to remain Provincial, which was disallowed, and he moved his episcopal residence to Clapham Common, near to St Mary's. He also made some difficulty about handing over necessary papers to the new Provincial.[106] Reviewing his achievements, his biographer contrasted the state of the Congregation in 1865 and 1882:

> In 1865 the Province had only three houses; now the number has doubled. A novitiate and a studentate in order. The missions and renewals in a flourishing state. Three teams of missioners in England, two in Scotland, and three or four in Ireland, each comprising between two and four fathers working ceaselessly for the most abandoned souls. In the three countries it is the

Congregation which has given the greatest number of retreats to clergy, the bishops, almost without exception, having the greatest confidence in the zeal and prudence of the sons of St Alphonsus.[107]

This general picture of the Institute's well-being was reflected in the leading Catholic national newspaper, which welcomed Coffin's elevation as the seal of approval on his seventeen years as head of the Redemptorists:

There is now scarcely any Order better known in these countries for the excellence of their public missions to the people and for their spiritual influence, exercised unobtrusively, and invited and courted by, rather than obtruded upon, the clergy. A Congregation which is notoriously still in its first fervour, and which confines itself closely to the special work to which it is consecrated, could not fail to win the confidence of the clergy and laity alike.[108]

3

Troubles and division, 1882-1898

Although it would appear that Coffin bequeathed a strong legacy to his successor, Hugh MacDonald, there was much underlying disquiet and disaffection in the Province, which Coffin's departure brought to the surface. It concerned his manner of government and the negative effect this was held to have had upon the life and work of the Institute in Britain and Ireland. One critic assessed that

> there is an almost universal sentiment of discontent among the fathers of the English Province that the Congregation has not done the work offered it by divine Providence. One senses that this diminution in the work of the Congregation has been caused by the manner of administration of this Province for many years by a single and the same Superior, an administration that has had the effect of diminishing the Congregation in terms of the number of subjects, of reducing the Province's financial resources, of discouraging individuals in particular, and in general of obstructing a great deal of good which could have been done for the good of souls.[1]

The result was that 'there was a great deal of suppressed thought and feeling in the Province, which was becoming very dangerous'.[2] It was not, however, so suppressed that the secular clergy did not catch word of it. Among the arguments adduced in the letter of the group of priests in the Southwark diocese requesting Coffin as their new bishop was one which told much about Coffin's public image and provides a clue to the unease of his confrères:

47

> Fr Coffin is already more of a bishop than a Redemptorist. He ceased to work as a missioner a long time ago, and the English Province of this Congregation has felt the effects of this; their work has declined, new vocations are rare, and numerous missions requested by our priests have been continually refused [on the grounds that the Congregation] is too small. A new superior would give a new thrust ('élan') to the Congregation in England, and help it to make the same progress there as all the other religious orders.[3]

The complaints of the Redemptorists about their former Superior's manner of government, about its tone and the directional trends he had initiated, were compounded by the frustration that was felt by his subjects with regard to the unassailable position into which Coffin had manoeuvred himself and the influence he exercised over the Rector Major, whereby he could do as he pleased; to have complained to Rome, it was felt, was not just useless but would have rebounded to the disgrace of the complainant.[4] Consequent upon this was the belief that, as the affairs of the Province were reported to Rome solely by Coffin, the Rector Major saw the Province only through the eyes of his Provincial; all contact with the Roman authorities was blocked, save through Coffin, and he communicated the decisions of Rome to the Province only selectively and partially.[5] Whatever the truth of these complaints, there had been a growing mistrust of, and lack of confidence in, the Provincial which developed into a groundswell of opinion among a large number of his subjects that he had abused his position, through the misuse of power, and that he had ruled despotically rather than authoritatively. Thus, there were accusations that he administered the Province independently of his consultors and the local rectors, destroying any local initiative by concentrating all policy and decision-making in his own hands, and imposing his will on the Province; that he ruled through a chosen band of favourites, mainly fellow-converts, thereby encouraging secrecy and scheming among others; that he employed a system of espionage; that he was ruthless in the suppression of dissident voices; that he was severe and unbending in the application to his subjects of the Rule and Constitutions, whilst lax himself in the keeping of them.[6]

The last criticism was admitted by Coffin,[7] while some of the other accusations were, doubtless, exaggerated; it is difficult, for instance, to draw a sharp line between espionage and that necessary surveillance which was urged on superiors.[8] Coffin's attitude to opposition, real or potential, does, however, tell against him. Individual opponents and difficult characters were summarily removed or edged out of the Province, and any incipient party hostile to the Provincial was speedily quashed. For example, when it was rumoured in 1872 that de Buggenoms was to return to the English Province from the West Indies, to which he had been seconded in 1858, Coffin wrote to Rome in agitation. He pointed out that de Buggenoms and Fr Lans 'are of the old regime, and too much given to secret confidences and, if it is not too harsh a word, to meddle in holy intrigues or mysticism and exaltation of the spirit'.[9] He even refused to allow de Buggenoms to stay at Bishop Eton in 1874 on a return trip to the West Indies because of 'his independent manner of acting, his great imprudence in conversation ... and besides that his tendency to plot in a certain sense'.[10] Whatever his faults, de Buggenoms deserved better than this of the English Provincial, who, one suspects, was motivated by old jealousies.

It was this relentless inability to forgive and accommodate himself to others, to brook no opposition whatsoever, that many of his subjects found so disturbing. Fr Van der Aa, Consultor to Coffin during his vice-provincialate, opposed Coffin on several issues and on the direction in which he was taking the Congregation. Van der Aa was joined in his opposition by other Belgian and Dutch fathers. There may be some truth in Coffin's assertion that his Consultor's objections were all general and difficult to pin down, that he lived in the past, and that he had 'certain fixed ideas about the Congregation, which he has had ever since I knew him, and which are as difficult to understand as they are to remove'.[11] Yet in asking for his removal from England, Coffin claimed that he took no interest in the affairs of the Vice-Province, and that he acted 'as head of a party, and is the model (beau-idéal) of a Redemptorist' to others.[12] He also castigated the other members of Van der Aa's 'party', one of whom complained to Rome that his good name had been traduced by Coffin.[13]

This tendency to slur the character and adequacy as religious of those who opposed him was also evident in his relations with William Plunkett. He was a loyal Irishman, a former army officer and member of the Irish aristocracy who had been a novice with Coffin and was sufficiently regarded in his own country to be considered as a possible coadjutor to the Bishop of Meath in 1864. True, he was somewhat vacillating and indecisive, apt to compromise easily, but he did not deserve the harsh reports which Coffin sent to Rome.[14] The fact that Plunkett was a possible Provincial Superior may have something to do with Coffin's denigration of him. Of Coffin's ploy of trying to pass on to other provinces those subjects who were a nuisance, mention should be made of Frs Hall and Arnoldy. Hall was a very strange character, almost a caricature of an enthusiast, who required very careful handling. He was persuaded of the superiority of his talents, which were not inconsiderable, for he was an immensely popular preacher. Coffin suggested that he would be better 'under another Provincial', and that Canada might find a use for his talents.[15] Fr Arnoldy was an eccentric lector in the studentate who was independently-minded and had a habit of reasoning away any order from a superior which he happened to find burdensome. Coffin did not appreciate this craftiness, accused him of having no practical judgement, refused to keep him with the students and, since he was said to have no talent for the pulpit or the confessional, expressed himself at a loss what to do with him.[16] Arnoldy's removal to the Austrian house of studies, where his peculiar character did not disbar his presence among young Redemptorists, was welcomed by the English Provincial.

Worse, perhaps, than any of his other faults was a fatal flaw in Coffin's character which had far-reaching consequences and put him out of sympathy with the majority of his subjects.

He was said to possess a domineering manner, typical of his nationality and class, allied with a haughtiness and arrogance towards, and prejudice against, foreigners.[17] In an international order, whose English-born members were vastly outnumbered by their continental and Irish confrères, this was disastrous. As early as 1861, Plunkett expressed disquiet at Coffin's Englishness and fear, not only for English-Irish relations, but also that all the foreign members of the Institute would return to the Continent unless there was an improvement.[18] The growing consensus of the Irish fathers that Coffin had no understanding of, still less sympathy for, Ireland and all its problems, generated a strong, suppressed sense of outrage, which was openly voiced in 1882. Once articulated, it grew into a movement for Irish separation within the Province, implying a strong criticism of the previous direction of the Congregation.

To set this in context, it has to be admitted that Coffin's task was not an easy one. He had, in effect, to govern 'two distinct nations';[19] to an Englishman, the Irish could appear as both incorrigible and unruly.[20] Nor should this cause surprise, for, as one Irish father recognised, 'the mischief of centuries cannot be undone'.[21] Coffin was obviously aware of the tense relations between the English and the Irish, both within the Congregation and outside, and of the difficulty for the Irish of abstracting themselves from the problems of their homeland. In recommending Bridgett for the vice-rectorship of Limerick in 1881, for example, he admitted the difficulty of placing there an Englishman 'pure and simple', but one who would sympathise 'much with the Irish in all that they have suffered from the bad and anti-Catholic government of England for three centuries, and [who] would never say a single word to offend the national susceptibilities of our Irish confrères and people'.[22] Equally, he recognised the need to mollify his Irish subjects and to provide signs of his impartiality between nationalities, as much to maintain an overall balance in the Province as to make the Irish feel that they were not excluded from positions of responsibility. Thus, in 1868, he proposed bringing Fr Harbison to Rome as his 'socius', as this would gratify the Irish fathers and help to ease tensions.[23] Ten years later, when appointing a Consultor for Kinnoull, he thought 'especially since the Irish element predominates in the Province, to nominate (nommer) Fr Johnson (Irish) and also to conserve the balance among the nationalities'.[24] Ironically, in view of complaints against himself, Coffin could criticise two of his subjects as 'excessively English',[25] while condemning, in very strong language, 'nationalism and so-called patriotism' as 'false [and] essentially opposed to and utterly destructive of the true spirit of the congregation'; Redemptorists, he argued, should be

> indifferent and supernaturally dead to all distinctions of race, country, political institutions, forms of government, questions of national independence and all other wordly elements, in order that free from these hindrances, savouring as they do, for the most part, of simple worldliness, and of the spirit of the prince of this world, they may be solely and wholly occupied in the things of God and in winning souls to the love and service of their Divine Master.[26]

Yet such sentiments could not repel the overriding impression that Coffin created of undermining the work of the Redemptorists in Ireland by displaying a reluctance to make a second Irish foundation, or to take up any of the various episcopal offers to establish the Redemptorists in their dioceses. In addition, there was his refusal to establish an Irish novitiate, or to have the house of studies in Ireland, and resentment against his supposed discouragement of Irish in favour of English vocations and his consistent promotion of Englishmen to the higher offices in the Province above qualified Irishmen. There was much sadness and exasperation behind the words of an anonymous memorialist:

> The Irish would be only too pleased to help the work in England, scarcely demanding a separate Province, but they believe that Ireland has been neglected and request a change ... Many Irish postulants have been refused by the Provincial; few English vocations are forthcoming;

in a short time the existing fathers will not be able to missionise and, not having replacements, the missions will come to be abandoned, as already the rectors must continually refuse them, and the Congregation will be incapable of existing.[27]

The outcome of such mounting criticism was that the last two decades of the century were filled with the forebodings of fragmentation for the Province, as positions hardened and the call for separation grew louder and more persistent. The natural jealousies and rivalries between the Irish and English members of the Congregation could not be healed; Coffin's provincialate had attempted to conceal them, but he had succeeded only in converting them into an open rift. It took several more years for the inevitably fissiparous consequences of that rift to be conceded and accepted. In the meantime, there was a depressive air over the Congregation's affairs, as this one issue came to dominate more and more the consciousness of the Redemptorists, and a resultant feeling of irreversible decline.

Hugh MacDonald, Provincial for eight years until his elevation to the see of Aberdeen in 1890, was a compromise candidate, being neither English nor Irish.[28] Humble and able, he was a pioneer of missions in the Gaelic-speaking parts of Scotland. More active than his predecessor, he travelled round the Province a good deal and continued to conduct missions. Writing to Mauron in 1885, he reported that:

> I am now for the fourth time on mission since the beginning of the year; perhaps, I do too much in this respect, but there is much to do, and so many of the fathers are ill, that it is difficult to stay at home. But it is also true that my disposition carries me thence, and perhaps, I do not sufficiently resist this temptation![29]

His period of government witnessed a continuing steady increase in the number of missions undertaken by the Province, an increase which the authorities in Rome viewed with contented pleasure: 'This table [the *Elenchus Laborum Apostolorum*] shows truly consoling results, especially with

53

regard to the small number of Fathers which your province can count upon'.[30] Nor was there any diminution in the popular esteem of the Redemptorists. The publication of the life of a beatified Redemptorist, for instance, elicited the press comment that 'the labours of the Redemptorist Fathers are too well known and appreciated by the masses of our people, for should not there exist a deep interest in all that concerns the growth and development of their congregation?'.[31]

One of MacDonald's first acts as Provincial was to respond to the Rector Major's request to establish a Juvenate, similar to that in the French and Dutch Provinces.[32] Intended as a junior seminary, the Juvenate was necessitated 'by the growing need of more subjects, the difficulty of finding young men sufficiently advanced in their studies to meet the requirements of our Constitutions, and uncontaminated by the wickedness of the world'.[33] It opened at Limerick in late 1884 with four boys, and it was hoped to recruit from all parts of Britain and Ireland. In addition to the wide distribution of a printed prospectus, the fathers on mission were urged to look out for youths 'with talent, good health, piety and signs of religious vocation, with a suitable degree of education and instruction'.[34] It was a moderate success; by 1887, there were eighteen boys, 'without room for a single other'[35], and of the hundred or so boys who passed through it in the first sixteen years of its existence, many went on to enter the Redemptorist novitiate.[36] Even here, however, there was a problem; nearly all the juvenists were Irish, and few English boys could be attracted.[37] The increasing consciousness and official acceptance of national sentiment's controlling force, which this one-sided recruitment further emphasised, was also voiced by the novice-master in his report for 1889.[38]

Although MacDonald could rejoice at the large amount of sickness and trouble in the Province, because, he believed, a more interior spirit was thereby fostered,[39] his final assessment of the Province must have made depressing reading in Rome. While noting the continued demand for missions, and the generally high estimate of the Redemptorists and their labours, he commented also on the declining quality of the mission work and the increase of obstacles to it, on the lack of zeal among the fathers for study and prayer, and the contentment with 'ordinary piety', on the neglect of the Rule and Constitutions, and, above all, on the predominance of exterior work over the interior life of both individuals and communities. Among the serious deficiencies which he noted was the lack of sermon preparation: 'At the beginning the young Fathers are industrious, but after several years, and having prepared the instructions and several sermons and having passably acquitted themselves in the confessional, they pay no more attention to perfecting their sermons'.[40] What linked all these observations was an overriding sense of jadedness about the Congregation, its members and work.

MacDonald was succeeded by another Scot, John Bennett, whom the former Provincial had described as 'the most capable Redemptorist in our Province'.[41] His four-year term of office saw no change in the discrepancy between the outward success and apparent well-being of the Congregation, masking much interior turmoil. There was, for example, building work at Clapham, Bishop Eton and Kinnoull, which bespoke prosperity. Yet, in view of later events, there was something almost perverse in Rome's opinion that 'an increasingly rich future is reserved to it. May the number of your subjects and of your houses ever increase, and at the same time may the good spirit [of religious observance] be maintained and perfected more and more'.[42] Bennett certainly took a more independent line of Rome than either of his predecessors and he wrote sparingly to his superiors; when he did, he was capable of criticism.[43]

In 1893, Mauron called the only General Chapter of his rector-majorate. Having died before it met in April 1894, the delegates' first task was to elect Mauron's successor, Matthias Raus. The calling of a General Chapter was a signal for the majority of the Irish fathers to demand a measure of self-government and autonomy. Talk of a separate Irish Province, or at least a Vice-Province, was widespread, and the Irish Capitular at the Chapter was charged to seek the necessary authorisation for some kind of division. The arguments were adduced afresh by the Irish fathers of the previous neglect of Ireland by the Province's superiors and they spoke openly of their desire to work in their native land. To these dissident voices was added a rising chorus of English protests, notably that the strong Irish flavour of the Institute discouraged English vocations.[44] Although the General Chapter seems to have acceded to the Irish demands, there were fears that a full division would seriously weaken the Congregation in England. Following a visitation of the Province by the Irish Consultor-General, John Magnier, which revealed some disturbing trends in the Province with regard to the conduct of missions and the spiritual qualities of the fathers, Raus decided against the creation of even an Irish Vice-Province.[45] Arguing that it would not be in the interests of either the Irish or English houses, which would both suffer if immediate division were effected, Raus urged charity on his subjects, while assuring them that the matter was still open. He also ordered the establishment of a Juvenate in England.[46] At the same time, Edmund Vaughan was recalled from Australia to take charge of the Province.

Raus's motives would appear to have sprung from the desire to see the Congregation strengthened in both countries before a division could be contemplated. His appointment of Vaughan as Provincial, an Englishman who was known to disapprove strongly of a division, was interpreted as Rome having set its face against Irish aspirations. It would be truer to say that the Rector Major refused to be rushed into a decision which he knew would have to be made one day. The stream of letters from Ireland, sometimes from a whole community, left him in no doubt of that. When Vaughan pleaded the impossibility of an English Juvenate, he was told to establish it forthwith at Perth and to order the teaching of Irish at Teignmouth.[47] At the same time, the Rector Major sanctioned the founding of one, or possibly two, new houses in Ireland, one of which could serve as a future house of studies. Several proposals for suitable sites were made, but they all came to nothing, either because of local opposition from the clergy, or because of the conditions imposed by the bishops.[48] More promising was the offer of the newly-consecrated Bishop of Down and Connor to establish the Redemptorists in Belfast, where they had been giving regular missions since 1871. The bishop wanted them in the Falls Road area of the city, where there were thirty thousand Catholics and insufficient church accommodation and priests. He proposed to evict the Bon Secours Sisters from their convent to make way for the Redemptorists; their refusal to move out in favour of the Redemptorists the bishop thought 'cranky'.[49] On 1 November 1896, the Redemptorists moved into Clonard House, where a chapel was opened to the public, as a prelude to the building of a temporary church in the following year. The new foundation was welcomed by the secular clergy, and the people who flocked to the temporary chapel 'kissed the habits of the fathers and, raising their hands to heaven, thank[ed] God that they had lived to see the day when we came amongst them'.[50] The search for another house continued, and in 1897 an Irish novitiate was established at Dundalk.

In the light of the new foundation in Belfast, it seemed that the day was drawing near when the Irish houses would form a separate Province. John Bennett believed that division 'is the only way out of our present troubles. There will never be any peace 'till it comes, and the present state of uncertainty is so bad for all that the sooner it comes the better'.[51] He believed that even those who had been against division in the past were now accepting its inevitability. Not so Fr Vaughan, however, who concurred with the description of a division as 'unnatural, inequitable and injurious to the Congregation and the work of souls', although admitting that it was

> the desire of the Irish portion of the Province — a desire which some years ago was that of a very few, has become within the last three or four *general*, if not almost universal, [resulting in] a loosening of the bonds of Fraternal Union and even Charity, that it would seem impossible to restore peace and mutual confidence in the Province.[52]

At the same time, he proved difficult and obstructive in furthering the objective of division. He argued that, as the great part of the Catholic population in England and Scotland was Irish, it would be wrong for the Irish fathers to abandon 'their fellow-countrymen in exile', especially as it was often claimed that the English priests were unsuited to Irish congregations. In addition, he pointed out that for over thirty years the Irish students had been supported by the patrimony of the English members of the Congregation, and he had never thought that

> some of those who owed their education in the Congregation entirely to the contribution of the English Fathers would later be the most forward in demanding a separation, or declare as one did recently that he thought it an injustice that the Irish Fathers should have to spend their strength on Missions in England.[53]

Bennett reported to Rome that 'we are woefully disappointed in Fr Provincial. He seems to be much harder and [more] unsympathetic than ever. He freezes people when they go to him for anything'.[54] Widespread unrest in the Province was so intense that he feared 'a breaking out like that of the Paulists', and asked for a general visitation of the Province.[55] This was granted, and the following year (1897), Fr Schwarz, one of the Consultors-General, undertook this visitation. In September, he held an extraordinary Provincial Consultation at Clapham to discuss details of the division. Although there was disagreement over the details, especially financial details, the fact of division was questioned by no one; even Vaughan grudgingly accepted its inevitability. When Schwarz informed the community at Clonard a month later of the division, the news was greeted as 'a much desired event', a sentiment echoed in the other Irish houses.[56] In January 1898, the deed of separation was drawn up, and the Irish Province came into existence on 1 April, with Andrew Boylan as the first Provincial. The Australian houses were constituted a Vice-Province under the Irish Provincial.[57] In the Irish Province, as a whole, there were fifty priests, fourteen lay brothers and twenty-nine students.

The much-reduced English Province, with thirty-six priests, twenty-three lay brothers and nine clerical students, was the smallest in the Congregation. One immediate result of the division was Vaughan's replacement by John Bennett and an attempt to counter the demoralisation that was inevitably felt among the priests and brothers. The presence of Irish students enabled the Studentate to continue for another two years, but the English Province could not maintain it once the Irish had been removed. Teignmouth was abandoned in 1900 and the English students were transferred to the Austrian house of studies at Mautern. New foundations were sought as a means of re-establishing morale and of galvanising the fathers into activity. Bishop's Stortford in Hertfordshire, Kingswood in Bristol and Monkwearmouth in Co. Durham were the chosen places for new Redemptorist houses. All of these foundations involved parochial cures, so that hope for the future lay in a paradoxical return to the origins of the Congregation in England; the early fathers had undertaken parochial work in order to establish themselves as a prelude to their proper apostolic labours. It is for the historian of the Institute in the twentieth century to follow the progress of these and of other foundations made in the early years of the new century. At the close of the old century, the return to parochial work betokened a weariness, a crisis of confidence and uncertainty for the future. The Congregation in England was described as being 'in a fossil state'.[58] It was a cause of grave concern to the Rector Major, who thought that the English Province was 'more needy than the Irish'.[59] Uncertainty lay in the future, but the past, if not quite glorious, was a source of consolation to the fathers. Their inspiration and source of renewal and hope was the same as that of their saint-founder who had told his early followers, 'Do not have any doubts (non dubitare); the Congregation will continue until the day of judgement because it is not my work but the work of God'.[60] If this was not sufficient, his spiritual sons had only to meditate upon, and apply to themselves, the motto, which Alphonsus had chosen for his Congregation: Copiosa apud Eum Redemptio (With Him there is plenteous Redemption).

4

The bishops
and the secular clergy

It had been the fear of the Redemptorist authorities in Rome that the discord in the early years between members of the Congregation and the English Hierarchy would blight any hope of future good relations, on which progress depended.[1] Conflict between bishops and religious was centuries old, revolving around the inevitable clash of their respective interests. The bishops' efforts to extend their ordinary jurisdiction presaged conflict with the religious orders, desirous to preserve intact, and live according to, their rules and constitutions, jealous to maintain all their rights and privileges and determined to take full advantage of papal grants of exemption by asserting their independence of episcopal control. Over and above all this was not a little human jealousy and obfuscation, together with difficulties arising from the clash of personalities. Relations in England were further complicated by the country's missionary status in the eyes of the Sacred Congregation 'de Propaganda Fide', and the corresponding probing and testing of the full extent and limits of their respective rights and powers by the bishops and religious orders. In the absence of a codified system of canon law, it was left to provincial synods to promulgate the disciplinary decrees of the Council of Trent and subsequent decisions of the Sacred Congregation, and to adapt them to contemporary local conditions. But that was to invite the obstruction of the religious orders at those points where their interests were threatened. Several problems arose which were not settled until the Apostolic Constitution *Romanos Pontifices* (1881) conclusively established the relations between the bishops and regulars in England and Scotland and resolved the vexed questions which had been thrown up in the previous thirty years.

The Redemptorists were aware of the ambiguity of the position of the religious orders vis-à-vis the bishops, and were drawn into the wider controversy. What is interesting is the small part they played in the conflict which forms one of the themes of nineteenth-century Catholic history. Partly, this was because many of the disputed issues were of little or no concern to the Congregation, and its members were not involved in the conflicts that arose. Largely, it was because the Redemptorist authorities determined, after the early troubles, to cultivate good relations with the episcopate by avoiding direct confrontation; it was felt that the Congregation would benefit more by gaining the bishops' goodwill than if it were seen to obstruct their authority, and the mission work (depending, as it did, on episcopal sympathy and favour) would correspondingly prosper. The confident tone of the Rector Major's response to the Secretary of Propaganda, regarding various questions ('dubbi') raised by the English and Scottish bishops, is testimony to the success of such a policy. He declared 'with a grateful heart' ('con grato animo') that the Congregation enjoyed the goodwill of the Archbishop of Westminster and of all the other English and Scottish bishops and was on the best of terms with them ('e sta con essi in ottime relazioni'). These prelates, he continued, freely availed themselves of the Redemptorists' services in giving missions to the people and retreats to the clergy, to ecclesiastical colleges and to religious communities. And he concluded with the olympian assurance that the present conflict between the episcopate and the regulars *(sic)* did not interest the Congregation in England and Scotland, nor in any other country of Europe.[2]

It was one of Coffin's achievements that he was able to win the confidence of the majority of the episcopate and to establish good relations with all the bishops wherever the Redemptorists laboured. This was achieved in part by a blandiloquent submissiveness. His letters to individual bishops, even though they may have been his penitents or friends, were marked by a reserved respect,[3] and he strove to create the impression that the Redemptorists were ever eager to be of greatest service to the bishops.[4] Creating a favourable impression, so that any sense of incipient rivalry was dissipated and the bishops well disposed to the Congregation, was also achieved by acquiescing in things that might be irritating or burdensome in themselves, but which did not impinge seriously on the Redemptorists' exemption or religious character. For example, although forbidden by the Rule to be ordinary confessors to other religious, it was undertaken 'as a special favour to the old Bishop of Plymouth' for the Benedictine nuns at Teignmouth, and the Clapham fathers were told to accept such a position in the case of some German nuns in London, if the Cardinal persisted in an earlier request.[5] Two years earlier (1886), the Scottish bishops had asked to hold their provincial synod at Kinnoull, and this was agreed to, because 'this charitable act will strengthen the good relations that exist between our Fathers and the Scottish prelates'.[6] Even the invasion of the enclosure by the bishop and his clergy was tolerated at Dundalk, despite the fathers' initial disquiet.[7]

There were, of course, dangers in apparently meek accommodation to the bishops' will. The Redemptorists could appear as pliant agents of the episcopate. As early as 1861, Richard Simpson regarded them as tools of the 'clique' which Wiseman had gathered round himself.[8] Coffin was aware that too close a relationship with the bishops, especially Manning, whom Coffin described as 'a true friend of the Congregation,[9] could easily draw the Congregation into the machinations of ecclesiastical politics.[10] On the whole, however, the use made of the Redemptorists by the bishops was regarded as a positive contribution to the work and progress of the Congregation. Thus, the use of individual Redemptorists as episcopal 'troubleshooters' was welcomed, such as the Bishop of Beverley's request in 1862 for Coffin to reform a difficult community of nuns in York,[11] or that of a Scottish bishop who called in the Redemptorists to salvage a mission station which the resident priest wanted to abandon as hopeless.[12] This availability consolidated the reputation of the Congregation and the good impressions created by its mission and retreat work. Bishop Goss, who made his own pre-consecration retreat at Bishop Eton, regarded the Redemptorists as the best spiritual guides for his priests; if one of them made a sincere retreat under their care, he believed, then his spiritual life would be healthy.[13] This opinion was shared by Goss's successor, who had confessed at Bishop Eton for twenty-two years prior to his elevation and was himself a Redemptorist Oblate, and who said that the fathers worked in the Liverpool diocese 'with truly the greatest fruit for religion and piety', the like of which he did not apply to the other religious working in the diocese.[14] Archbishop Cullen welcomed a Redemptorist retreat to his clergy in 1864 as 'one of the best retreats he had heard' and as 'the only retreat which can truly be called a retreat since he came to Ireland'.[15] Similarly, the enthusiasm for Redemptorist missions, which the Bishop of Cork expressed in 1854,[16] continued to be shown throughout the century, and was occasionally conveyed to Rome; Bishop Grant's enthusiastic reports to Propaganda of Redemptorist missions in 1862, 1863, 1865 and 1868 were echoed as late as 1890 by the Archbishop of Armagh and the Bishop of Limerick.[17] The Bishop of Ferns would have only Redemptorist missions in his diocese and the Bishop of Kilmore stated in 1868 that of all the missions in his diocese, those of the Redemptorists were easily the best ('facile princeps').[18]

If the Redemptorists managed to secure the high regard of the bishops by the quality of their apostolic labours and their deferential manner, this also reflected the measure of success with which they projected their self-image upon the episcopate. It did not mean that the Redemptorists were wholly creatures of the bishops, unwilling or unable to take a contrary line. When Bishop Goss asked the fathers at Bishop Eton for a detailed report of their labours and for an assessment of the priests in the parishes where they had undertaken missions, it was recognised that this 'would undoubtedly end by the exclusion of the missioners from every parish';[19] the request was refused, and the bishop apologised.[20] Nor was the

Redemptorists' accommodation without an eye to the advantages that would accrue to them. When considering the appointment of a new Rector of Limerick in 1871, for example, Coffin advised that it would be a good idea to leave Fr Harbison on the missions, because it was in that capacity that 'he is so highly esteemed by the bishops and does honour to the Congregation'.[21] Although they managed to create a strong psychological impression of unity and concord with the bishops, the Redemptorists were well aware that it did not do to become too closely identified with them, and that a healthy distance was necessary. This awareness was neatly captured by Fr Douglas in 1879, shortly after the restoration of the Scottish Hierarchy. Writing of the decision to make Dunkeld a see-city in preference to Perth, as had originally been mooted, he noted that 'it will be better for us at Kinnoull to have [the bishop] at a little distance'.[22]

More importantly, whenever the position of the Institute or the work of the fathers was threatened, the Redemptorists were as jealous of their privileges, and as active in obstructing the bishops, as any other religious order. It was the determination to live according to the Rule, and to preserve their distinct identity, that had occasioned the withdrawal from the mission stations and chaplaincy work in 1850, even at the expense of incurring the bishops' wrath. Some bishops were initially surprised at the extent and scope of the privileges which the Redemptorists claimed, and needed to be persuaded of their authenticity.[23] The vehemence with which episcopal interference was resisted when it seemed to threaten the Redemptorists' privileged position, was evident in the Vicar General's remarks about a privilege which Bishop Grant acquired in Rome for the Clapham fathers in 1853, a privilege the Redemptorists already enjoyed:

> It is evident that the concession which Monsignor the Bishop believes he has obtained for us, far from being a favour, would be rather a disfavour, a punishment, an odious exception to the common rule ('du droit commun'), against which we must defend ourselves with all force.[24]

The strength of Smetana's words is surprising in view of Grant's expressed favour of the Redemptorists and his benign intentions. Yet it provides an insight into the embittered attitude which lay beneath the cultured affability of surface appearances. Indeed, problems to do with privileges merged into the wider question of the Redemptorists' status as an order exempt from episcopal authority and interference, and goes some way to explaining the acerbity of Smetana's remarks.[25]

At the first Provincial Synod of Westminster (1852), the bishops decreed that all mission and public churches served by regulars were subject to episcopal visitation, and asked the superiors of the religious orders to act cordially with them in the appointment and removal of subjects from such churches.[26] In so decreeing, reference was made to a decision of Propaganda, dated 30 September 1848, regarding the mission stations in China served by religious, in which the care of souls was said to be undertaken not only 'ex caritate', but even 'ex justitia'.[27] As the only community of male religious in the diocese of Southwark prior to 1857 serving a parochial district, albeit from charity and temporarily for the sole purpose of the cure of souls ('ex caritate et temporarie solum modo curam animarum'),[28] the Redemptorists were drawn into the protest that arose among the religious orders over the Synod's decree, when Wiseman claimed for Grant the same rights in the parish and the same obligations on the part of the fathers as would apply in the case of diocesan priests.[29] Smetana made a separate protest on behalf of his subjects both to the Cardinal and to Propaganda, pleading the demands of the Rule, which forbade the Redemptorists to undertake the cure of souls, and the extraordinary circum-stances and conditions in which, and under which, the Clapham mission had been accepted.[30] A temporary solution to the problem was found by side-stepping the issue of principle and appointing a secular priest to look after the parish. This arrangement lasted until 1857. The following year, the bishop re-opened the question of the basis on which the Redemptorists held the cure of souls, and Coffin wrote to Rome for clarification.[31] What is surprising about the ensuing correspondence is the absence of mutual misunderstanding and acrimony which soured the relations between bishops and religious in the second half of the century. Indeed, Grant stressed 'how grateful I am to the Fathers, and how anxious I am to preserve their privileges'.[32] When Coffin informed the bishop that the Redemptorist authorities in Rome had suggested that the Clapham fathers should withdraw from any parochial work, Grant was sufficiently worried to answer that 'if any other plan can be derived to reconcile your Rule and parochial work, I should be happy to further its adoption if all agree upon it'.[33] The outcome was a formal declaration that the Redemptorists held the parish and the cure of souls 'non quidem ex justitia, sed ex solo titulo caritatis cum obligatione tamen servandi ex quae praescripta inveniuntur in Caput XXVII Primae Synodi Provincialis'.[34]

This settled the principle in the Redemptorists' favour. They were thus saved from the arguments surrounding *Romanos Pontifices*; when it was issued, Mauron confidently informed Coffin that it changed 'nothing in our situation. The quasi-parochial district of Clapham is and will be served by the Community "titulo caritatis". Not being missionary rectors (curés missionaires), as such, we cannot be made to attend the [diocesan] Synod'.[35] After 1859, the Redemptorists made sure that the episcopal approbation of subsequent foundations contained the phrase 'without the ordinary cure of souls', according to the Rule of Benedict XIV; at Kinnoull, for instance, a formal document was obtained, whereby the bishop agreed that the house was undertaken strictly according to the Constitutions, and that the Redemptorists were free to follow their Rule 'and could devote themselves to giving missions and Spiritual Exercises at home and abroad in our Vicariate'.[36] These approbations were produced whenever the bishop sought to overstep what the Redemptorists considered was the due exercise of his authority, as happened at Kinnoull in 1889 and at Clapham in 1892.[37] The Redemptorists' exemption, as Mauron had pointed out to Coffin, extended to attendance at the diocesan synods and theological conferences. Here again, the practice was to insist upon a recognition of their exemption, but also to compromise by a gracious token attendance. This solution was adopted as early as 1853 at Liverpool, although the appointment of Fr Lans as Synodical Examiner was forbidden by the Provincial.[38] Douglas advised Coffin to stay away from the Southwark diocesan synod, 'as it establishes always more clearly the fact that we are not parish priests of Clapham'.[39] The wisdom of this advice was proved in 1878 when, following Coffin's attendance the previous year, Bishop Butt questioned the exemption from attendance of the Provincial and his subjects.[40] Butt tried again in 1888, pleading that the fathers now came under the provisions of *Romanos Pontifices,* but he was again repulsed on the grounds that they were not ordinary pastors and thus subject to its provisions. Similarly, the Bishop of Plymouth's request to attend his synod in 1878 and 1895 was politely, but firmly, refused.[41]

There was even more reluctance to attend the theological conferences, since the Redemptorists held their own domestic conferences. On the whole this was recognised by the bishops, although there were exceptions. Cullen, for instance, regarded the fathers' attendance in Ireland as necessary so that a united policy could be effected with regard to secret societies.[42] While admitting the need for guidance on this subject, Coffin resisted the Cardinal's attempts to get a ruling from Propaganda in his favour.[43] Unlike attendance at the diocesan synods, the Redemptorist authorities consistently refused to compromise on this issue, with one notable exception.[44]

That exception concerned Bishop Butler, Auxiliary of Limerick, whose relations with the Redemptorists deserve to be examined at length, for they are illustrative of the Redemptorists' handling of difficulties. Butler was determined to exert his authority as soon as he was consecrated, and the early years of his episcopate were marked by a series of trials for the Redemptorists, which tested their usual equanimity with the bishops to the limit. Butler began by summoning the Limerick fathers to the diocesan theological conferences. The advice of Rome was that the Rector of Limerick should inform the bishop that, although not bound to attend the conferences, the fathers had no objection to attending from time to time in order to give pleasure to his lordship. This was clearly an attempt to temporise: 'If we can pass the matter with good grace, it will be a gain ... it is clear the less such questions are brought out, the better for us'.[45] The bishop, however, was not so easily satisfied and made known his intention to take up the matter with the relevant authority in Rome, which he was soon to visit. Coffin wrote to Mauron, urging him to counter-lobby in the corridors of Propaganda in order to forestall the bishop's manoeuvre. At the same time, he warned that 'we must be prepared any day for a Crusade'.[46] The Rector Major took the opportunity of the bishop's stay in Rome to woo him:

> The Rector Major has had two *firm* interviews with Dr Butler, which he hopes will contribute to the peace of the ff at Limerick ... [and urges you] to satisfy the Bishop's desires in all that is conformable with our order, and to treat him invariably with deference, not disputing with him on any question.[47]

Thus, although the Limerick fathers were advised to go to four or five of the bishop's conferences a year, it was as much to forestall him taking further action with the Congregation of Bishops and Regulars as a desire for genuine compromise.

The Redemptorists had misjudged their man if they thought his appetite had been satisfied. The new Redemptorist church in Limerick was soon to be solemnly opened and Butler began to express himself in proprietorial terms over it, giving instructions for the order of service and the choice of preacher. Coffin felt that the Rector, Fr Plunkett, was being too weak with the bishop and counselled a firmer line, at the same time ordering him to defer the opening of the church and to inform Butler of this, without giving any reason. In an uncharacteristic outburst, Coffin highlighted the issues at stake:

> I fear we are gradually and yet more surely slipping into the hands of Dr Butler, forfeiting our independent position as a Religious Order, and creating difficulties for

ourselves and for our successors from which years and years may not release us ... I will never consent, for the honour of the Congregation, for the peace of our successors, and for my own conscience's sake, to be his trainbearer ... our position as Redemptorists is at stake, and our religious liberty endangered.[48]

Tempers were now frayed, and Butler continued to show himself a determined and potentially dangerous adversary: expressing his aversion to the non-Irish fathers and the dependence of the Limerick house on England; making trouble over the clergy retreat in the house, calling in Bishop Moriarty of Kerry to conduct it instead of the Redemptorists; forbidding the fathers to hear cases of reserved sins in their church or in the diocese; prohibiting them from blessing and distributing the brown scapular.[49] All this represented the most concerted and sustained attack made upon the Redemptorists of the English Province by a bishop in the whole of the nineteenth century. When Coffin remonstrated to Mauron, he was told to put up with the vexations, though if anything was demanded by the bishop which conflicted with the Rule and Constitutions, Coffin was to advise the bishop that the matter would have to be referred to his superiors.[50] This meek and submissive attitude defused the mushrooming tension between the two parties and, in less than three years, the bishop restored the right to give absolution in cases of reserved sin as a mark of his confidence in the Redemptorists, and Coffin could report that Butler was now calling him 'Father Provincial', and not just 'Coffin' as hitherto.[51] Thenceforth, there were no serious ruptures between Butler and the Redemptorists in the remaining twenty years of his episcopate.

The clear lesson of this episode was that patience, rather than the abrasive assertion of rights, eventually won the day. Although as determined as any other group of religious to preserve their independence, the Redemptorists preserved principle by proceeding cautiously, with patience and moderation, and so avoided alienating the bishops. Throughout the century, the relevant officials were busy in Rome extending and confirming the Redemptorists' privileges,

Thomas Edward Bridgett (1829-1889). One of the first English Redemptorists, and like Coffin, an Oxford convert. He was a prodigious writer and pioneer of the apostolate of the pen.

thus providing the necessary armour for any stand against the bishops. This was very much a last resort, and it says much for the Redemptorist authorities that they resisted the temptation to strive for pyrrhic victories in the short-term at the expense of winning the overall contest.

It is more difficult to assess the relations between the Redemptorists and the secular clergy as a whole; the fragmentary nature of the evidence, comprising mainly letters from individual priests and mission reports which cannot be used to construct general theories, makes any assessment both tentative and impressionistic. Clerical jealousy between religious and seculars was traditional, with the seculars resenting both the privileged position of the regulars, which enabled them to elude the burdensome nature of episcopal authority, and the prima donna-ish behaviour of many religious which attracted the laity and encouraged odious comparison between the two groups.

The Redemptorists were, of course, sensitive to the seculars' touchiness and the need to proceed cautiously whenever they might be thought to be encroaching on the seculars' territory. When there were plans to build a new German Chapel in London, de Buggenoms asked Wiseman to launch an appeal in his name, 'because if it were made in our name with the approbation of your Eminence only, it would raise many objections and excite the antipathies on the part of many who [loath?] our name and that of the Jesuits, and would say that this appeal is intended only to promote our Establishment in London'.[52] Equally, the danger of good relations with the episcopate could easily excite the seculars' suspicions; hence, the swift and vehement opposition to episcopal suggestions that the Redemptorists spy on the seculars.[53] It took a long time, and much tact, to break down hostility. At St Patrick's, Soho in 1861, for instance, where the Redemptorists had worked from an early date, the priests were still 'cold and indifferent, only seeing the missioners when they met in the sacristy, and finding more occasions of censure than approbation'.[54] Two years earlier, before the first clergy retreat in the Limerick house, the bishop wrote to say that the clergy were 'jealous of the great name you have among the people; they accuse you of being too liberal and easy in your treatment of great sinners, and too severe in your remarks and your doctrine of the duties of secular priests'.[55] In the face of such reactions, the Redemptorists could merely persevere, while attempting to remove any cause of friction, and try to win over the secular priests through being friendly but reserved, dignified but deferential, and so avoid any criticism. These were the behavioural qualities that were repeatedly urged upon the fathers during the missions by their superiors.

More persistently difficult, as the above example from Limerick illustrates, were the relations with the diocesan clergy where the Redemptorists had a house with an attached public church. Because of the indulgences attached to many of the privileges they could confer, the genuine popularity of Redemptorist preaching, and of their confraternities, and the high liturgical standards, lay people were inevitably drawn to Redemptorist churches in large numbers. This often meant a corresponding decline in surrounding churches served by seculars, and a consequent loss of income, as well as popular esteem and prestige. At Clapham there were no churches with which to compete in the vicinity, although as the century wore on, beginning in 1866, new parishes were carved out of the district originally served by the Redemptorists. A letter from the end of the century suggests that there was some rivalry between the Redemptorists and the local clergy as a result of the new arrangements.[56] On the whole, however, there is little to indicate that the secular priests felt either belittled or undermined by the presence of the Redemptorists; it may be the case that by serving a parish some of the criticism which might have been expected from the secular clergy was mitigated.[57] At Limerick, the secular clergy had originally opposed the Redemptorist foundation; when complaints against the fathers continued, Bishop Ryan defended them by saying, 'I think the Fathers know better than you what they ought to do'.[58] When a confraternity was begun in the church, the director was careful to ensure that the members continued to attend their parish churches. In Liverpool, there is no evidence of relations between the Redemptorists and other clergy, although the enthusiasm of Bishops Goss and O'Reilly may have muted the seculars' criticism. At Kinnoull, the isolated position of the house outside the town did not threaten the town clergy's interest, or provide any spirit of competition. Similarly, at Teignmouth, the smallness of the public chapel did not menace the diocesan clergy, who welcomed the foundation.[59]

At Dundalk, it is possible to get a clearer picture of clerical jealousy and opposition, and to analyse its depth. The archbishop had reported that the secular clergy were 'not unfriendly' to a Redemptorist establishment in the town, and did not anticipate 'any murmuring against your Foundation'.[60] However, the opposition of the clergy, not only of Dundalk, but also of the greater part of County Louth, was both strong and constant. Fr McCann, Administrator of the parish church of St Patrick, expressed eloquently the reason for this clerical opposition: 'Unless those who have to render an account to God for the souls of their flock have a paramount influence in a parish, there cannot be order, and consequently there will not be real piety'.[61] Misgivings that the Redemptorists' presence would undermine the influence and authority of the secular clergy were heightened by the sense of unfair competition which the seculars now felt. Arguing that the Redemptorists would inevitably draw folk away from St Patrick's and the other churches, even though the Redemptorists had offered to have their public Mass at an early hour, McCann complained bitterly that 'those who come to a feast of Rhetoric in the morning, will scarcely have a stomach for our dull homilies at noon'. The upshot was that the Redemptorists were ignored completely by the secular clergy for over five years; the first time that any of them even replied to the many invitations to attend functions in the monastery was in 1883.[62] The Redemptorist authorities, as ever, counselled caution and the avoidance of anything that could aggravate hostility, while expressing confidence that the secular clergy had given 'proofs of a really bad spirit and a block-headed ignorance (une sotte ignorance)', which would lose them the confidence of the people.[63]

The vast majority of the secular clergy knew of the Redemptorists merely by repute and what they read of them in the Catholic newspapers; it was only in the course of their apostolic labours that direct contact was made. Whenever the fathers preached a successful mission, the local clergy were both gratified by the results and favourably disposed to the Redemptorists. A small mission in Warwick Street Chapel, London, in 1856 for example, was deemed to have given 'great satisfaction to the clergy, and has caused a favourable opinion of our missions'.[64] This was repeated elsewhere and had a cumulative effect in establishing the high opinion of the Redemptorists among the clergy. It also helped to further the work of the missions. Thus, a successful mission at Fort William in 1874, it was held, 'will persuade neighbouring parish priests to ask for missions'.[65] Missions could also convert those who were otherwise opposed to the Congregation; for instance, the Vicar General of Dundee had been so disenchanted with missions given by others that he was hostile to the Redemptorists when they came to conduct a mission in St Mary's in 1867. He was sufficiently impressed with their labours to support the possibility of a Redemptorist foundation in the district, and Coffin reported that he and the other clergy were 'very well disposed in our favour; they have asked for missions … and they urge us greatly not to defer the establishment of the Congregation in their country'.[66] There were those who felt that the Redemptorists did more good than any other missionary order. At Leamington, Warwickshire in 1866, the priest said that the missioners of no other order produced such fruit, and the parish priest of St Chad's, Manchester in 1862 compared the Redemptorists' assiduity in the confessional with that of other missioners, and concluded that 'they not only made plenty of work, but did it'.[67] Bishop Herbert Vaughan found that on asking the clergy at the end of a large general mission in the churches of Manchester, 'he finds it the general opinion that *our* missioners do their work more thoroughly than any others'.[68] In expressing their thanks for a mission, few priests can have gone to the lengths of those in St Mary's, Hartlepool in 1863, who 'bade adieu to the Fathers with abundance of tears, kissing their hands and humbly on their knees soliciting their blessing'.[69] There were, however, many who were stimulated 'to new earnestness in the discharge of our duty' by the Redemptorists' labours.[70]

The status of the Redemptorists as the spiritual sons and heirs of St Alphonsus was an added advantage in that they were associated from the mid-1850s with the successful attempts to establish the dominance of the saint's moral theology. As early as 1849, Wiseman asked Fr de Held to take part in clergy conferences in order that the priests might gain a correct and familiar knowledge of Alphonsus's moral theology and thus be led to a more professional and disciplined approach to their work in the confessional.[71] The Redemptorists were also said to have been instrumental in helping to dispel the spirit of Gallicanism which was supposed to infect St Edmund's, Ware, Ushaw and Maynooth.[72] Thereafter, those who had been trained on Alphonsian manuals had a reverence for the Congregation's founder which overflowed to his sons. The Redemptorists managed to influence seminarians through retreats, and this was also the instrument through which they sought to continue and expand that influence. Throughout Britain and Ireland between 1850 and 1900, the Redemptorists conducted over six hundred retreats for clergy and seminarians, a figure unsurpassed by any other religious order.

Retreat work, as part of the Redemptorist apostolate, was of equal importance with the work of the missions since they depended for their effectiveness not only upon the sympathy and cooperation of the secular clergy but also upon a shared zeal and apostolic fervour. Although recognising the goodness of the four priests at St Joseph's, Liverpool in 1865, the Redemptorist Chronicler observed that 'there is a total lack of that energy, system and united effort, which would be desirable and absolutely necessary to effect and keep up any good commensurate at all with the needs of so great and such a population'.[73] Retreats were one possible remedy of such defects.

The object of a Redemptorist retreat was to share a priestly ideal, to give priests a sense of their dignity and the value of their work in order to stimulate in them a missionary zeal. Thus, Fr Bridgett told his retreatants that their principal purpose was not to set themselves right with God by a good confession, nor to learn anything new about their duties (although both these things might be a result of the retreat), but 'to stir up the grace that is in us by virtue of our ordination ... to renew our ecclesiastical spirit'.[74] This he defined as 'being every inch a priest', cultivating a love and esteem for their vocation, with all its demands, performing their pastoral tasks with a zest, an enthusiasm, which was not of obligation.[75] This was in conformity with what St Alphonsus had set out in his *Selva*, in which he outlined a priestly ideal, for which the clergy were encouraged to strive.[76] In addition, retreats attempted to raise standards among the clergy by impressing upon them 'the spirit of sacrifice, the necessity of Ecclesiastical Science, and a spirit of recollection and prayer and union with God'.[77] Thus a standard feature of Redemptorist retreats, in addition to the series of meditations and instructions on the dignity, sanctity, duties and dangers of the priesthood, was the discussion of moral cases and the practice of liturgical rubrics, with a view to ensuring high standards in conformity with Roman norms.

The large number of Redemptorist retreats to clergy is striking evidence of the confidence placed in the Congregation by bishops and clergy alike, and contributed much to good relations. Following a retreat to the clergy of the Westminster diocese, Cardinal Manning wrote to the conductor, 'O Father, you have made me and my clergy so happy in our vocation'.[78] Many who were hostile to the Congregation were converted to it by a clergy retreat. The Limerick clergy, who were suspicious of the Redemptorists before their first retreat in 1859, were so pleased afterwards that they asked to come again, while the parish priest of Ballingarry was so well known as an enemy of the Congregation, mocking and ridiculing the fathers, that he felt compelled to record his reversal of opinion in writing.[79] In the early years, retreats were also useful in converting priests to the idea of a mission; after a retreat at St Peter's College, Wexford in 1853 for fifty priests, Fr Prost received several requests for missions.[80] The reason for the popularity of Redemptorist retreats was their quality and the sympathetic tone which they imparted to the retreatants. It was said of Coffin that he was able to sympathise so readily with the misery and weakness of secular priests that he won their immediate confidence; he did not dwell on the great dangers of the priesthood and the difficulty of priests' salvation, a difficulty so insurmountable that the only recourse was to the religious life, as did the religious of some other orders. Rather, it was said, he showed how, despite all the obstacles, they could be sanctified and be good priests.[81] Coffin was certainly in heavy demand as a retreat conductor, 'refreshing and strengthening and consoling [the clergy] in their lonely and heavy trials'.[82] In a telling phrase, he summarised both the method and intention of Redemptorist retreat work: 'To tell the truth, I taught them nothing other than to live as a really good Redemptorist (de vivre en vrai bon Rédemptoriste) like us in the world'.[83]

It will not do to strain this fragmentary evidence and to construct a full-blown thesis on the relations between the Redemptorists and the secular clergy. It is possible, however, to suggest that in the absence of significant causes of division, and without the abrasive assertiveness of certain other orders, combining with the positive work and reputation of their mission and retreat work, the Redemptorists were regarded by the secular clergy with equanimity, if not enthusiasm, mixed, at times, with awe and respectful admiration.

5

Preparing for the harvest: vocation and apostolate

Save as a term of abuse, the inelegant title of 'Liguorians' was never applied to the Redemptorists in Great Britain and Ireland in the last century, as was the case in France and Italy. They were themselves, however, in no doubt as to the constant source of their inspiration; as spiritual sons of St Alphonsus, the Redemptorists stood in the same relation to their founder as the first followers: 'The Spirit of the Congregation of the Most Holy Redeemer is the perpetual Spirit of St Alphonsus in the hearts of his sons'.[1] That spirit, or characteristic mark of the Congregation in contradistinction with other religious orders, was to be found in the saint's life and example, was enshrined in his works and was encapsulated in the Rule and Constitutions, which he had largely formulated. Affection for, and loyalty to the memory of, St Alphonsus was more than an expression of filial piety. By sharing the saint's vision, through reading his works, as well as in the oral tradition, the Redemptorists' religious vocation was sharpened, and the Gospel took on a new closeness and compelling reality. This was the reason why anything associated with the founder was held to be sacrosanct. The papally-approved Rule of 1749, for instance, had been amplified, explained and glossed by the General Chapter of 1764, which had added nearly fourteen hundred Constitutions, defining the peculiar aim of the Congregation and determining its definite way of life. Since these Constitutions were drawn up during the saint's lifetime, under his aegis, and represented the collective wisdom of the primitive group that surrounded Alphonsus, there was bequeathed to future generations a vision of apostolic life and work, tried and tested in difficult circumstances, which was not of the remote past, but was adapted and suited to the needs of the contemporary Church. Although rooted in an age-old spiritual tradition, the Redemptorists were recognisably one of the 'two greatest of modern Orders'.[2]

The Rule and Constitutions, then, were the essential framework around which, and by means of which, the Redemptorists were to be moulded; exact observance of them was enjoined on all who wished to be worthy sons of the Congregation.[3] Similarly, the works of Alphonsus were deemed to be a compendium of all that was necessary for a Redemptorist in his religious life and work; they provided a boundlessly rich mine of spiritual and practical wisdom which every Redemptorist was meant to imbibe, and in them was distilled the essence of what it meant to be a member of his Institute. Not only were the Redemptorists always to be reading one of the saint's works, but they also received constant exhortations from their superiors on every aspect of their vocation, culled and derived from, or based on the words of, Alphonsus. The intention was not merely that the disciples would be soaked in the master's ideas, but that by studying his works, they would be led to acquire his virtues and be so much of one mind with him as to adopt his methods, so that 'in preaching the Word of God, in hearing holy confessions, they put on the mantle of the apostolic spirit of Alphonsus (Alphonsi spiritum apostolicum induunt), and follow his doctrine with his method and style'.[4]

It was impossible for the Redemptorist to escape the influence and brooding presence of the saint, even had he so desired, since Alphonsus was the model all were called to emulate. Thus, the priests' *Manuale* was commended to the English Province as 'the means of advancement in the spirit of true Redemptorist piety, and of a greater knowledge of Our Holy Father Alphonsus's works, who in the "True Redemptorist" and in his "Circular Letters" still speaks to us, and lives as it were in the midst of us'.[5] St Alphonsus was 'our *negotiator in caelis* (advocate in heaven). He loves the Congñ far more now on his throne in heaven than he did when upon earth'.[6]

In a somewhat romanticised portrait, an English member of the Congregation described the Redemptorists as 'God's gypsies, providentially appointed to roam hither and thither, with no definite flock or fixed sheep-fold, to deliver a special message, to do a special work for God and then to hurry on to other sheep and other pastures'.[7] This interesting self-image does illustrate how vocation and apostolate were inextricably linked. The intention was to combine an active apostolate and a contemplative religious life, in which the life of Christ and his apostles were mirrored: 'This imitation of Christ is the most important (principalissima) of all our Rules; in it consists the proper spirit of our Institute'.[8] The desire merely to engage in apostolic work did not make a Redemptorist:

> And, therefore, let him who would enter the Congregation principally in order to give missions, to preach, &c., not think of entering, because this is not the spirit of the Institute ... Much less should anyone think of joining the Congregation only with the intention of learning in it how to preach, and to hear confessions, &c.[9]

Before anything else, the Redemptorist was required to look to his own sanctification and salvation, recalling the words of Alphonsus, 'God has called us into the Congregation to become saints and save ourselves as saints. As for him who would simply save his soul in the Congregation, and not become a saint, I do not know if he will be saved at all!'[10] A consequence of this call to sanctity was the stipulation that no Redemptorist was to be employed in the active apostolate for more than six months of the year, and that he must spend at least half of the year at home with the community. Here, the provision of a strict ascetic regime, entailing a virtually enclosed monastic life, was designed to promote the cultivation of apostolic virtues, by means of which character and personality would be moulded. This regime, extensive in its all-embracing nature and intensive in the cultivation of piety, was highly regulated; the life of the Redemptorist was governed by a mass of rescripts, ranging from the Rule and Constitutions to the decisions of the Rector Major and the recesses left after the annual canonical visitation of each community. It was a life in which nothing was left to chance or to personal decision and individual will: 'In the home life of the Redemptorist, rule and rote are the commanding forces. From the moment he awakes in the morning, till he retires at night, his rule has something to say about nearly every movement he makes'.[11]

The Redemptorist's devotional life and daily spiritual exercises, his dress, diet, penances, reading material and manner of celebrating Mass were all minutely prescribed and ordered according to rule, custom and the devout usage of Alphonsus. Any deviation from established norms was quickly checked: 'We seriously disapprove and forbid a *habit of practical jokes either in word or action* [which] leads to a diminution of fraternal charity and mutual respect, and levity of conduct, which is contrary to the priestly and religious state'.[12] The pressure to conform to the model of what was considered to be the proper Redemptorist character was great, and the upholding of a rather rigid ideal of priestly character was considered to be especially important in the context of apostolic work: 'We pretend to be models for the Clergy. The Clergy expect us to be so, they come to us for retreats, that from us they may gain somewhat more of the Ecclesiastical and Priestly Spirit'.[13] The Redemptorists were meant, and were expected by their superiors, to epitomise that priestly ideal which they fostered in others; failure to do so would result in a loss of regard for them and for their apostolic labours. On missions, the Redemptorists were required 'to be more guarded, more circumspect, more religious ... than in our houses'.[14] This is why they were forbidden to mix with the local clergy on mission, to discuss with them any matter unconnected with the mission, to take walks or to go sightseeing or to engage in anything that could be construed as a misuse of their time and of a frivolous nature. The success of the mission work depended, as it was felt, upon conformity to the Alphonsian,

81

priestly ideal. So, writing to the fathers at Limerick, Coffin opined that 'the great success which accompanies all the works of the Congregation in Ireland is in great measure due to the care which you take not to commit any wilful fault against the religious spirit which would mar the work and withhold from it the fulness of Divine Blessing'.[15] The discipline and uniformity of the Redemptorists' religious formation was also important so that they would work in concert:

> On Missions we work not as isolated Priests but as members of a body, and, therefore, we must work together and, in so far as may be, in perfect accordance with one another. We are called to attack the strongholds of sin and of deep moral degradation, but we must attack in rank and file, in one common order, conjointly and not individually, in ways and with ideas of our own, which vary with caprice and the heat of the moment or of our own particular character.[16]

In the last resort, the first purpose of the Institute, the gaining of personal salvation, was bound up with the second, missionary purpose. Holiness was meant to be contagious; contact with a holy missioner was intended to quicken the desire for holiness in his listeners. Thus, his actions and demeanour had to suggest an interior sanctity that provided a pattern for others, be it dignified behaviour in church or never spending less than fifteen minutes in thanksgiving after Mass. The Redemptorists of the English Province were reminded that

> the Missioners are looked upon by the people as saints, and as men dead to all things of this world, as if they had neither flesh nor feeling; hence, any action of theirs which does not seem to the beholder holy is a cause of astonishment and scandal.[17]

The whole of their training and life-style was geared towards the missionary apostolate. Although retreat work was included in this apostolate, parochial missions were considered the real *métier* of the Redemptorist: 'It is when giving a mission that a son of St Alphonsus is completely in his element'.[18] So much was this the case, that a man's apostolic ministry was measured by the number of missions in which he was involved.[19]

Writing to Fr Lans in 1859, when the first attempt was made to establish an English novitiate, the Belgian Provincial urged the need 'to make men of prayer, mortification and zeal for the salvation of souls, but they must not be solitaries but apostles'.[20] The novitiate was meant to be a severe testing ground of a man's vocation, a period of probation and preparation, in which the novice was introduced to the theoretical and practical art of leading an interior life, and in which clear signs were expected of his suitability. The novices had a Rule of their own, in which stricter discipline was prescribed than for the professed members of the Congregation, although it was not physically harsh, and excess of bodily mortification was discouraged. The Constitutions stressed the need to effect a complete reformation of the interior man, and for the novices to be imbued 'with a spirit of mortification ... and to value for itself a holy hatred of self, the common life and strict poverty, a spirit of submission and blind obedience, the love of [religious] observance and a hatred of every exception'.[21] The day he donned the Redemptorist habit, the novice was deemed to have put off the old man and to have put on the new. All contact with the outside world was now ended. The dramatic break with his former life was the beginning of the formation of a new character, a new identity. Describing his clothing as 'a liberation', George Stebbing nonetheless recalled, in a telling phrase, that his novitiate was 'constant tension and strain. There was no relief, no attempt to win me by affectionateness, no attempt to find out my mind and my inner thoughts'.[22] Sheer determination to get through was the instrument of his perseverance. Similarly, thirty years earlier, John Gibson had been singularly unimpressed by the lack of interest shown in him, and of recognition of the sacrifice he had made to become a Redemptorist, when he first entered the novitiate at St Trond; only 'the example of so many fervent novices, eager for mortification and humiliation was a powerful stimulus, and after a little time I entered into the spirit of the Novitiate'.[23]

The cold, calculated, almost inhuman regime of the novitiate was based on the assumption that it was both possible and necessary to break down previous habits and temperament, and to re-fashion men according to the Alphonsian model. This explains the harsh treatment of priest-novices, who had, perforce, more developed personalities than younger men, and had to be moulded in the short space of a year's novitiate and the six months spent in the studentate studying moral theology. The first requirement of the novice was that he love the Congregation with the best affection of his heart, 'as a mother, of whom he is spiritually born'.[24] Like the professed members of the Institute, the novices were constantly reminded that a good Redemptorist was one who obtained the spirit of St Alphonsus by assimilating large portions of his writings, and of the Congregation by esteeming everything in it, especially its Rule and Constitutions, 'the means by which we are to arrive at perfection'.[25] Similarly, the life of the novice was regulated to the last detail. His dress, deportment and washing habits were keenly observed and criticised; he was told how to conduct himself towards his superiors, how to lie in bed at night; even the rules of politeness were written down for his instruction. Much of the day was spent in chapel, and every action of the day — even the unfolding of his table napkin — was accompanied by prayer. He was required to kiss the hand of the novice master whenever he received anything from him, as at High Mass, so that the whole of his life was set in a quasi-liturgical context.

The cultivation of an introspective, demonstrative, occasionally oppressive, piety was a primary charge on the novice; a piety based on official forms, which grew by feeding on itself and informed the mentality and ecclesiastical outlook of the novice, as well as providing the basis for his later missionary career. George Stebbing was not peculiar in imposing on himself thirty-three separate devotions to the Blessed Virgin during the month of May, and proved himself a model novice in making monthly resolutions to acquire certain virtues. Among these was to make a novena of communions on nine successive first Fridays in honour of the Sacred Heart for the grace of final perseverance and to obtain the sacraments of the Church before dying, to salute the Guardian Angels whenever he entered a room, to renew his vows continually throughout the day, to say an *Ave* whenever a clock struck, before and after every action, on entering and leaving a room or when passing before our Lady's statue and before every canonical hour. Above all, he determined to begin life anew each day and to fight continually to give the first thought to God:

> I ought to consider Our Lord as speaking to me from the tabernacle personally and face-to-face, and telling me that He wills that I serve Him in the Congregation. Hence the Rule is to me the Will of God, and the gaining of the Spirit of the Congregation my work ... I take for *my Hero, Our Holy Father Alphonsus* — studying, honouring and imitating him in his *Life* (my Legend), his *Works* (my Encyclopaedia) and *Institute* (my Charter) and his *Patrons* (especially *St Theresa*), his *Companions* and his *Sons*.[26]

Such an insight into the mentality of a novice is rare. Much more common are surviving reports of the Novice Master, made every four months to the Provincial, who sent on the Novice Master's final recommendation to the Rector Major at the end of the year, with whom rested the final decision about profession. These reports give a clear indication of the qualities required of a Redemptorist. Typical among them was the assessment of David Joseph Patridge:

> Without having noticed anything extraordinary in him, I can nevertheless say with conviction that he possesses the qualities to be a good religious, i.e. he is pious — he loves prayer and the other spiritual exercises; he is attached to his vocation ... He has observed the rules well and striven ... to acquire the spirit of abnegation and the other qualities which the religious life demands. He is singularly docile and obedient'.[27]

At the end of the day, what was looked for from the novices were signs of future promise, especially 'a strong determination to give themselves to God and [the Congregation's] service without reserve or condition'.[28]

Regular reports on each subject continued to be made throughout the six years of theological study and to reflect the primary concern of superiors for piety and conformity to the Redemptorist ideal. Thus, in commending to the Rector Major the student William Owen, Coffin wrote of 'his true and solid piety — his preferred devotions are all those of the Congregation' and of his 'great spirit of faith, which is displayed above all by his obedience'; great affection and esteem for his vocation was said to cause him to be fervent, obedient and observant of the Rule, while his simplicity and trouble-free nature sprang from 'a truly perfect clothing (couverture) of the heart', which caused him also to be obedient to his superiors.[29] The academic progress of this perfect student was not even mentioned. Indeed, provided that performance in the annual examinations was satisfactory, academic ability appears to have occupied a relatively minor place in the concern of superiors. In part, this was because the Redemptorists were not an intellectual order; it was, for instance, admitted that one man was a Redemptorist because he was too stupid to be a Jesuit.[30] In part also, theological studies were subservient to the end of the Institute and never unrelated to the apostolate in view; the canon law classes, for example, dealt with little more than the Redemptorist privileges and exemptions and with what was required in the confessional, while moral theology was little more than a regurgitation of St Alphonsus and was, again, concerned with the equipping of confessors.[31] Although the reports of the students give the impression that a desultory prayer life, lack of zeal for their vocation, or anything deemed to be unRedemptorist, were of more concern to superiors, it should not be thought that study was unimportant or that academic standards were low. The need for an apostolate of the pen was recognised, albeit grudgingly, and was ably served by some members of the English Province, and application to study, 'especially to studies which would prove useful in the mission work', was a requirement of all students.[32]

The years in the novitiate and studentate were supposed to stamp a man with the hallmark of the Congregation and make him a living likeness of his divine model, the Most Holy Redeemer. To underline the comparison, no Redemptorist could begin his mission work until he had attained the age of thirty, the same as Christ when he had begun his public ministry. The preparation for the work of the missions had, of course, commenced in the house of studies, where regular academies of missions were held, designed to provide an introduction and to relate book-learning to the work of the missions. Academies of missions were a regular feature of all Redemptorist houses, when every detail of the missions and of preaching was discussed and analysed in the light of the pattern established by St Alphonsus. The proven worth of his methods, techniques and preaching style were a powerful stimulus to preserve intact the type of mission and the pulpit oratory that he had evolved. Believing that these could not be improved, and that the spiritual wants of British and Irish Catholics 'called for very little change, if any, from the soul-stirring topics and the wise methods pursued by St Alphonsus in Italy',[33] the members of the Congregation were bidden to show 'no desire for useless and wanton innovations, but to preserve and apply zealously the principles and methods of St Alphonsus'.[34]

Because their founder was 'the very doctor and prophet of missions [who] has reduced mission-giving to a regular art, and compiled the most particular rules for each exercise of the mission',[35] the Redemptorists had the clearest-cut ideas of what their apostolate entailed and how it was to be effected. The constant reminder of these ideas was a chief purpose of the circular letters which issued from the Rector Major, the authentic voice of St Alphonsus speaking to his spiritual sons and urging them to guard and maintain the apostolic tradition that their founder had consolidated. With regard to the preaching of the Word of God, for instance, Mauron impressed upon his English subjects that 'we must follow scrupulously

[Alphonsus's] maxims', urging them to eschew 'a low and trivial manner of preaching ... extravagant and florid language, affected pronunciation, arguments above the level of reasoning of the ordinary faithful (des raisonnements au dessus de la partie du common des fidèles), too long or studied pauses'.[36] This was in conformity with the advice of the founder and the requirements of the Constitutions, which forbade affected delivery, the transposing of words, and long and intricate sentences. Rather, the fathers were to preach Christ crucified 'in the apostolic manner (more apostolico), by simple and popular speech'.[37]

If the admonition and exhortation of rectors major and the Constitutions were insufficient, there were other means to promote and preserve the full measure of professionalism on which the Redemptorists prided themselves. Before the publication of the *Directory of the Missions* in 1877, it was common for the Provincial to issue reminders to the missioners regarding the proper order and other details of the missions, and large or important missions were often prefaced by special instructions. The general mission to five churches in Belfast in 1872, for example, described as 'the most important mission which the Congñ has ever yet given in these countries', prompted Coffin to remind the missioners that all the instructions 'should be characterised by solid, dogmatic and didactic matter. Barren and noisy declamations must be avoided; great discretion and prudence must be used in the selection of examples, stories and supernatural facts'.[38] In like manner, the missioners at St Chad's, Birmingham in October 1869 had been told to make their sermons 'solid and instructive', and to make the acts of reparation in the sermons on the Blessed Sacrament and Blessed Virgin 'short and concise, carefully worked out beforehand, and not left to feeling and the excitement of the moment'.[39]

Such instructions were necessitated by the fathers' temptation to wander from the narrow, approved path. One way of recalling them, reprimanding the past decline in standards and re-asserting the ideal, was by means of the Provincial's circular letters. Thus, in urging the avoidance 'of all mere sensational excitement in your manner of treating and developing the Eternal Truths', Coffin recalled that the object of Redemptorist preaching was 'to root out sin from the souls of all to whom [the missioners] are sent and to plant in them the love of Jesus'.[40] The aim of reconciling men to God could be effaced by failures in the contents of the sermons and in their manner of delivery. A common fault in the early years of the Province was 'poverty of matter in the sermons: points not well worked-out, a want of preparation is visible, and too much trafficking in old sermons preached years ago'. Such sermons, Coffin complained, were 'preached incoherently and in a slovenly manner and, instead of giving [the people] good, solid matter, well thought-out and well worked-out, [the preacher] will string together a series of unmeaning generalities, which will neither convince nor persuade'. Control of the voice was also criticised: 'Some begin to scream and shout from the commencement, whilst others speak in a monotone … and [others] tend to add a vowel at the end of words, which makes a painful impression'. The instructions and explanation of the mysteries of the rosary required 'more sinew and nerve … and far less exclamation, accumulation of epithets, repetition of the same idea and mere platitudes'. Nor was attention paid to the proper time for working on the affections and passions; this was to be done during the peroration, which had, perforce, to be short. Reminding his subjects that the first object of the mission sermon and all the instructions 'is to convince the understanding and then to move the will', Coffin concluded that a sermon or instruction, 'which is nothing but a series of exclamations and appeals to the passions, necessarily fails in one of the chief ends for which it is delivered'.[41]

In order to remedy these faults, and to forestall any further occurrence, the younger fathers were expected to write out sample sermons and instructions and to have them scrutinised by their seniors.[42] John Gibson recalled that he was 'imperfectly furnished with mission sermons' when he began his apostolic ministry, and he sought to remedy this defect by building up a full series.[43] Patrick Sampson felt no such compunction; arguing that 'the Province was in its infancy', there seemed little point 'in preparing remedies till we knew the nature of the disease ... I wrote all my sermons, or nearly all, in full, only after some years' experience ... and [they] were in great measure taken from the discourses of experienced fathers'.[44] In any case, a young missioner was never allowed to preach the large mission sermons; he began his mission career by taking his turn in the confessional, by reciting and explaining the mysteries of the rosary, and by giving a few instructions. Coffin warned the young priests that they should 'be on their guard against the natural but foolish desire of wishing to become preachers of the great sermons', and he admonished them to listen to, and learn from, their elders.[45] Such apprenticeship was not possible in the early years of the missions, when resources were overstretched and the young missioners had to be given more responsibility than their lack of experience sometimes warranted.[46]

As conditions improved in the Province, it became possible to institute the second novitiate, according to the Constitutions.[47] It was first held at Kinnoull in 1870, and was designed to make the young priests 'better trained and more strictly established in the practice of all the virtues of our apostolic ministry'.[48] Here again, the success of the missions was seen to depend upon the quality of an individual's religious life. The second novitiate took the form of a long retreat, and during its six months' duration it was hoped to renew newly-ordained priests in the spirit of piety and to prepare them more solidly for the work of a missioner. The first three months were spent in making plans of missions, retreats and renewals, and the novices were required to make written sketches of the instructions that they would give on these occasions, which could then be discussed and criticised. The latter part of the second novitiate was spent in producing sample sermons, which were often delivered before, and commented upon by, the whole community. In addition to sermon preparation, the ceremonies of the Church were practised, especially those in which the young missioners would be directly involved, such as the necessary formulae for the blessing of scapulars or proclaiming a plenary indulgence, as well as the more strictly liturgical matters, such as acts of reparation to the Blessed Sacrament. Nor was the work of the confessional neglected. There was discussion of the categories of penitent and of moral cases, together with instruction on the techniques and qualities required by the confessor and the appropriateness of specified penances. Binding all this training together were the spiritual conferences, in which the virtues of a good missioner were set forth and the opposing dangers and faults outlined. Thus, even preaching was placed firmly in a spiritual context: 'Love Jesus well, and you will preach well. Be a good religious — an interior man — a man of prayer and you will be powerful in the Word of God and true apostles'.[49]

The second novitiate did help to form the young missioners and to set before them guidelines which they were expected to follow throughout their ministry. Patrick Sampson, a member of the 1870 novitiate, recalled that it caused 'a fluster of excitement among the twelve young priests who comprised it', and he envinced, as its lasting fruits, 'renewal of the spirit of our vocation and of prayer, improved health and great zeal for the Irish language among some of us'.[50] Not everyone was as enthusiastic. A young priest who attended the second novitiate in 1883, brought suddenly to an end because one of the fathers contracted typhus fever, complained that as the Prefect (Bridgett) 'never made his own 2nd Novitiate, he gave us (as we found afterwards) "his own" views rather than "the traditional" ones of the CSSR on some points'.[51]

Fr Somers' concern for 'the traditional' ways of the Congregation, and its concomitant suspicion of anything that smacked of innovation, is testimony to the success of his early training. Yet the danger was that the spiritual demands that were a constant feature of Redemptorist life could produce ethereal characters, plaster-saints, oppressed by the mould into which they were forced, as much as they were made by it. The maintenance of high spiritual standards was possible only through unrelenting admonition, exhortation and prescription. It did have its amusing side, as in the prohibition of the ministers at High Mass to take snuff,[52] or in the correspondence with Rome over the propriety of allowing the students to read the novels of Dickens and Walter Scott, and the decision that to prevent it would brand the Redemptorists as 'rustics'.[53] And there is something almost preposterous about the Rector Major's prohibition of turkey-red pocket handkerchiefs and electro-plated cutlery.[54] Such a degree of interference and concern for the minutiae of religious observance was bound to have an adverse effect, for it destroyed any local and personal initiative. There is, for instance, a pathetic tone to a series of questions put by the Provincial to Mauron in 1886, which included the request to begin the greater silence at the end of Evening Prayer instead of five minutes before supper, and clarification of the point whether black coffee should be taken on the fasts before the seven principal feasts of the Virgin, as on days of ecclesiastical fasting, or white coffee, as on ordinary fast days.[55] There may be a reflection of the resentment felt by the fathers at continued interference in the canonical recess left at Limerick in 1871, where 'the want of knowledge with regard to Documents which come from the H. See or from the Most R$^{\underline{d}}$ Fr General' was because the 'chronista' and librarian no longer bothered to leave them out for perusal by the community.[56] A few years later, a member of the same community left the Congregation, having rebelled against 'the slavish work', which resulted from 'new regulations every time there is a canonical visitation, which makes one a slave, [and] is unbearable'.[57]

Even the Provincial was forced to complain to Rome about the secret codes invented by the Consultor-General, which were easily broken and would bring the Congregation into disrepute.[58] More seriously, such a regime, which encouraged secrecy, undue dependence on central authority, and repressed both natural feeling and local and personal enterprise, could result in immaturity of decision and a lack of self-confidence which bespoke arrested emotional development. Fr Urquhart, who left the Congregation to become a Benedictine in 1891, was repelled by the constant impregnation of 'the apostolic spirit and "Redemptorist simplicity'', under which I class chiefly the prevalent disesteem for esoteric knowledge and speculative subjects, the preference that exists for weak, popular devotions rather than for liturgy, and lastly the spirit of those childish feast-day observances'.[59]

The preference for 'weak, popular devotions', which so disgusted Urquhart, identified the Redemptorists as firm supporters of the school of Ultramontane sympathisers that argued that 'showy', populist, slightly vulgar, pietistical exercises were both a consequence of abandonment to divine love which Alphonsus had so recommended, and the means to form people in firm habits and the practice of prayer. Enthusiasm for exuberant forms of devotion sprang from the belief that they were good in themselves, as expressing Catholic belief, and that they were the means to consolidate the hold of Catholicism upon the people by providing a substitute cultural expression and identity that would help to banish any pagan or Protestant cultural influence. It served to satisfy all the emotional and spiritual needs of those who were drawn into the ambit of their influence, including those who propagated the devotions. The struggle to establish new devotional customs which underpinned the theological ideas of the Ultramontane Movement could be presented in terms of the battle for truth against semi-Catholic compromise, which merely encouraged Protestants. The 'anti-Catholic spirit of opposition' to Marian devotion which had been evinced by a knot of York Catholics during a Redemptorist mission in 1861, for instance, was noted to have 'altogether disappeared' by 1864, and this was regarded as the most satisfactory outcome of the 1861 mission.[60] Newspaper accounts of the early missions often mentioned the introduction of new devotions which were to change the face of Catholicism at the popular level and were the means of asserting those doctrinal emphases that marked out Ultramontane Catholicism from the more restrained type of Catholicism which had hitherto prevailed. At Droylsden, Lancashire, in 1858, for example, it was reported that 'great is the devotion to our dear Mother Mary which these holy missioners have inspired. I do not think that now there is one who attended the Mission who does not wear the holy Scapular and use his rosary'.[61]

The Redemptorists had a clear idea of themselves as pioneers of the new Ultramontane devotions and of all that they entailed. Not all of them were as mischievous as Fr Gibson. Giving a mission in Maudsley, Lancashire in 1858, he found that the parish priest was 'of the old school, and objected to what he called "new-fangled" devotions. He would give us no help in erecting an altar for the statue of our Blessed Lady, but with the aid of some books from his library, which we took the liberty of borrowing, we built up an altar and decorated it with candles and flowers, for the ceremony of consecration to our Lady'.[62] Fr Prost was less inventive, but nonetheless insistent that proper belief, true prayer and right devotion were bound together. The introduction of the hitherto-unknown delights of extra-liturgical devotions was part of his mission brief and, during his early missions in Ireland, he carried about with him 'a ciborium, monstrance, vestments, chalice, thurible, purificators and corporals', since he knew that he would not find some of these items in the parishes, and if he did, that they would be unworthy.[63] The fact that people, for the most part, wallowed in these novelties confirmed the Redemptorists in their belief that they were essential to the preaching of the faith itself. In turn, they were captivated by what they fed to others, believing that Catholics were to be renewed by re-forming the outward appearance of their religion. Fr Johnson, writing from the novitiate in Wittem, expatiated on the parish pilgrimages, the Blessed Sacrament processions and the rule of fortnightly communion which he encountered for the first time among continental Catholicism, and concluded that 'the best-regulated and most fervent parish in the diocese of Ferns is very much behind the parishes in general here ... What it is to come among a really Catholic people!'.[64]

Believing that they were involved in the task of making a really Catholic people, the Redemptorists' sympathies were wholly with that devotional spirit that animated the Roman see in the pontificate of Pius IX. Liturgical extravaganzas were a means of raising the spirits, confirming people's allegiance to, and dependence upon, the Church, and provided an emotional spiritual outlet that was refreshing in the humdrum of ordinary life. They were also community celebrations, helping to form, as much as to express, community-sense and identity. Thus, the Blessed Sacrament procession on Lady's Island, Co. Wexford in 1864 involved eight thousand people, with a hundred acolytes in cottas and a hundred girls, dressed in white, each carrying a bouquet of flowers and banners, and the circuit of the island was matched by a flotilla of small craft.[65] Within a few years, such spectacles were common among Catholics both in Ireland and in Britain and did not call for special comment or the self-conscious pioneering mentality. Thenceforth, the emphasis changed to one of consolidation. After 1867, the Redemptorists did this through fostering devotion and encouraging novenas of prayer to the Virgin under the title of Our Lady of Perpetual Succour. Copies of the miraculous image, housed in the church of S. Alfonso in Rome, were set up in many churches, and within a few years the dioceses of Leeds and Middlesborough were dedicated to our Lady under this title. A translation of a French manual of devotion to our Lady of Perpetual Succour sold so well that it went through three editions in two years.[66] Small copies of the image also sold well; at Middlesborough in November 1882, for example, nine hundred pictures were bought by the people, who were encouraged by the missioners to say the family rosary before it, and it was noted that

> the difference between those who had kept up the practice of saying the rosary 'coram Imagine', and those who neglected it, was like the difference between the elect and the reprobate, as shown in the perseverance, the family union, and the general Christian lives of the former, and the all-too often shameless and scandalous relapse of the latter.[67]

If the miraculous qualities of the original were deemed to infect all copies, it was also important that the image was indulgenced, so that its possession was held to confer real

95

spiritual benefits. The Redemptorists' privilege of bestowing the four scapulars, the ability to establish the Society of the Holy Rosary, to bless crosses for the Stations of the Infant Jesus and the Immaculate Virgin, and to perform many other spiritual works, including the absolution from papal censures, meant, not only that they could call upon the rich treasury of merit and confer some of its riches to the people, but that they also had a vested interest in exalting the authority of Rome as the dispenser of all these privileges. Indeed, enthusiasm for lavish devotions was but one sign of the Redemptorists' identity with the cause of Ultramontane Catholicism. The other was fierce loyalty for, and obedience to, the Roman see. It was recorded of Coffin that he loved 'to see the Church's ornaments rich, in good taste, and always, *à la Romaine'* and that he was 'the indefatigable propagator in England during his whole life of this Roman Spirit'.[68] When, in 1864, Rome forbade the use of Gothic vestments, the Redemptorist authorities ordered the immediate implementation of the ban, and Coffin complied by forbidding their use and ordering their alteration to conform to Rome's decree; in so doing, he informed his subjects that 'in this as in all other matters of like nature we might be doing what was most pleasing to the Holy See'.[69]

In like manner, when the Vatican Council defined the dogma of papal infallibility, Coffin ordered that the constitution *Pastor Aeternus* should be read and explained to the faithful in St Mary's, Clapham. Having informed the people that they were bound by it, the expositor was told to conclude with 'an exhortation of thanksgiving, submission to the Voice of God and a mark of love to Our Divine Lord' for the dogma.[70] Even before the definition, the Redemptorists strongly maintained belief in papal infallibility, and would have extended the dogmatic definition to include the temporal power of the papacy. When Petcherine spoke against this power, he was severely reprimanded and forbidden, not only to speak on the subject, but even to read any book or publication against the civil government of the pope: 'A son of the Church who holds only what is a dogma, is not a good

son of his holy Mother ... to pronounce against the universal
sentiment of the Church, no, my [dear] father, I cannot permit
it to a son of St Alphonsus'.[71]

If the Redemptorists regarded themselves as in the vanguard of the religious movements of the day, it was because
they believed that their founder had epitomised all that was
noblest and best in the Catholic tradition, and they strove to
imitate him. He was their inspirational ideal and constant
source of reference; every aspect of their religious life and
apostolic work was judged in the light of the ideals which he
had set before his subjects. These ideals were clear; it remains
to be seen how far they were realised in Great Britain and
Ireland in the last century.

6

Workers in the vineyard

Uncertain of the direction of his religious vocation, the young Cyril Dodsworth sought the advice of Monsignor Manning. He directed Dodsworth to the Redemptorists since, in his estimate, they were 'the most evangelical men I know'.[1] The Redemptorists had a reputation that was scarcely rivalled by other religious. Alexander Goss, for example, declared that Bishop Eton was 'the only truly religious community of men under his jurisdiction, all the other religious orders being more secular priests than religious'.[2] Highly favourable estimates of the Congregation and its work confirm the good favour in which it was held by contemporary Catholics, while even antagonists were forced to recognise it as

> the most aggressive order the Church of Rome can produce ... [its members] are reputed as great preachers, holding and teaching the most subtle and obnoxious doctrines of the Church. Being disciples of Liguori, you may know that they are a most dangerous class of men in any country.[3]

The relevance and clarity of the apostolate combined with the declared fervour and dedication of its members to draw men to the Congregation. Fr Harbison, writing to his parents from the novitiate at St Trond in 1853, enthused

> the more I see and know of the spirit and life and manners of the Redemptorists, the more do they approve themselves to my judgement and to my heart ... [in the Congregation] I feel such a certainty both of saving my

own soul and of doing an immensity of good to my poor brethren in Ireland.[4]

Richard Crofts, who entered the novitiate in 1862, was similarly moved by the thought of saving his own soul:

> I could form no hopes of happiness from anything the world can give. I would not become a secular priest because the position of secular priests in the world did not correspond to my dispositions. I would not join any of the old religious orders, for I did not feel safe, and did not look for an active employment, except in a modern missionary order. I then began to consider and review in my mind all that I knew of the Oblates, the Vincentians, the Jesuits and the Redemptorists. Though I admired the first three, I could never so satisfy my mind with regard to them, as to be willing to join any of them. On the other hand, everything that I heard or knew concerning the Redemptorists was in perfect accordance to the bent of my mind, and it seemed to me that there was no better or safer path in life for me than that which is to be found in the Congregation.[5]

William Owen, Novice Master from 1872 to 1874, used to tell his charges that 'one good Redemptorist in his "yes" was equal to thousands of persons in the world'.[6] A former Oratorian likewise felt that the Congregation's disciplined interior life and its external labours provided all that was needed 'to be led to as high a degree of perfection as God's grace will enable me to attain'.[7]

The call to sanctity, in fulfilment of the first end of the Institute, was not an invitation to seek a secluded refuge or retreat from the world, but was quickly followed by the evangelical imperative. Fr Edward O'Donnell's ascetical intentions were thwarted by the labours in which he was engaged: 'I came to the Congregation to hide myself and the more I sought to be unknown the more I was made to appear'.[8] Conversely, Fr Somers' joy and gratitude to God for calling him to the Redemptorist life was born of the realisation 'at once that a member CSSR does, as our H[oly]

F[ather] says in "True Redemptorist", more good in *one year* than he could do on the Secular Mission in *ten years'*.[9] The Redemptorists' sense of purpose was captured hyperbolically by de Held when he wrote, 'I would not change my habit for a royal mantle, nor my cross of missioner for the Tiara of the Pope'.[10]

Compelling certainty of a religious vocation sometimes outstripped the practical difficulties and obstacles that stood in its way, and some aspirants had to overcome these before they could achieve their ambition. Francis Hall, for example, was only fourteen when, as a result of attending a Redemptorist mission at St Oswald's, Old Swan, Liverpool in October 1850, he conceived the burning desire to join the Congregation. His father took a dim view of his adolescent son's yearnings and did all he could to frustrate them. He was, however, out-manoeuvred by the determined boy, who persuaded his father to allow him to finish his education at the Jesuit College in Liège, 'which was chosen to get me far away from the fathers, my father fancying there were no Redemptorists in Belgium'. The impressionable Francis spent much of his time there in the Redemptorist church, wallowing in the liturgical extravaganzas, which he detailed in the effusively pious letters that he wrote to his mother, who seems to have been more sympathetic than his father to the idea of his religious vocation and to have been an accomplice in the deception. Two-and-a-half years' daily contact with the Redemptorists confirmed Hall's intentions and, on his return to England, he ran away from home to the Congregation's house at Clapham. His father directed repeated tirades against 'that rascally body ... those miscreants at Clapham', whose 'monstrous malpractices' and 'kidnapping system' were blamed for having turned the boy against his father. Faced with the threat of being disowned by his father, and after pleas from other members of his family, Hall returned home. He did not remain long. He remade the acquaintance of George Corbishley, whom he introduced to the Congregation. When Corbishley entered the novitiate soon after, Hall renewed his determination to become a Redemptorist and set to work on his father, who was sufficiently weakened to allow his son to enter the novitiate in November 1855. He was professed in January 1857 and was later to have an eventful, if somewhat idiosyncratic, career.[11]

John Magnier's problems were of a different order, although he displayed a similar degree of perseverance. As a layman, Magnier obtained a copy of the *Redemptorist Mission Book* and adopted the rule of life it suggested. A retreat at the Redemptorist house in Limerick confirmed his developing vocation: 'I came to the Supper-room, and, being alone, I felt a happiness I cannot describe. The very pictures of the room seemed to share my feelings'.[12] His lack of studies, however, precluded his entering the Congregation. During the two years of hard study that followed, 'the one great dominating thought remained — that it was God's will that I should be a Redemptorist'.[13] Professed in 1867, Magnier referred to his clothing in the Redemptorist habit as 'a second Baptism'.[14]

The initial joy of entering the novitiate was not sufficient to sustain a man throughout his religious life. He entered a world that was wholly contained and, for the most part, impenetrable to the vulgar gaze. Contentment came only through the assumption of the Redemptorist 'persona', with its consequent subsuming of individual personality. Some glimpses of this are caught in the extant letters of Redemptorists to their relations. John Magnier's letters to his younger brothers, for instance, are little sermons on the need to pray and receive communion frequently. To his father, he confessed that 'my Christmas letter is an exhortation',[15] while on another occasion he could opine,

> I expect our Blessed Lady will pull me up to Heaven by means of a very long Rosary, which I wear hanging at my side. Well, as I pray continually that she may obtain the same grace for you, dear father, I must give you the same means. See, I enclose a Rosary.[16]

It was in urging his family to pray and read the works of St Alphonsus that Magnier provides a clue to the understanding, not only of this kind of spiritual admonition, but also of the working of his mind and its subsumption in the officially-approved line. After a short time, he told them, they would begin to think like Alphonsus and, in their own way, act like him.[17] Holiness, to which every member of the Congregation was called, meant, as we have seen, to act like St Alphonsus, to have his mind, so that the holy missioner might become a miniature, contemporary Alphonsus in all his relations and contacts with the outside world.

Those who did not persevere in their vocation were judged not merely to have failed to be true sons of their spiritual father, but, as a consequence, to have lost altogether any hope of salvation.[18] They were considered as traitors, and the fate of some — apostasy, lunacy, unhappiness, the lack of worldly success, the loss of spiritual charisma — was recorded with scandalised, but smug, satisfaction.[19] Some of these, of course, if not deserving their fate, were at least responsible for it.[20] For others, it was their inability to live out the Redemptorist vocation in the officially-approved way, and the need to preserve the other members of the Institute from contamination, which resulted in their exclusion from the select band of Redemptorist missionaries. Fr Jacobs, for example, was described as 'of a restless, impetuous disposition; vain, impulsive and irascible, self-opinionated and impatient of contradiction', all of which characteristics had not prevented him from being professed. However, grace could not perfect unredeemed nature in his case, for on the missions he was 'very polite with people of the higher class and with ladies, but hard and rough with the poor and ignorant'.[21] It was the threat which he posed to the Redemptorist self-image as impartial and above worldly concerns that ensured his expulsion. Three years previously, the suspension of a priest from mission work who was guilty of 'violence and severity coupled with abusive language' in the confessional, resulted from the belief that 'it was productive of immense harm to the Congregation as well as to souls'.[22] Similarly, the Provincial considered that Fr McLaughlin 'does not have the spirit of the Congregation. He is not simple; he is vain and conceited ... His outward demeanour, and especially his manner of preaching, is full of vanity'. He suggested that if the door of the Congregation were opened to him, 'the Congregation would be free of a difficult and scarcely edifying subject'. Yet what caused his superior to apply pressure on him to seek a dispensation from his vows was not deficiency of character, but the fact that he owed money to a secular priest and threatened, thereby, to bring the Congregation into bad repute.[23] Fr Edward Swainson was regarded by Coffin as 'a good religious, very pious, greatly attached to his vocation; good spirit and very capable'. Yet within three years, 'mental aberrations' were detected and he was forced to leave the Congregation.[24] The main complaint against him was that he was not acting like a Redemptorist on mission, and, in particular, that he drank and mixed with the local clergy.[25]

It is in this context of public image, and the fear that it might be tarnished, that the preference for avoiding publicity should be viewed. It was Coffin's boast that the Redemptorists were called to work 'under ground, without noise or show (sans bruit ni parade), and always without the glory that comes from men; it is rare that mention is made of us in the Catholic newspapers'.[26] In *The Tablet* account of a general mission in Leeds in 1880, for example, the part of the fifteen Redemptorist fathers was completely unmentioned: 'We were left completely in the shade, no doubt "cooperante S.P.N. Alphonsi"'.[27] Such expressions of humility should be understood as more than a devout desire to be thought of as of no account in the Lord's vineyard; Redemptorist comparisons of their labours with those of other religious orders, which occur quite often in the mission chronicles, will blunt such a pious interpretation. Nor was publicity unwelcome if, despite the temporary difficulties it caused, it ultimately reflected to the Congregation's honour. So, when the Pope announced publicly in Rome that the English Redemptorists had converted eight hundred Protestants, Mauron wrote to Coffin that such news would scarcely help the Institute in England.[28] Coffin's reply displayed a remarkably unruffled indifferentism:

> As for the '800 abjurations', this news has also made the rounds here of the English press — doubtless, we should have preferred to have been spared this publicity, but it

will soon be forgotten, like everything else of this
nature.[29]

Few and occasional reports helped to sustain admiration and
had the psychological effect of enhancing the Congregation's
mystery and remoteness, indistinguishable in the Catholic
mind from other-worldliness and holiness. But there was no
toleration for anyone whose individualism threatened to
bedim the missionary ideal.

One would expect Fr John Furniss to have had a trouble-
free career as a Redemptorist. He was, after all, the pioneer
of children's missions in the English Vice-Province and was
given the title of 'apostolus parvulorum' by his confrères.
Missions to children were his great forte, and he acted the part
of holy missioner to great effect. He knew that he had to
convey an abstract ideal to the children, the ideal of Catholic
holiness, which would inspire them to live it out through and
by means of the practical acts he suggested to them during
the course of the mission. Admittedly, he was a somewhat
eccentric character, but there was also a great deal of deliberate
cultivation of the role of children's missioner which he
assumed. His ascetic appearance, for example — thin, worn,
emaciated — caused people to ask whether he did not live on
bread and water. His clothes were old and shabby, sometimes
dirty, and ill-fitting, while his manner was such that he gave
the impression of great antiquity; although only 53 when he
finished his labours, he was believed to be 107! In his
appearance and manner Furniss embodied the ideal of the
Holy, in the garb of holy poverty, which he hoped to convey
to his hearers. The result was that the children were fascinated
at the mere sight of him, interpreting the physical oddity as
holiness, and regarding him as a saint before ever he opened
his mouth.[30] Furniss was thus in himself a statement about
the mission and its ultimate purpose; he enshrined those
qualities of character and Catholic spirit which he sought to
induce in the children through exhortation. His Redemptorist
contemporaries, however, were far from convinced of his
missionary qualities, methods and practices and feared that
he would bring the Congregation into disrepute, if not ridicule.

Vladimir Petcherine (1807-1885). An exile from Russia, he became one of the most popular Redemptorist preachers in Ireland. He subsequently left the Congregation and spent his last years as chaplain in the Mater Misericordiae Hospital, Dublin.

Bernard Hafkenscheid (1807-1865), Superior of the Missions in England and Ireland from 1853 to 1855, after which he returned to Germany.

The Superior of the Missions, Fr Hafkenscheid, doubted the propriety of separate children's missions, and his Provincial wrote of Furniss that 'I see nothing of the Redemptorist in him but the habit'.[31] Although some of his methods were approved by the Roman authorities, suspicion of others continued, especially with regard to the incredulity of some of his stories and his over-excitement of the children. Furniss complained that he had found in the Congregation 'a harsh mother (une marâtre) and among his confrères 'so much persecution', and he seems to have contemplated leaving the Institute.[32]

As is suggested by the example of Furniss and of those who were forced to leave the Congregation, individuality was tolerated only in so far as it dovetailed into, and did not threaten, the well-being of the Congregation or overstep the declared limits of acceptable religious behaviour. The missioners were to be walking sacraments; their outward behaviour and professional repose was intended to reflect the interior that was supposedly theirs through their religious vocation. Much of the difficulty with Vladimir Petcherine, for example, was that his enthusiasm for the oppressed Irish and his politically liberal views could not be contained within the rigidly narrow spiritual limits of the order to which he belonged, and the effectiveness of which depended upon its remoteness from the maelstrom of life and its ordinary concerns.

Petcherine was an academic who had become an exile from tzarist Russia because of his liberal views, had converted from a nominal Orthodoxy to Catholicism and joined the Redemptorists in Belgium. Ordained in 1843, he came to England in 1845 and worked in Falmouth and later in Clapham. His facility for languages and oratorical skills gained him great popularity as a preacher. He was the first Redemptorist to work in Ireland and he fell in love with the country and its people. What excited his passion was the old hatred for tyranny which he had gained in imperial Russia and he became a great champion of the Irish cause, openly sympathising with an oppressed people against their foreign overlords, of whom he was critical in his sermons. His popularity among the Irish increased in proportion to his reputation for his vehemence for justice, and in 1855 the public rejoicings which accompanied his acquittal of the charge of Bible-burning in Kingstown confirmed this popularity even more. His superiors were less enamoured of his popularity and were worried by his political opinions, especially when they spilled over into criticism of the Pope's temporal power. He was called to Rome, ostensibly to preach a course of sermons in the Russian church, but he hated the experience and found himself under increasing pressure from the Redemptorist authorities to temper his enthusiasm, behaviour and expressed sympathies. In 1861 he sought leave to join a more austere order, a permission that was readily and speedily granted. Although he soon realised his mistake, he was not allowed to rejoin the Congregation, and for over twenty years, until his death in 1885, he lived in obscurity as chaplain to the Mater Misericordiae Hospital in Dublin.[33] His story is particularly sad because, whatever his excesses, he was consistently misunderstood by his superiors, who insisted on treating his passionate love for justice as an embarrassment to the Congregation, expressive of a lack of obedience and humility, and failed altogether to appreciate his real intellectual gifts and political discernment. It was the same rigidity and lack of imagination on the part of superiors that lost Isaac Hecker, founder of the Paulists.

In like manner, the strength of character which Francis Hall had displayed as a young man was not weakened by his years in the Congregation. Although eulogised after his death by the *Freeman's Journal* as 'a splendid orator, [who] imbued the listening congregations with a devout feeling, to an extent to which few missioners succeed',[34] his superiors were less enamoured of his abilities. Coffin reported to Rome that Hall

> is causing me much difficulty by his extravagant views and opinions on Ireland and the Irish, Patriotism, the Political-Religious aspects of the Papacy and Temporal Sovereignty, the Zouaves and fighting, and the use of

blood ... Hall thinks it is his duty to keep alive the Irish patriotic spirit.[35]

Although the Provincial lamented that 'his present position in our midst is that of poor Petcherine all over again — a craze about the Irish leading to principles [which are] utterly opposed to the teaching of the Holy See, the wishes of the Irish Hierarchy and, above all, to the spirit of St Alphonsus and the Congñ', his 'obstinate democratic views' were not the only danger.[36] Equally serious were the style and content of his mission preaching. At a mission in Thurles, for example, he preached for one and three-quarter hours, while the bishop had to wait to give Benediction. At the close of the mission, he 'made the women shout out loudly, clap their hands several times, jumping up and down etc., all with the Blessed Sacrament exposed and the Archbishop kneeling in the sanctuary'.[37] The vexed prelate asked why a madman had been allowed on mission and forbade him to enter his diocese again.[38] On the other hand, the archdeacon of Drogheda specifically asked for his services for a renewal, and Hall always attracted many penitents.

The examples of Hall and Petcherine illustrate the great fear of singularity which marked all Catholic orders in the last century. When Mauron told Coffin to accept as Redemptorists only those 'with the right abilities, talents and intellectual ability', and that 'it is better to have a few of these than many without',[39] he was appealing for stolid, practical characters, who were prepared to operate within the narrow, specified limits of correctly-defined behaviour and showed no inclination to dissidence. Yet Mauron's advice flew in the face of reality, and it is noteworthy that several professed members of the Congregation showed very clear signs of mental instability. Fr Lempfried was not the only Belgian Redemptorist who was recalled because of this. There was also Fr Rudeau, who conceived the reading in the refectory of the curses pronounced against the Egyptians in the Book of Exodus as a personal attack on him by the lector. He awaited his opportunity for revenge, and when the community was in the chapel after the meal, singing the *Te Deum*, he struck the lector a violent blow and laid him out.[40] Years later, a candidate for the priesthood, John Sampson, became so mad after his novitiate that he had to be kept under restraint at Bishop Eton. However, he periodically escaped and informed passers-by that he was being kept a prisoner against his will. This was too much of an embarrassment to the Redemptorists, who eventually had him confined to a lunatic asylum, where 'he resigned himself to the will of God'.[41] Fr Albert Barry was also deranged, though he was kept in check. All of these men, and others, proceeded through the novitiate without problems; if they already showed the signs of later mental trouble, it was not discovered there. Similarly, there were those who were discovered to be quite unsuited to be Redemptorists, like Fr Cyril Ryder, who joined the Congregation from the Oblates of St Charles in 1883 and whom the Provincial accused sixteen years later of caring 'nothing for the ways and traditions of the Congregation'.[42]

The biggest surprise is that many Redemptorists were, in fact, unfitted for the specific work of their order. Fr de Buggenoms was not considered a good mission preacher, 'nor did he excel in his retreats to clergy, which were rather a source of mortification to him, but he was a very spiritual man and excelled especially in the direction of nuns'.[43] Fr Bradshaw had such a dread of preaching that in his later years he only heard confessions and recited the rosary on missions,[44] while Fr Gibson

> was not spoken of as a very great Missionary, or as an eloquent preacher. His sermons were well composed and delivered with earnestness; and his enunciation was distinct, and his voice penetrating; but there was evidence of studied preparation and some appearance of restraint.[45]

Andrew Boylan, who was to become the first Irish Provincial, was commended as 'a most industrious missioner', but 'on account of his inflexible voice and a certain rapidity of communication, he may not be a good preacher'.[46] Even those in major positions of responsibility were not always of

William Plunkett (1824-1900) in old age. He was the first Irish-born Redemptorist to join the English Province and was Rector of Mount St Alphonsus, Limerick in the early 1860s and of St Mary's, Clapham from 1868 to 1871.

*Andrew Boylan (1842-1910), first Provincial of the Irish Province, 1898.
He was later appointed Bishop of Kilmore.*

the right calibre. Thus, for instance, Fr Stevens as Novice Master was 'so irregular and indulgent in his own manner of life; he makes such pets of certain Novices, so that it makes many of our best Fathers think it would be impossible for him really to train our Novices properly in the Spirit of the Congregation and the practice of at least some of the Religious Virtues, e.g., that of mortification'.[47]

The greatest factor working against the Alphonsian ideal was the force of nationalism within the Congregation. As early as 1849, Fr Hëilig warned his subjects that they should scrupulously avoid any talk or discussion which might be thought offensive by brethren from another country,[48] and Coffin was forced to remind the missioners that 'our work is to preach to the people as Catholics, as members of the Holy Church, and not as belonging to this or that country'.[49] Yet the Redemptorists could not be so olympian with regard to the problems associated with nationalist sentiment; although there was much good intention to heed the advice of Provincials,[50] nationalism could not be effaced and was the source of repeated admonitions.[51] It provided, as we have seen, a focus for agitation and discontent within the Province, which in turn led to heightened criticism of superior authority. The tight rein that Coffin exercised over the Province would admit of no serious problems; his reports to Rome, for instance, contained criticism of individuals, but always gave a good picture of the life of the Province. His successors were more expressive of difficulties and less prone to give Rome what it wanted to hear. It may also be true that they did not possess the same ruthlessness to check abuses and maintain standards; the repeated attention which had to be drawn to such things as the prohibition of smoking is an indication of this.[52]

To some extent, the problems within the Province were the result of its isolation. In 1886, when there was a possibility that Mauron might visit England, the Provincial wrote to him that

> we are so isolated in these islands that we are in danger of losing the spirit of St Alphonsus, or at least its fullness,

at once so strong and sweet. But a single visit of the head (Chef) of the Congregation, of him who wears the mantle (porte le manteau) of our Holy Father himself, would compensate much for all this.[53]

Allowing for the exaggerated flattery implicit in this statement, MacDonald was not wholly wide of the mark, although there were other factors to consider. After the establishment of the studentate, for example, intellectual isolation and non-exposure to the cultural ethos of a Catholic country combined to confirm the nationalist tendencies already at work in the Province. The Extraordinary Visitation of the Province in 1894 revealed some disturbing results of its isolation. A 'decay of the spirit of obedience and the growing loss of love for Superiors and trust in them' was noted, while the works of St Alphonsus, it was claimed, were not read as much as hitherto, so that 'many in the Congregation have not mastered the Spirit, nor the *Works* of St Alphonsus, but have avoided him'. Indeed, criticism of Alphonsus was not unknown: 'We don't live in the last century; we are not in Naples; we must keep pace with the age ... St Alphonsus was no doubt the man of his day, but not the man of our age. His views are antiquated, unfit for our times, and we, though his children, ought not to follow him'. The Visitor concluded that St Alphonsus was 'no longer loved, nor looked up to as a guide with the boundless veneration and affection of earlier days'. Rather, in the argument that Alphonsus's meditations were fine for Neapolitan communities, but that in England more intelligent meat was required, and that his Marian devotion was 'too sensational, extreme, untheological — injurious to the one Mediator — shocking to Protestants', the Visitor bewailed the fact that 'worshippers of Newman rather than of Our Holy Father are found in the Province', and that 'new ideas are creeping in amongst a certain and daily increasing number of our fathers about preaching not only at home, but also on the missions. Intellectual lectures, essays, dissertations, newspaper articles, or what just sounds like them, are beginning to appear and to be approved'.[54] There was criticism, too, of the missions, particularly the neglect of children's missions and of missions in country places. The inadequate number of men sent on missions of inadequate length, the neglect of study, the amount of time the fathers spent on missions in excess of the permitted six months of the year were also highlighted by Fr Magnier. Much of the last criticism was unavoidable, as Magnier was forced to concede; at Limerick, for example, there was enough work to keep twelve missioners continually busy, but there were only four of them. There was much that was hopeful; analysis and assessment of individual fathers' character and missionary capability spoke well of the Province's personnel, and the novitiate was considered strong, but the general tone of the report was unfavourable to the Province.[55]

Although the judgement of the Visitor was questioned,[56] his was not the only voice raised in anxiety at the drifting trends of the Province away from the Alphonsian ideal. Fr Geoghegan wrote to the Rector Major expressing his disquiet that the missions in the Province were lacking both in depth and in time to do any good.[57] He bemoaned the failure to hear all the parishioners' confessions during the course of a mission and the tendency for retreats to confraternities to become quasi-missions for the whole parish, and he argued that instead of accepting any and every mission offered by bishops and parish priests on their terms, missions should be refused unless regular conditions could be insisted upon. These abuses were particularly prevalent in Ireland, and Geoghegan pinpointed the root cause as a failure of nerve and lack of strength on the part of Redemptorist rectors: 'to please them [i.e. parish priests] is the root of [our] evils (vitiorum principium), but it is the principle that obtains much among us'. Elsewhere, he observed that 'the greater part of our work has been in *towns* and in better-off places; with the result that the poorer and more remote country places — particularly in Ireland — are left comparatively unmissioned. It is a remarkable fact', he continued

> that though [in Ireland] for the last 45 years, we have left the poorer, the mountainous, and the more remote places comparatively unmissioned, although it was for

115

such places that the Congñ was specially founded; and although in addition to the plea of their poverty and greater spiritual want, the people were emigrating in large numbers to different parts of the world.[58]

In the letter to Raus, he went on to argue that too much money was being spent on buildings that were too far from the centres of population. Grinding the Irish axe, he bewailed the fact that of all the religious orders, only the Redemptorists had made no foundation in the west of Ireland and were content to supply from England, with the result, for example, that in the fifty-three parishes of the diocese of Tuam, the Redemptorists had given only two missions in forty years. Having outlined the lack of common discipline and practice, he concluded that

we have for [our] founder a great Doctor of the Church; therefore, his Rule and Constitutions ought not to be changed at the will of the Rectors, Superiors of the Missions or Provincials. Yet that is what happens in this Province, as I have shown.[59]

Of themselves, Geoghegan's complaints would command little attention, and some of them were both unfair and exaggerated. In so far as they accord with, and contribute to, the picture of the Province's decline given in Magnier's visitation report, they are of more than passing interest. Certainly, the Roman authorities were sufficiently worried to order a Provincial Consultation with the object of drawing up a set of Provincial Statutes, in which clear and unequivocal guidelines for the conduct of the missions would be laid down and Alphonsian methods and techniques reasserted. Recognising that there was 'an undertone grumble' throughout the Province that the Rule and Constitutions with regard to making a strict Redemptorist spiritual life had not been sufficiently adhered to, the Provincial Consultation showed also that theological studies were 'somewhat shallow' and 'kicked aside by us'. The need to read more of St Alphonsus, and be imbued with those principles that he taught and prescribed, was admitted, as was the fact that some fathers, though of many years' standing as missioners, were not supplied with several of the important mission sermons and instructions. Recreation after dinner with the secular clergy was said to be gaining ground on the missions, as was the purchase of papers and periodicals by the fathers as they travelled to, and during the course of, the mission, some of which 'offend public modesty', while grumbling about food and drink was on the increase.[60] Even so, the Provincial considered that 'spirituality is more wanting with us than knowledge of the missions'.[61] Yet the problem was more than could be encompassed by such a remark. What Magnier had sensed in the disregard for St Alphonsus was an insidious and, perhaps, unclearly-defined lack of conviction in the relevance and effectiveness of the original apostolate which had inspired and sustained the early Redemptorist pioneers in Britain and Ireland. Fr Livius expressed what few others were either prepared or courageous enough to admit, when he argued that the Redemptorists must diversify in their apostolate and even undertake parochial work:

> It often seems to me that the old missions in England at least have almost run their day. The circumstances of the parishes, priests and Catholics generally are so much changed from what they were 40 or 50 years ago. And now in most places the priests call in the Fathers only to bring up the outstanders every 3 or 4 years to their Easter and annual duties, whilst in some parts of England the Fathers give hardly any missions.[62]

It remains to be seen if analysis of the Redemptorists' mission work in the last two decades of the century bears out Livius's assertion. Whatever the misgivings about the general drift of the Province, the degree of self-criticism that abounded was an encouraging sign of its ability to reform and adapt, and outside the Congregation little was known of its inner turmoil. The fact that the order could contain and hold together so many talents and contrasting personalities, all of them stamped with the Redemptorist mark, is testimony to their training and life-style. It is also testimony to their own individual dedication to their religious calling and identity. The reputation of the

Congregation in Britain and Ireland was built upon succeeding generations' experience of individual missioners. It was not necessarily their piety or holiness that impressed — though there are examples of both — but their unfussy professionalism. Patrick Sampson recalled Fathers Theunis and Schneider as belonging 'to that category of apostolic men who do steady, solid work in the pulpit and sacred tribunal, but who do not set the world on fire', and he considered them 'models of the ordinary, solid and effective missionary'.[63] Many of the early missioners were foreigners who spoke English imperfectly but were able to win the people by their earnestness, zeal and unction. Thus, after a mission in Kilkenny in December 1858, the people gave a formal address to the missioners, thanking them for 'the eminent services you have rendered to religion in this city', and noting that 'you have laboured with a truly apostolic zeal'. The people, the address continued,

> will, with God's blessing, never forget the lively faith, the firm hope and the ardent charity you have impressed upon them ... Would that we could find words to do justice to your merits, and to express their feelings towards you — to tell you of their respect for your sacred character, their appreciation of your pious labours, and their unbounded gratitude for the blessings you have conferred upon them. Three weeks ago we were strangers to each other, but within that short period you have laid the foundations of a friendship which shall be as lasting as life itself.[64]

Reporting the mission in Carndonagh, Co. Donegal earlier in the same year, a correspondent wrote of 'being carried back to the days of Bossuet and Massillon and the Augustan age of French eloquence'. He noted that 'the good Fathers have the secret of true eloquence; they feel themselves, and can make others feel. They are convinced of the importance of their mission, and carry with them the zeal of their great founder'.[65] The examples of Kilkenny and Carndonagh go a long way to answering the questions put to its readers by the

Wexford People, reporting the wild scenes of the Redemptorists' departure from Hook, Co. Wexford, and the affectionate expressions of the people: 'What has produced this strong attachment? How have four poor strange priests, without scrip or staff, gained in one short month such an ascendancy over the people? Have the missioners of any other denomination ever produced such wonderful effects? Never!'.[66] A few years later, a reporter marvelled that the Redemptorist missioners at Emly, Co. Tipperary 'worked daily and nightly with a zeal that showed no limit, with a vigilance that knew no sleep, with a devotion which is known only to those men who are inspired by the loftiest motives, and who look for reward not to the praises of mortals'.[67] The passage of time did not bedim such a reputation. Thus, the missioners at Kanturk, Co. Cork in 1878 were said to have been characterised by 'an eloquence in the pulpit of the most touching and convincing nature and by a zeal and perseverance in the confessionals that knew no cost'.[68] In the Highlands of Scotland in the 1880s, missions were given in quarries and on the mountainside, in music halls and masonic lodges, Mass being offered in attics and basements 'and all sorts of holes and corners'.[69] If this shows that the pioneering spirit was not lost, the Redemptorists' reputation was gained and sustained because they were regarded as plain, unfastidious preachers of the eternal truths: 'The fathers of the Redemptorist Order are well-known for their piety, zeal and humility in preaching the truths of the Gospel. Their names are now almost a household word throughout the Catholic world'.[70]

Individual fathers received similar, affectionate praise from the newspapers. Edward O'Donnell, Rector of Limerick for eleven years until his death in 1878, was called 'this splendid specimen of the national priesthood' by a local newspaper, and the widespread lament at his death was occasioned by the sense of loss of one said to have been marked by 'unbounded charity, deep humility, earnest piety and a wonderful zeal for the salvation of souls and invariable equanimity of temper and unvarying kindness of heart'.[71] If

119

this represented local praise, fulsome obituaries were not uncommon in the Irish national press. Fr Johnson, erstwhile editor of the *Wexford People,* was hailed as 'a zealous and widely-esteemed priest … [who] leaves behind him a godly record of solid work done for faith and country … He has preached and left memorials of his ardent zeal in nearly every portion of Ireland'.[72] Whatever his nuisance to the Redemptorist authorities, Francis Hall was similarly eulogised, and when news of his death was received in Dundalk, bunting was displayed at half-mast on the quays.[73]

Few missioners were as highly praised and widely esteemed as Father Harbison. Coffin described him as 'the Irish Father Bernard … solidly pious and virtuous … he it is who directs almost all the large missions in Ireland; the bishops request him for the retreats to the clergy [and] to seminarians … He is the great missionary of the country'.[74] In 1876, when he left Limerick to found the Dundalk house, the *Limerick Reporter* lamented his departure, attributing to him 'that firm hold of the citizens', which had 'won for the Redemptorist Fathers the large place in the hearts' best affections of the great bulk of the people from which it is impossible to displace them'.[75] Patrick Sampson recorded that Harbison was known as 'the parish priest of Ireland', and noted that while there was little material in his sermons, the power and converting force and success of his oratory came with the peroration at their end.[76] In these perorations, 'his burning words, his quivering voice, his flashing eye, his animated gestures, and whole exterior bearing, displayed the interior emotions of his heart for the conversion and salvation of his auditors'.[77] In fact, during the course of his missionary career, Harbison gave seven large missions in St Nicholas's, Dublin and never changed a word in his discourses, but it was said that every discourse was heard by the people as eagerly as the first occasion when it had been preached.[78] After his death, among the many obituaries that appeared in the Irish press, the *Morning News* opined that 'no missionary of recent times worked more earnestly or with equal depth of pious devotion', and compared him favourably with the great Father Tom

Burke, O.P. '[whom] he rivalled and excelled'.[79]

If much of the Redemptorists' reputation was built around the heroic impression created by such pioneers, which allowed the ascription of titles like 'martyr of the confessional',[80] the affectionate necrologies of deceased confrères contribute to the picture of the qualities and worth of individual fathers. Fr Gibson, for instance, was said to be a model of regular observance and obedience to his superiors, a man of simple piety and of a perfect religious spirit, of unfailing kindness and genial, child-like gaiety, which caused him to be 'a treasure in every community which had the happiness of possessing him'.[81] At the same time, his faults were not passed over without comment; it is this critical element that gives value to the necrologies, which otherwise would excite sceptical suspicion on the part of the historian. Fr Roes, who went to Limerick as Superior in 1857, was thus described as 'austere and unkind by nature', although 'he did all in his power to overcome this natural disposition'.[82] He obviously succeeded, for when the young Patrick Sampson encountered Roes, he considered him 'an image of Our Lord'.[83] The sense of loss felt in Wexford at the death of Fr Van Antwerpen in 1853 was reported by a member of another religious order to have been 'as if some dear parent had been snatched away by sudden death from an affectionate family'.[84] His zeal for sinners and his indefatigable missionary labours were such that

> he made great and truly stupendous (magnos atque revera stupendos) fruits of penitence everywhere, he achieved outstanding (insignes) conversions of sinners, and for that reason he had won to himself the estimation and affection of of the people (et eoque aestimationem et affectionē populorum sibi captaverat), so that he was called everywhere by no other name than Good Father John.[85]

Such qualities were not confined to the early years; Fr Lubienski, for example, was described as 'an eloquent and earnest preacher and a very fire of zeal in all other walks of the apostolic life. Wherever he has given missions, his memory is still held in benediction by all who knew him. At home he was in all things a model religious, observant, humble, mortified, charitable'.[86]

The peculiar stamp that was impressed upon Redemptorist priests by their religious formation was intended to produce a love for the Institute, out of which grew apostolic zeal and longing for holiness. John O'Connor, who died as a professed student, was said to have had a deep love for the Rule which reflected 'his deep love for his vocation, having continually in his mouth words of thanksgiving for having been called to the Congregation'.[87] Fr Leo Van der Stickele, who died in 1887, was 'regarded by his confrères as a saint', and undertook great acts of mortification, such as cleaning the shoes of the community.[88] Called by Bishop O'Reilly of Liverpool 'the apostle of the diocese', his preaching was described as 'simplicity itself, but there was an earnestness and an unction about it that changed and won hearts'.[89] Of course, it is easy to be charitable after someone's death; those characteristics which are eulogised may well have been the source of difficulty in life. Fr Lans, for example, was a man 'of great force of character, of firm decision, of resolution, ardent courage and practical energy', which qualities brought him into conflict with Coffin at various times. But they also had the effect 'of inspiring to a singular degree, the hearts and minds of others with something of his own sentiments. Many came to Father Lans for direction, counsel and consolation in their difficulties and trials'.[90] When he was too old to go on mission, Lans was assiduous in visiting the sick and assisting the dying, including condemned prisoners in Walton (Liverpool) gaol.[91]

Sufficient has been written to show that the members of the Institute in Britain and Ireland in the last century were not unworthy sons of St Alphonsus. Although we have been concerned with the priests of the Congregation, final mention should be made of the lay brothers, who performed the domestic chores that released their priest-confrères to do their apostolic work. Often, they served as an example and inspiration to the ordained brethren by the sanctity of their lives and their devotion to duty. Two lay brothers who played an important part in the establishment of the Congregation in England lived long lives and were greatly mourned after their deaths. Stephen Senegres, who lived at Bishop Eton for forty years until his death in 1892, was esteemed as 'a truly holy brother, [who] edified the community by his spirit of prayer and recollection'.[92] After Felician Dubucquoi's death in 1897 at Limerick, where he had been sacristan of the church for forty-one years, it was written of him that

> throughout the whole course of his religious life, his conduct was exemplary — exemplary in his respect for Superiors, and for the Fathers, and exemplary in his kindness to his confrères — exemplary in his politeness to strangers and in his charity to the poor — exemplary in his untiring labour. He never spared himself — he was beloved and esteemed by all.[93]

Whatever the shortcomings of their religious formation, of the rigid ideal to which they were expected to conform, it remains true that the Redemptorists managed to maintain a high level of esteem on the part of the Catholic public. Although, towards the end of the century, especially in England, doubts were raised about the relevance of the apostolate and the clarity of their vocation, they were not sufficient to blight the reputation or the self-image of the Redemptorists as epitomisers of a confident, aggressive Catholicism. In the final analysis, members of religious orders are to be judged in the light of their fidelity to their founder and his ideals. By this standard, the Redemptorists in Britain and Ireland in the last century were, on the whole, not lacking.

7

Mission background

The Redemptorists had come to Britain and Ireland in order to conduct missions and retreats. The development of the Institute and the formation of its members were directed to facilitate this end, which was shared by other Counter-Reformation orders. Parochial missions were a hallmark of the reformed Catholicism which had its roots in the early sixteenth century and received its ideological formulation at the Council of Trent.[1] They were thus symptomatic of a Church on the offensive against Protestantism, ignorance and spiritual neglect. With varying degrees of success in the late sixteenth and throughout the seventeenth century parochial missions helped to christianise the masses in the Catholic lands of Europe.[2] In the Age of Enlightenment they suffered an eclipse, prolonged during the revolutionary and Napoleonic wars. As the old order sought to recover, and the Church emerged from the turmoil with a new missionary zeal to restore what had been lost by Enlightenment and Revolution, parochial missions returned to favour and became a standard feature of nineteenth-century Catholicism throughout the world.[3]

Their return to favour resulted from the conviction that they were a valuable means of forming and consolidating strong Catholic communities by confirming the resolute, reviving the languid faith of the spiritually negligent, recalling the lapsed, evangelising the ignorant. This was felt to be all the more important as the Church came to feel itself increasingly under siege from the forces of liberalism, religious indifference and immoral secularism. The fostering of a resistant, local Catholic identity in a hostile world was not merely a reaction or counterblast to these destructive forces, but was also intended to protect and preserve intact the edifice of Faith. This was conceived as a battle for survival; its apocalyptic implications were not wholly articulated, but they were hinted at in the rallying-cries to flee the contamination of the world and in the frenetic efforts that were expended to gather as many as possible into the Ark of the Church before the inevitable, calamitous storms which were brewing all around, finally broke. Beneath all this activity was an underlying integralist ideology, which, in contrast with other forms of religious influence, sought to integrate Catholics into their (at least in Britain) largely urban, working-class environment, while at the same time 'supernaturalising' their lives, providing a substitute culture, so that they did not become wholly of their environment.[4]

The work of parochial missions in helping to establish this Catholic identity was an essential prelude, as well as contribution, to the building-up of parishes and the cementation of regular parochial life, on which the long-term success of the missions depended. Without the superstructure of parish organisation and parochial enterprises, missions would have been little more than episodic revivalist campaigns, after the manner of Protestant equivalents. Catholic missions were intended in the first place to reach those who were otherwise beyond the Church's reach and to put them into touch, or greater touch, with the institutional Church; without such a superstructure to assimilate them, parochial missions would have been futile.[5] In England by 1886 it was held that Jesuit, Passionist and Redemptorist missions 'have, perhaps, had a greater influence upon Catholics ... than any other of the many good things which God has bestowed upon us in these our days'.[6] Commentators might give priority to such other ventures as the network of Catholic schools, but there was widespread agreement that parochial missions did much to avert the loss to the Church of many Catholics and to recall them to the practice of their faith.[7] In their reports to Propaganda, the bishops mentioned regular parochial missions, together with sodalities, the increase in school accommodation, the provision of better seminary training, and the like, both as a normal feature of their dioceses and as having a beneficial effect in terms of preserving and increasing the faith of Catholics.[8]

Somewhat prosaically, an Irish Redemptorist described a parochial mission as 'a sending forth of men, divinely chosen to teach and to save, to enlighten the mind, to move the heart and to cleanse the soul from sin'.[9] The Constitutions of the Congregation envisaged missions as

> nothing else than a continual Redemption, which, by means of His ministers, the Son of God is always effecting in the world. They, in a certain sense, support the Church, preserve her fervour, separate the tares from the wheat, give strength to the weak, confirm the strong, raise up the fallen, banish evil, and overcome the wiles of the devil. In a word, we should think of Missions as the chief, not to say the only, defence and aid for preserving the faith and for establishing it firmly on the Rock, which is Christ.[10]

The mission was to be 'an intense "all-out" effort to strengthen the life of grace in every soul' to whom it was preached.[11] Indeed, it was

> an extraordinary grace. The time of a MISSION is the time of mercy and blessing. A MISSION is a message from Almighty God to His children, to put them in mind that there is 'but one thing necessary' and that that 'one thing' is the salvation of their souls. Many who are now in Heaven are there because they took advantage of this extraordinary grace, and many are lost because they were careless to avail themselves of it. God calls *me* to the mission — what must I do? I must attend to it as well as I can — Daily, if possible — I must listen to all the Instructions and Sermons — I must prepare to return to God by making a good, humble Confession — I must begin at once to pray that I may have the grace to break off directly the habits of sin, or of tepidity, to make a good MISSION, and save my soul.[12]

Through the preaching of Christ crucified and the use of revivalist techniques, the mission sought to inure people in their belief in Christ and the Church, to teach them sound principles of morality and to re-establish the regular frequentation of the sacraments. This spiritual intent was basic to all missions, but behind every request for a mission was a general, and sometimes a particular, situation, which the mission was designed to meet. In general, there was the difficulty of keeping Catholics up to the mark, of translating nominal faith into the firm habits of prayer, piety and practice which the institutional Church deemed necessary and to which its efforts were directed. To this was added the difficulty of maintaining and perpetuating the faith of Catholics against a background of Protestantism or even of religious indifference, combining with such debilitating social problems as those associated with poor housing and drink and with the moral turpitude which many religious observers believed infected especially the urban proletariat, among whom the majority of Catholics were to be found. The missions were thus part, and particular instances, of a wider, universal apostolate. The call for a mission could also be precipitated by a particular situation which it was intended to resolve. Thus, speaking at the opening of the Redemptorist mission house in Dundalk in August 1876, Archbishop McGettigan reflected on the missionary calls which the fathers would receive:

> One parish priest will come to them and say, 'I have some proselytising ministers and Bible readers in my parish. I fear that they may do harm to some of my little ones. Oh! do come and give a mission to the children. Instruct them practically and well, give them a lively interest in everything which concerns the faith and obligations of religion'. Another will come and say, 'There are some secret society men in my parish who are leading others astray, and producing insubordination to all lawful authority. They will not dispose themselves, nor allow others to dispose themselves for the worthy reception of the sacraments. Do, Father, come and give my parish a

good mission'. Another will say, 'Many of my people have been careless and lukewarm, others are addicted to drink, others after promising often to amend return to their bad habits. For the love of God, come and help. Nothing can save them but a good mission'.[13]

Before each mission, the Redemptorists themselves ascertained the spiritual state of the parish and any particular abuses, which were recorded in the mission chronicles. Typical of these was the following estimate of Callan, Co. Kilkenny in 1887: 'The people were in a rather indifferent state before the mission and, according to the local clergy, factions, old family quarrels, neglect of religious duties, drink, company-keeping were prevalent abuses; add to these a spirit of independence and contempt for ecclesiastical authority — fruits of the ''O'Keefe scandal'' '.[14]

In tackling such problems and coming to the aid of the ordinary pastors of the Church, the mission was intended to supply a degree of spiritual intensity that was not normally experienced or otherwise sustainable, such that it could be described as 'an assault on the soul'.[15] This assault was meant to enliven the whole parish community and to be the means of a new start for everyone; an early Redemptorist mission in Douglas, Isle of Man, was thus 'not so much a regular mission as a stirring-up of a kind of apathy of the whole place on account of the priest being infirm and being at variance with a good many of his parishioners'.[16] Often it was felt that only a mission could provide the necessary remedy for a parish's ills. Describing the situation in Ireland in the early years of the mission, Fr Van der Aa wrote that the country was full of abandoned souls and that the priests did not know what to do with the ignorant and lapsed. They were, therefore, happy that the missions caused people to come to instruction and that they were there prepared for the sacraments, thus relieving the priests of a terrible burden. Van der Aa believed that the circumstances of persecution, emigration, poverty and, consequently, of ignorance and negligence were such that only the grace of a mission could avail the people.[17] Nor did this conviction that a mission was the essential, indeed almost panacean, means of grace to remedy spiritual neglect and abuse diminish with the passage of time. Before relating the success of a mission in Kilmallock, Co. Limerick in 1883, the Redemptorist Chronicler analysed the 'not remarkably flourishing' spiritual state of the people. Although the greater number of parishioners were in the habit of going to the sacraments, they did so infrequently, 'i.e. they were satisfied with Christmas and Easter'. As to abuses in the parish,

> we may mention that of drunkenness on the occasion of fairs and visits to different towns, such as Limerick, Cork and Tipperary, to sell their farm produce. In addition to this, it was a public fact that several young women of the place had disgraced their sex of late by having illegitimate children; which fact certainly reveals the truth that the standard of morality is not altogether what it ought to be in Kilmallock.[18]

In similar fashion, a mission in Ilkestone, Derbyshire in 1887, where the bad attendance at the sacraments caused by the pastor's neglect and by a mission preached ten years previously by a severe Cistercian, who had succeeded only in frightening the people, was remedied and 'gave the people a new start. Nothing but a mission could have done this work'.[19] Summarising such benefits, a newspaper reported that the advantages of a mission could not be overrated 'when it is considered how potently it operates in arousing many out of their spiritual slothfulness and in bringing absentees into active communion with the flock'.[20]

If the parish mission was both an example and demonstration of grace, it was not meant merely to convert individuals and to encourage them to a frequent reception of the sacraments, the performance of the duties of their particular state and the avoidance of sin. The assault was intended to confirm the separation of Catholics from their non-Catholic neighbours by drawing them deeper into the life of the Church, making it the dominant force in their lives, and thereby consolidate the Catholic ghetto as a bastion against the malign influences of wider society. By thus removing people from the immoral ambience of secular influence, it was hoped that those contaminating forces that were destructive of true religious feeling would be effectively neutralised and the Catholic community immured against them. In this respect, there was no difference between missions in Ireland, where Catholics were in the majority, and those in Britain. Although the missions were directed to the needs of a particular parish community, which made for certain differences between Irish and British missions, the overriding call to holiness was intended to effect the psychological separation of Catholics, wherever they might be, from whatever the Church deemed to be detrimental to the faith. What marked a good mission was not just the attraction of large numbers to the confessional and altar-rail, although this was important as indicative of their conversion; it was also the dissolution or resolution of null or mixed marriages, the removal of children from Protestant schools and institutions, the implanted desire to shun the occasions and places of sin, such as beer-houses, wakes, music halls, the destruction of secret societies and, within the Catholic community, the reconciliation of enemies, the restoration of good relations between bishop and priest and people. These were the areas of danger which ecclesiastical authority regarded as inhibitors of Catholicism's proper progress and destructive of its essential solidarity. The missions were in the vanguard of the fight that was common to the whole Church, and which the whole Church was increasingly geared up to undertake, a fight against the contrary social and religious forces and the creation of favourable conditions according to which the Catholic masses could be reclaimed and retained within a Catholic sub-culture. Missions were the means to convert and draw into the nexus of Catholic institutional life those who formed part of the Catholic community but stood on its fringes, and to enclose them, together with those who were already converted and persuaded, in their own religious and social world. Paradoxically, despite its universal claims, the Catholic Church opted for the homogeneity of the sect, with its alienation from the outside world, in much the same way as other denominations, though on a larger scale and, ultimately, more successfully.

The main difficulty of achieving these aims, and working against them, was the political, social, cultural and moral background against which Catholics were meant to preserve their faith and adhere ever closer to a Church which was making strenuous efforts to serve their needs. The course and content of the missions, which will be the subject of the next chapter, can be understood and appreciated only within the context in which they operated and which they were meant to help to answer. Something of the difficulty of reaching those for whom the missions were intended is reflected in a report of the missions in the dioceses of Westminster and Southwark in the late 1860s. Although he felt that in each mission the fathers did much good, and that there were 'most consoling cases', Coffin lamented that

> the Catholics are poor and scattered among an immense population and there is no *esprit de corps:* poverty and incessant labour and materialism and indifference which surrounds them does much harm, and in consequence it is difficult to get to them, to get them to the mission and to take a true interest in their spiritual welfare.[21]

A mission in 1862 at St James's, Spanish Place found that 'here as throughout the great towns of England the mass of the Catholic population is composed of Irish poor living in the courts, the garrets and cellars', but they were found to be buried in grosser neglect and ignorance of religion than in the larger towns of Lancashire.[22] The problems of the metropolis, however, merely foreshadowed those of the large centres of population in Britain. The missioners at St Catherine's, Sheffield in 1888, for instance, found that the scattered Catholics had 'no spirit in them' and were 'half-ashamed of being Catholics'.[23] Writing towards the end of the century about Scotland and its inhabitants, whom he described as 'a most drunken and impure people', a Redemptorist priest felt that the poor state of the 350,000 Catholics was due to the combination of their indifference, as a result of daily contact with infidelity and heresy, and the great evil of drink ('diluvium ebrietatis'). The faithful he found hard to instruct, difficult to move for the better, 'and those who are moved do not persevere in what is good'; although there was much good done in many places, most of those who came to the mission, he believed, 'return to their vomit'. He concluded that if this state of affairs were to continue, it would be impossible to preserve the faith.[24]

This pessimistic account illustrates one of the most serious problems among the Victorian working-class, what one bishop described as 'the national evil'.[25] It was not just that drunkenness led its victims to neglect their religious duties, but that it resulted in the neglect, destitution and break-up of families, in greater poverty, and in brawling, which earned Catholics a bad name.[26] In short, it was 'the source and origin of many of the gravest ills'.[27] Thus, the condition of Catholics all around Glasgow was found by the Redemptorists to be 'the worst of all' because 'drunkenness and all the consequences were in abundance', and they found it hard to break through the spiritual and material myopia which this caused.[28] Drunkenness was, of course, a solacing response to the appalling conditions of life in which many working-class people found themselves, both in Ireland and in Britain, affecting both sexes from an early age.[29] Against it much effort was expended by the Catholic Church, ranging from the crusades of Fr Mathew in the 1830s and 1840s through the Catholic Association for the Suppression of Drunkenness and the many Temperance Associations to Cardinal Manning's Catholic Total Abstinence League of the Cross (1873). The results of such activity, however, were not encouraging. In his *relatio* of 1887, Bishop O'Reilly of Liverpool echoed the opinion of other churchmen that drink was the origin of many ills, and he continued:

> It causes me shame to admit that no efficacious remedy has been found applicable (adhiberi potuisse) to this evil. By every means, and everywhere, in the countryside as well as in towns, diocesan priests have sought by private exhortation, sermons, sodalities, and all other means to

expunge this pernicious evil of the faithful (pestem tam
perniciossam venis fidelium expellere studuerint).[30]

It was a standard feature of most missions that the pledge
would be given and encouragement made to refrain from drink
at least on specified days or such traditionally rowdy occasions
as the St Patrick's Day celebrations. At Airdrie, Lanarkshire
in April 1866, for instance, a thousand men took the 'Truce
of God', which obliged them not to enter public houses on
Saturdays, Sundays, New Year's Day, or during the local
races.[31] Occasionally, the large-scale incidence of alcohol
abuse lay behind the request for a mission, as at Clone, Co.
Wexford in November 1885, where the parish priest invited
the Redemptorists 'for the sole purpose of establishing a
"Temperance Sodality" for both sexes, though really the
women did not need it'.[32] Whether a sodality was
established or not, the evils of drink were referred to in many
sermons throughout the course of the mission, as well as in
a specific sermon on what came to be regarded as the greatest
social evil of the day. At St Vincent's, Liverpool in March 1858,
an instruction to married women encouraged them to take the
pledge for one week and to urge their husbands to attend the
sermon on drunkenness at which they would be asked to take
the same pledge, which covered St Patrick's Day, although
the women were told not to inform their menfolk about the
pledge![33] Traditional habits, however, were hard to
eradicate, and an Irish Redemptorist recalled a contemporary
mission in Hospital, Co. Limerick, at which a discussion broke
out among the men from outside the parish who had attended
the mission as to whether the pledge was binding on them;
they decided that it was not.[34] Nevertheless, the drive
against drunkenness was part of the missioner's endeavour,
and the widespread and deeply-ingrained habit of drink was
a constant irritant and obstacle against which they had to
battle.

Trying to persuade men to abandon the beer-shop meant
asking them to abandon a whole complex of recreational
behaviour and companionship, thereby further emphasising
the separation from their religiously-indifferent or non-teetotal

Protestant neighbours. In this context should also be seen the vigorous campaigns that were launched against mixed marriages. Here again, the emphasis on maintaining group solidarity in their marriage patterns was a means of preserving the Catholic community intact and of assisting the influence of the Church over its members. Dispensations for mixed marriages were given only after strict assurances were obtained from the non-Catholic partner, but mixed marriages were seen as a prime factor in the drifting away from the faith of many Catholics and the slide into indifference with which their children were infected.[35] Those who married a Protestant were themselves deemed to be semi-Protestant,[36] and their betrayal was compounded if their marriages were technically invalid because contracted in a registry office or before a Protestant minister, which usually led to their children being baptised 'in heretical churches' and educated 'in heretical schools'.[37] Of course, a mixed marriage could result in the conversion of the Protestant partner or in the children receiving a Catholic upbringing.[38] Thus, in 1893 mixed marriages in the diocese of Liverpool resulted in 2,333 conversions. At the same time, however, there were 804 apostasies directly attributable to marriage.[39] Such danger from apostasy was thought to be more prevalent in rural than in urban communities, as the Bishop of Galloway reported to Propaganda in 1885:

> It is certain that in the towns, where Catholics are united in large numbers with several churches, schools and priests, they support each other; their faith is in proportion more firm, stronger, and more fervent. They encourage and associate with one other. In addition, mixed marriages are proportionally rare among them. But it is otherwise where Catholics are few [in number] and dispersed in a large Protestant district. Sadly, such is the case in this diocese.[40]

The result was indifference, 'religious defections and deplorable apostasies'.[41]

In the towns and cities of Britain, habitual contact with non-

Catholics was thought to have an inevitably corrosive effect. A mission report concerning Blackley, Manchester in 1868 stated that it was no wonder there were so many abuses and deplorable indifference to their religious obligations among the Catholics since they lived 'in the midst of heretics'.[42] In such circumstances, mixed marriages were unavoidable, as were the consequences; so, the spiritual state of the people of St Mary and St Joseph's, Carlisle in 1892 was 'exceptionally bad owing to mixed marriages, company-keeping of the most disorderly nature', which led to 'coldness of faith which saps the whole parish of all love and respect for their religion'.[43] Although it was admitted that the people of St Mary and St Michael's, Commercial Road, East London seemed to have plenty of faith and that they were 'much weighed down with poverty and the hard times', it was the large incidence of mixed marriages which was said to provide 'great deadness and heaviness in them'.[44] The frequency with which mixed marriages, together with the problem of 'concubinage', are mentioned in the bishops' reports to Propaganda, as though they were one and the same problem, illustrates the size and intractable nature of this obstacle to Catholicism. A Redemptorist neatly summarised what was considered to be the result: 'Some members of the family go one way, others another, and many are too cold and indifferent to go anywhere'.[45] The solution, he felt, was to deplore any company-keeping with non-Catholics and to urge Catholics to seek relationships only with their co-religionists. Through the missions, the Redemptorists hoped to appeal to those who had fallen away as a result of a mixed marriage and, if possible, to attract their partners to the faith.

The Bishop of Plymouth, bemoaning the number of nominal Catholics who disobeyed the precepts of the Church, did not hear Sunday Mass or perform their Easter duties, was sure of the reason: 'they enter into civil marriage, like their neighbours (Protestants or infidels) without any spiritual sense, and later imitate [them] in morals'.[46] It was little comfort that 'in danger of death they seek the ministry of a priest', for such residual faith was often not transmitted to their offspring, who were largely ignorant of, and correspondingly indifferent to, the Catholic religion.[47] Bishop O'Reilly estimated in 1894 that of the 15,745 children of 7,153 mixed marriages in his diocese, half were in great danger of being lost altogether to the faith, together with a further 8,369 children of irreligious parents who never went to church.[48] The need to enliven the faith of such children and to rescue them for the faith was the motivating force behind the programme of school-building and the plethora of Catholic reformatories, orphanages and other institutions that burgeoned as the century progressed, together with the determined efforts to ensure that Catholic children in workhouses were properly catechised and protected from the influence of proselytisers. Often, during the course of a mission, provision was made for a missioner to visit the local workhouse and give instruction to the Catholic children. A particular feature of the Redemptorist apostolate in the 1850s was the large number of children's missions, which accounted for between one-third and one-half of all their labours, but which declined during the course of the century.[49] These were intended

> to attract together numbers, especially of poor abandoned children, who in consequence of their circumstances, have scarcely any knowledge of, still less love of religion, and to interest them in religion, and to let them see that it can be accommodated to their circumstances.[50]

In particular, the missions appealed to children over the ages of eight years, and 'principally those boys and girls at work up to the age of seventeen and eighteen, especially those brought up in much ignorance and neglect of religion'.[51] The aim was to enkindle faith and a religious spirit by attracting children who would not otherwise have attended the Catholic chapel. Children's missions were not intended to convert Protestants on a large scale, but to instil a strong self-identity among Catholic children, to bring them together under the knowledge and influence of their pastors, to whom belonged the long-term work of keeping them within the practice and household of the faith. In reclaiming the children of Catholics, it was hoped to appeal to their parents, and children's missions served as a preparation for many adult missions.

It was, however, a fact that in spite of all efforts to the contrary, many children were lost to the Catholic faith through the circumstances of their lives and their daily contact in such institutions as board schools, 'where Catholic children mix daily with non-Catholics; they become worse by their [i.e. non-Catholics] bad example, and drink the lethal poison of indifferentism (venenum indifferentismi lethiferum)'.[52] A Redemptorist chronicler bemoaned the great number of children who were brought up as heathens ('quos Arabes'),[53] while another observed of a mission in Wigan in 1886 that 'many, especially the young men, never came to the mission — children of mixed marriages or bad parents brought up to no religion and hardly to be called Catholics'.[54] Nor did working conditions assist; at Standish, near Wigan twelve-year-old boys went down the mines 'and thus in gross ignorance and without the sacraments spend their youth, and then, contracting marriages with non-Catholics, they easily fall away from their faith'.[55] And at Heckmondwike in Yorkshire in June 1889, the missioners noted 'a great loss of faith among the pitboys apprenticed out from Chadwell Industrial School among the Methodists'.[56] Later still, a successful children's mission at St Alphonsus's, Liverpool, nevertheless 'scarcely touched those for whom such a mission is necessary, viz. the bigger boys and girls, who have left school and are engaged at work or at business in shops and offices'.[57]

Many children were, of course, second and third generation Irish immigrants. Where they retained close contacts and a sense of identity with the Irish immigrant community and were not absorbed in the host community, it was easier for the Church to appeal to their traditional Catholic identity. Ironically, an important counterweight to the Church's influence both in Ireland itself and among the immigrants was the strength of nationalist feeling. On the whole, this presented few problems in the sense that the sympathies of many ecclesiastics were with the plight of the Irish. There were, however, certain political issues on which disagreement was inevitable. The parliamentary elections of 1880, for example, were said to have caused much damage between the priests and people of Athlone, Co. Westmeath,[58] and Fr Harbison considered that missions in Ireland were 'more necessary than ever owing to this miserable national and land-league politics'.[59] Rome's disapproval of the Land League and its condemnation of the 'Plan of Campaign' in 1888 did not lessen the support for Parnell and for the boycotting of rents.[60] Years of tenant agitation and grievances over land reform created a hardened political climate which it was difficult to break through in order to appeal to people's religious susceptibilities. A Redemptorist mission in late 1889 in Kilnish, Co. Limerick, where the land question had greatly agitated the people, who were united in boycotting their landlords, was ineffective because it was 'difficult to work the people up to such a pitch of fervour as to give up spite'.[61] On the other hand, at Tulla, Co. Clare in 1892 the missioners did manage to ease the tension between landlords and tenants and even to persuade the landlords not to carry out some of their threatened evictions.[62] And a year later, the people of Tralee, Co. Kerry were said 'to long for something spiritual after the long struggle of the Land League'.[63]

Politics were never far beneath the surface of Irish life. Thus, at Enniscorthy, Co. Wexford in 1883, where missions and retreats had been given regularly for twenty-five years, and where the priests were said to be zealous, 'political agitation had disturbed the people and caused some estrangement between them and the clergy. It was said that secret societies were making progress and the temperance movement had received a decided check at the time of the late elections'.[64] The clerical reaction against Parnell was to cause even more resentment and prove a fresh obstacle to the missions. The Bishop of Kerry reported to Propaganda that the greatest danger in his diocese was 'a spirit of hatred and rebellion against the civil power' and that all clerics were classed as traitors by the people.[65] Five years later, the Bishop of

Elphin, in reporting the good and tranquil state of his diocese, nevertheless noted the large-scale support for 'Parnellism' and that 'priests who are opposed to the principles of this political system experience at some time opposition and contradictions'.[66] 'Parnellism' and opposition to priests were often regarded as synonymous,[67] and the rift could lead to alienation from the Church.[68] In these years, the missions were often intended to counteract this danger by cutting through the political agitation into which the parochial clergy were inevitably drawn and recall the people to their religious duties. Thus, at Ballivor, Co. Meath in 1896 the mission's objective was 'to break down the evil effect of the last political agitation. Parnellism destroyed the whole parish, it left its evil mark impressed upon the people ... in rebellion against ecclesiastical authority'. The 'old ascendancy' of religion over 'political blindness' was achieved by the fathers 'touching delicately on everything so as to give no offence. We confined ourselves to the one great thing: we preached the Word of God — the faith was there: we warmed it: we kindled it: grace worked and they came in crowds to the Mission'.[69]

The great fear of political agitation was that it led not only to rebellion against ecclesiastical authority but also to extremism, to revolutionary violence and support for secret societies, especially for Fenianism. Archbishop Croke believed that the great bulk of the Catholic population of Ireland was Fenian 'in heart and sympathy', although its influence could be contained.[70] Fenianism was condemned by name in Rome in 1870, but this did not destroy support for its ideas and objectives, albeit in a mitigated form.[71] Active support was more widespread in England and Scotland than in Ireland itself, though its importance was more as a social focus for Irish political cohesion.[72] Nevertheless, it was regarded as a great impediment to the progress of religion: 'In all the large towns [of England] Fenianism is now as great an obstacle as drunkenness to the full success of our missions'.[73] Fenianism was a self-proclaimed revolutionary and republican movement, yet in Rome all political agitation tended to be viewed in this light, and all Hibernians and Ribbonmen as variants of a

European-wide revolutionary freemasonry, dedicated to the destruction of the Church. In fact, they were nothing of the kind; unlike the Irish Republican Brotherhood, membership of these secret societies was open only to Catholics, and they grew out of the self-protection against Orangeism in Ulster and, later, in northern England and western Scotland in the one case, and out of agrarian outrages in the landlord-tenant agitation in Ireland in the other, merging with the mindless tradition of faction-fighting that was especially prevalent in Munster. Nevertheless, their secrecy was a challenge to the Church, enticing their members away from the loyalty they owed and the dominant influence which it was supposed to exercise in their lives, encouraging them to question the subservience taught by the Church, offering a secular, this-worldly salvation and an alternative brotherhood, as well as encouraging their members to violence as a political solution. This explains the strenuous efforts to eradicate them, which became more pronounced as people matured politically. Fr Harbison noted that while in the rural areas of Ireland the confessionals were well-attended by 'poor peasants', in towns 'among the artisans, servant boys, young sons of Farmers, it is not so — they often do not go, when they go they do not tell they are members of secret societies and do not generally give up their craft'.[74] From the Church's point of view, it was a case of no-one being able to serve two masters and of there being no doubt as to which of the two demanded obedience.

The charge and incidence of secret society membership could be exaggerated, as the Redemptorist missioners found in Mullingar, Co. Westmeath in 1872, a town which had a bad name for secret societies. In fact, the men were found to have a great love for Ireland 'and neither the bishop nor the missioners saw any reason to impede this'.[75] Even so, the continued existence of secret societies contributed to the Catholic authorities' fear of 'the spirit of Revolution which in these days animates all people'.[76] Irish agitation and expressed distaste for British government stimulated in many English and Scottish people both an anti-Irish and an anti-Catholic reaction.[77] The immigrants themselves were not unaware of such feelings, and it is interesting that the main problem which faced the general mission in Leeds in 1886 was that the (mainly Irish) people felt that the bishop (Cornthwaite) and his predominantly-English priests were anti-Irish.[78] At St Patrick's, Nottingham two years later, the missioners found that the animosity between the English and Irish communities resulted in the latter not coming to church.[79]

Another feature of the Irish was a *joie de vivre*, which did not always coincide with the Church's notions of decorum and correct behaviour. The Catholic Church sought to inculcate sobriety among its adherents, a task in which it was only partly successful, by suggesting a heavy investment in those spiritual values that would inhibit the natural proclivity to sin and control their wildness, and by providing substitute forms of social and recreational pleasure. The Church was concerned not merely to oppose itself to the peccadillos of its members, in the fear that they would lead to greater immorality, but also to provide an alternative culture, centred on piety and the performance of religious duty, to the alluring, ungodly world against which it was battling for the souls of men. Immorality was but the most obvious manifestation of that slide into religious indifference, which sounded the death-knell of the Church's influence, and from which people had to be retrieved. The people of Blaydon-on-the-Tyne were found by the Redemptorist missioners in 1889 to be 'pagans in religion, Turks in morals. The young people care for nothing but dogs and pigeons, and the idea of religion is ... almost extinct'.[80] A few years later, the Irish in Sunderland were said to be 'scarcely humanised yet'.[81] The missions sought to tackle depravity and attempted to bring people once more under the Church's spiritual and moral umbrella. Thus, when the missioners at Clonmany, Co. Donegal encountered the 'really *sinful* abuse ... by no means an *innocent* pastime of "kalying", i.e. meeting of boys and girls, especially on Sunday evenings in houses and elsewhere for dancing, drinking (though not to excess) and *this, that and the other'*, the intention was not just to put a stop to what elsewhere were called 'the usual concomitants', but to any social intercourse which fell outside the Church's approved guidelines.[82] Such restrictions came under the category of avoiding the occasions and places of sin; at Lisdoonvarna, Co. Clare in 1892, for example, this was identified as 'spending whole nights in the houses of neighbours emigrating to America and dancing till morning'.[83] There was no suggestion of immorality, it was just not proper behaviour for decent Catholics.

The unconducive moral climate reinforced ecclesiastics in the conviction and determination to gather in the faithful to protect them from the harmful effects of a wicked world. Although poverty was idealised as a spiritual blessing, as a result of which God came close to the poor, who were consequently nearer to him than were the materially better-off, the depressive and degrading effects of poverty sapped the energies and motivations of many, who drifted away from the faith: 'Poor people for the most part neglected their religion'.[84] The great difficulty was reaching them in order to appeal to such religious susceptibilities as they retained. Describing the recent mission in Birmingham, Fr Vaughan reported that the people were 'very apathetic and the distress and misery among the poor was such that numbers had parted with clothes and goods to support life. And when we went among them we found they were rather expecting tickets for the Relief Fund or alms than an invitation to the Church'.[85] In many places throughout Britain and Ireland it was reported that people were ashamed to attend the mission in their poor clothes,[86] and sometimes the missioners 'had to beg or borrow clothes for the poor to attend'.[87] It was even suggested that the mission renewals should be given in the winter months so that the darkness would hide the bad clothes of those who attended.

The difficulty of reaching the poor was compounded by the sabotage wrought on the missions by those priests who saw them as a means of raising money in excess of the missioners' expenses, usually by charging an admission fee.[88] This was a problem from the earliest days of the mission, and the result was to keep out many people, even when the charge was optional.[89] In Glasgow, for example, 'the asking (if not demanding) of money at the church door' was a standard feature of missions and an obstacle to their success.[90] At Brosna, Co. Kerry in 1892, the missioners found that poor people were turned away even at Mass if they could not pay.[91] Such charges were a source of friction between priests and missioners and sometimes led to the parochial clergy refusing to co-operate with the mission, as at Knocknagoshel, Co. Kerry in 1892, where alienation was caused by the Redemptorists' refusal to 'help [the clergy] screw money out of the poor people'.[92] There were, of course, always parish priests who resented the missions, like the pastor of Banhead in Scotland, who regarded the mission as 'a necessary evil and the sooner over the better', and the octogenarian priest at Tipperary, who viewed the 1878 mission as a disturbance in his parish.[93] Elsewhere, the priests took no interest in the mission, and at Warwick Street Chapel, London in 1864, they went on holiday during its course.[94] More persistent was the interference from priests during the course of the mission, particularly those who continued to hear confessions, instead of leaving the missioners a clear field, and those who wanted to keep control over the course of the mission.[95]

All of these factors represented obstacles to the work of the missions and to their success and underlined the immense and wide-ranging nature of the missioners' task to create and consolidate strong, resistant and resilient, local Catholic communities. This task was not the Redemptorists' alone, but was shared with other missionary bodies and with the whole Church, and their contribution was one among many. The value and effectiveness of that contribution will be assessed in due course. To reinforce the point that parochial missions were intended as consolidators of the Catholic community, it should be stressed that they were not designed as agents of proselytism. They were directed 'to those of the household of the Faith', and the missioners were, in general, forbidden 'to undertake the instruction, confession and abjuration of those who are drawn to the Faith simply by attending the Mission', which was left to the parochial clergy after the mission.[96] During the course of the mission, contentious sermons that attacked Protestants or their beliefs, or were designed to exasperate them, were forbidden.[97] The Redemptorists had to proceed cautiously: in Lancashire and western Scotland, where there were many missions, there was a strong, Protestant culture, and in Britain generally, latent anti-Catholic feeling could easily have been aroused by fierce proselytism on the part of the missioners; even in Ireland, outside the Protestant-majority North, the Redemptorists had to have an eye to the Protestant Ascendancy. The spate of anti-Alphonsian literature in the late 1850s and 1860s was occasioned by the Redemptorists' missionary labours and provided the staple diet of Protestant harangue against the missions.[98] This is what happened at Kilaveny, Co. Wicklow in 1859, when the Church of Ireland incumbent held a counter-mission and challenged the Redemptorists to public controversy, vilifying St Alphonsus, his doctrine and moral theology, and resorting 'to every kind of calumny and scurrility of the lowest kind'.[99] The following year, at Ballingarry, Co. Limerick, the same tactics were employed, with pickets carrying anti-Catholic placards outside the Catholic church and the local newspaper campaigning against the mission.[100] At Barton, near Manchester and Douglas, Isle of Man, in 1860 the Redemptorists encountered similar opposition.[101]

Opposition was not only vociferous. The first Redemptorist missioners on the Isle of Man were met by 'a growling crowd of Islanders, who threatened to oppose the mission by violence and drive them into the sea if they did not at once take ship for home'.[102] The hooting and insults that were thrown at the missioners in Peel, Isle of Man, were also accompanied by stones, but they were saved by the protection of a man 'of Herculean strength', dreaded by the Protestants, whose strongest man he had beaten in a fair fight.[103] The most fierce opposition and greatest physical danger came during missions in strong Orange areas. At Portadown, Co. Armagh in 1876, a group of Orangemen banged drums in order to drown the voice of the Redemptorist missioner.[104] Five years later, in the same place, 'since violent disturbances from heretics were feared, the mission was given the name of Exercises and the morning instruction for workers was omitted'.[105] At St Andrew's, Dundee in 1868, stones were thrown at the doors, while at St Matthew's, Belfast in 1885, shots were fired into the church and a riot threatened.[106] So menacing was the Orangemen's threat that Fr Somers recalled being given a loaded revolver to keep by his bed during a mission at Ballynahinch, Co. Down in 1887.[107]

This does not mean that the Redemptorists were inhibited from pursuing and developing their apostolic labours, and it was recognised that a certain number of Protestants would be attracted to a mission, often out of sheer curiosity.[108] At Tarbert, Co. Kerry in 1859, a recent published attack on Alphonsus's moral theology was sufficient to ensure a large crowd of Protestants, although none of them was converted.[109] The great numbers who attended the mission in the Guardian Angels, Mile End, East London in 1872 did not necessarily realise that it had been converted from its former use as an Independent chapel.[110] Occasionally, Protestant interest could be genuine, as at Canterbury, Cowes, Isle of Wight in 1889, when a large number of Protestants were said to have been attracted 'both by the lovingly persuasive and singularly winning discourse of Fr MacDonald and by the moving eloquence of Fr Bridgett'.[111] Some years earlier, an exasperated writer complained to his local newspaper about 'the large numbers of Protestants [who] are habitually flocking to these papal meetings to hear their Saviour and their religion reviled, to see poor pitiable Ignorance imposed upon them by the clap-trap of [a] scowling priesthood'.[112] Indeed, the number of interested non-Catholics was sufficient as early as 1868 for special instructions to be instituted for them.[113] Towards the close of the century it was proposed that at some of the missions, perhaps running concurrently with the children's missions, there should be a course of general, apologetic and dogmatic sermons for non-Catholics with a minimum of moral teaching.[114]

One consequence of attracting Protestants was, of course, their conversion, and occasionally the numbers were quite large: ninety at Sunderland in 1859, for example, and a further

150 at North Shields.[115] In total, between 1855, when figures become available, and 1900 the Redemptorists claimed to have received 23,446 converts from heresy, as follows:

Table I: Number of converts, 1855-1900[116]

Clapham

1855-64	at home and on the missions	406
1865-1900	at home	1443
	on the missions	2677

Bishop Eton

1855-66	at home and on the missions	3574
1867-1900	at home	180
	on the missions	5645

Limerick

1855-64	at home and on the missions	559
1865-97	at home	310
	on the missions	396

Kinnoull

1867-1900	at home	203
	on the missions	5645

Dundalk

1877-97	at home	3
	on the missions	285

Teignmouth

1875-1900	at home	33
	on the missions	62

Belfast

1896-1900	at home	22
	on the missions	2

Other   2001

As one would expect, the number of converts in Ireland, apart from the early years in Limerick, was comparatively low, especially in the North.[117] The mission figures for Bishop Eton and Kinnoull, representing missions largely in the lowlands of Scotland, the north and west of England, are certainly impressive. It should be borne in mind, however, that the number of converts is not qualified and that non-Catholic partners and children of mixed marriages would form a high percentage of the figures.[118] The fact that the Redemptorist chronicles recorded conversions from Protestantism does not indicate that such converts were active church-goers before their conversion to Catholicism, nor that they remained practising Catholics.[119]

The mission field was certainly great and the work was sufficient to keep not only the Redemptorists but all the missionary orders busy. Redemptorist missions were geographically widespread as well as numerous. By the end of the century, it could be said that hardly a town or village in Ireland had not been visited by the Redemptorists at some time for the preaching of a mission or confraternity retreat.[120] No major city or town in England, and few in Scotland, escaped a Redemptorist mission, and their activity extended to the Western Isles and the Channel Islands. Fr Stebbing spoke in 1899 of the Clapham fathers 'sallying forth in twos and threes to give missions in the slums of East London, and in the quiet villages of Sussex and Kent, and even further afield to the busy human hives of the North'.[121] Many places were visited more than once and Redemptorist missions in a particular church were interspersed with missions by other orders. Between 1848 and 1900 the Redemptorists gave 3,215 missions and renewals, ranging from a yearly average of 21.5 in the 1850s to 112.3 in the 1890s. The following tables give a clearer picture:

Table II: Missions and Renewals, 1854-1900*

Clapham	495	Limerick	506
Bishop Eton	923	Kinnoull	872
Dundalk	281	Belfast	5
Teignmouth	17	Province	90

* Between 1848 and 1853 there were 26 missions which were not assigned to a particular house.

Table III: Number of Missions and Renewals, 1848-1900

1848-54	39	1875-79	330
1855-59	176	1880-84	423
1860-64	220	1885-89	457
1865-69	200	1890-94	556
1870-74	247	1895-1900	567

Bare figures tell little of the scope and force of the mission, which must first be analysed before assessing their effectiveness and influence upon the Catholic Church.

8

Mission
course and content

Like a military offensive, a Redemptorist mission was planned
to the last detail and deviation from the Alphonsian model
was not countenanced. Preparation began a week or so
beforehand when the Rector of the house from which the
mission was being given would select the fathers to conduct
it and appoint one of them as Superior. It was then his
responsibility to draw up a plan of the course of the mission
sermons and instructions, assigning specific tasks to each of
his companions, who were then expected to prepare their
material. The Superior would also appoint one of the number
as Prefect of the church where the mission was to be given;
it was his responsibility to make the liturgical arrangements,
especially for the special services and acts of devotion during
the mission, and to give the alarum to signal the end of each
sermon and exercise. On the day of their departure, the fathers
would assemble in the oratory to recite the *Itinerarium* and to
receive a blessing from the Rector, who would delegate to the
Superior of the Mission all the necessary faculties and grant
any dispensations from the Divine Office or the laws of fasting
and give any advice he might deem expedient. In particular,
he urged on the missioners complete and absolute obedience
to the Superior, without which 'all will be disorder, confusion
and disturbance, and the Mission will have but slight
success'.[1] Thus armed with their missionary faculties, a
supply of tracts, medals, rosaries, holy pictures and crucifixes,
and third-class railway tickets, the missioners sallied forth. On
arrival at their destination, they would spend a day in retreat.

Every mission was requested by the local priest or, in the
case of a general mission in several churches, by the bishop,

and it was expected that prior advertising of the mission would have been made from the pulpit and by means of handbills and mission leaflets.[2] This preparation could be crucial, as at Carlisle in 1876 when the resident clergy were said to have made every effort to ensure the complete success of the mission 'both by public exhortation and prayers, and by house to house visitation throughout the whole city'.[3] Such visiting helped to bring up 'outstanders and those who would otherwise have let the mission by'.[4] At St Vincent's, Liverpool in 1865, the domiciliary visits of the clergy through the whole of the parish some few days before and during the course of the mission were of added benefit because they left 'confession cards', which ensured that priority would be given in the confessionals to parishioners, for whom the mission was intended, a practice which was repeated elsewhere.[5] Conversely, the lack of preparation by the clergy could place the mission at a disadvantage from which it could not recover; as one missioner ruefully remarked, 'if the local clergyman had prepared his flock better, it would have been better disposed'.[6]

In the early years, when missions were something of a novelty, those who attended the exercises were told to inform those who had not as yet come of the content of the sermons and instructions in order to attract them.[7] As missions became more commonplace, and the reputation of the Redemptorists spread, this was not as necessary.[8] Street-preaching, *sentimenti* or *svegliarini*, was very rare and confined to a few examples in the first years of the missions.[9] More usual was the visitation performed by the missioners themselves in the first few days of the mission, especially to those who had failed to respond to the pleas of their pastors and would not attend the mission without this further inducement: 'The Fathers were obliged, as usual, to sally forth in pursuit of laggards'.[10] Although this time-consuming exercise was meant to be discontinued when the mission was under way, its extension sometimes proved necessary. Fr Gibson recalled a prolonged visiting campaign during a mission in the Guardian Angels, Mile End, East London in

1872, a church newly-converted to Catholic worship from an Independent, Salem chapel, where the usual channels of parish communication had not as yet been developed and there was no tradition of missions in that part of the district.[11]

Visiting was sometimes the only way to reach certain groups or 'the most abandoned souls',[12] or to stir up any enthusiasm for the mission.[13] Occasionally, especially if the resident clergy had not done much visiting beforehand, the missioners visited every house in the parish, as at Latchford, Cheshire in 1893, where 'we visited every house in the town and country to beat up the people', as a result of which 'comparatively few threw the grace of the Mission away, except those who have completely lost the Faith'.[14] The key to the missioners' success among the poor and negligent was sometimes ascribed to the domiciliary visits they paid among the courts and back streets.[15] Where such visiting was not possible, it was felt that many failed to make the mission who might otherwise have been persuaded.[16] On the other hand, visiting by the missioners was intended to supplement, not to be a substitute for, efforts by the local clergy to prepare people for the mission. Towards the end of the century the complaint was made that too much time was spent on missions in 'useless visiting' of the negligent, which should have been performed by the secular clergy,[17] and this is borne out by the irritated report of a mission in Smethwick, Staffordshire in 1895, when 'the great part of the Fathers' time was spent in ... visiting, visiting, visiting, and sometimes not ten confessions were heard in a day by the two Missioners!!!'.[18]

Notwithstanding such exertions, there was an optimistic expectation that the mission would act like a magnet and irresistibly draw people, who, once drawn, would succumb to the spiritual and psychological pressure there exhibited:

> None but those who have the experience of it can understand the effect of listening, night after night, to the mission sermons on the Eternal Truths, or of living in the mission atmosphere, which begins to pervade the entire parish soon after the Mission opens. It enters into

every house, fills every soul, stirs every conscience, seeking even, and finding an entrance into the hardened hearts of those who at first stay away determined to resist God and the graces of the Mission.[19]

That this was not just wishful idealism is evidenced by the effect that a mission could have in a community. At Carndonagh, Co. Donegal in 1858, 'the ordinary business of life seemed to have been suspended for a time and the fifteen days of the Mission were kept almost as one long continued religious festival throughout the entire barony'.[20] Twenty years later, 'the spirit sent abroad by the good fathers travelled into every homestead in Dunhallow, and from its farthest confines representatives came to join in the services, and by their numbers and example to magnify them into grand religious demonstrations'.[21] Both these examples come from Ireland, where the open and widespread enthusiasm for a mission was less restrained and more enduring than in the cities and towns of Britain. The Redemptorists had a high expectation that the Irish, whether in their native land or among the diaspora, would avail themselves of the mission. The Limerick Chronicler remarked rather petulantly that two out of a population of 2,500 kept away from the mission in Kildorrery, Co. Cork in 1883; although he admitted that both were unable to walk, 'still, at the same time, it is equally true that having, as they really had, a "mint of money", they could easily have hired a horse and car'.[22] He did not record of them the terrible fate, seen as divine judgement, which betook others who neglected the mission.[23]

The chronicler did, however, give particular evidence of the zeal which was displayed for the benefits of a mission, like the men of Tipperary, who began queuing at the confessionals at one o'clock in the morning,[24] and the men of Kilmallock, Co. Limerick, who, as late as 1883, climbed over the walls and gates of the chapel-yard in the middle of the night and got into the chapel through the windows to get a place in the confessionals next day. After a while, the church was left open all night, and men remained after the evening sermon until the next day. To keep themselves awake, they marched around with lighted candles in their hands, saying the rosary. Those who did not make the sacrifice of their night's rest, it was said, had very little chance of getting to confession that day.[25] Of course, such enthusiasm was not shown everywhere, and some missions were decidedly slow to get off the ground: 'The first week went on in a very dead and heartless way and we were beginning to get a little discouraged, but we made a great attack by word and by prayer too I hope, on the second Sunday, and from that day the face of things changed completely'.[26] Divine Providence was seen to be at work here, as it was in Monagea, Co. Limerick, where a severe thunderstorm and heavy rain after the first week of the mission in 1890 put the fear of God into those who had held back, and who now came.[27]

Redemptorist missions usually lasted from two to four weeks, depending on the size of the parish, the number of missioners, the time of year or the request of the local clergy. This meant that there had to be a certain amount of flexibility in the content of the mission, a telescoping of sermons and themes in the shorter missions, although certain sermons and ceremonies were never omitted, and the general character remained constant. Some plans, drawn up for men in the second novitiate in 1881 (see Appendix), reflect the settled pattern of mission-giving, appropriate to contemporary conditions, which remained unaltered in substance throughout the second half of the nineteenth century.[28] Normally, the mission began on Saturday evening, so that the missioners could address the people at the early Masses on Sunday morning and invite them to the mission. Where this was not possible, it began before the High Mass on Sunday. The missioners processed into the church, the Superior carrying a large mission crucifix, while the *Benedictus* or *Litany of Our Lady* was sung. The mission crucifix was placed in a prominent place and remained throughout the mission as a symbol of it and as a visual aid, to which the preachers often referred. The parish priest would briefly introduce the missioners, one of whom, usually the Superior, then preached the opening sermon.

MISSION FOR MEN.

A Mission for MEN will be Opened

BY THE

REDEMPTORIST FATHERS,

IN THE CHURCH OF ST. ALPHONSUS

On the 1st of January, 1868, at $7\frac{1}{2}$, P. M.

ORDER OF EXERCISES:

SUNDAYS.	WEEK DAYS.	FEAST OF EPIPHANY
A.M.	A.M.	A.M. (6TH JAN.)
6 Holy Mass	$5\frac{1}{2}$ H. Mass with INSTRUCTION FOR MEN.	$5\frac{1}{2}$ H. Mass, with Instruction.
7 H. Mass with INSTRUCTION FOR MEN,	$6\frac{1}{2}$ H. Mass.	$6\frac{1}{2}$ H. Mass.
$8\frac{1}{2}$ H. Mass.	7 H. Mass.	7 H. Mass.
11 H. Mass and Sermon.	8 H. Mass.	8 H. Mass.
		11 High Mass and Sermon.
P.M.	P.M.	P.M.
$3\frac{1}{2}$ Sermon and Benediction, for men only	$7\frac{1}{2}$ Rosary, Sermon and Benediction, for men only.	$3\frac{1}{2}$ Devotions and Benediction for all.
7 Usual Devotions for all.		$7\frac{1}{2}$ Rosary, Sermon and Benediction for men only

Kirby Brothers, Machine Printers, 39, Patrick-street, Limerick

Announcing a mission in Limerick, New Year's Day, 1868.

Each day, Mass was said at an hour most suited to the convenience of working people, usually 5 a.m. The instruction that followed was not to exceed thirty minutes, although it could be repeated later in the morning and extended by a further ten minutes. It was preceded by an *Ave* (in Ireland, by the 'Morning Offering'), and concluded with Acts of Faith, Hope and Charity according to the form used in the diocese (and in Ireland, three *Aves* were added). The missioner gave

154

the instruction seated, in an informal manner, and its purpose was purely didactic. The principal exercise of the mission was in the evening, normally at 7 p.m. Its importance was emphasised by the attendance of all the missioners in choir and the suspension of confessions. On the first evening after the opening of the mission, an introduction to the devotion of the rosary of a quarter-of-an-hour's duration was followed by the recitation of five decades. On the following nights, each of the five mysteries proper to the day would be proposed according to the method of St Alphonsus.[29] The object was to introduce and commend to the faithful the practice of reciting the rosary, the importance of which became more apparent as the mission progressed and the theme of perseverance was introduced. Equally important, the explanation and meditations on the rosary were a means of conveying the principal doctrines of the Church, so that, together with the morning instructions, this constituted the catechetical element of the mission.

The rosary devotion would be followed by a hymn, during the last stanza of which the preacher would ascend the pulpit and give out any special notices. If the church did not contain an adequate pulpit, or if the mission sermon were delivered out-of-doors, a platform was specially constructed, on which were a table, chair, large crucifix and, if possible, a statue of the Virgin. The sermon was preceded by the Daily Acts, which the people repeated after the preacher, who was to recite them always 'with earnestness and animation, and in a manner calculated to interest the people and excite them to pray'.[30] The sermon lasted for no more than fifty minutes, although the Constitutions stipulated that it should last an hour, and an order from Rome in 1883 restored the hour-long sermon in the English Province.[31] The sermon ended, an act of contrition before the crucifix was made, followed by Benediction of the Blessed Sacrament and the recitation of five *Paters* and five *Aves* in honour of the five sacred wounds and for the conversion of sinners.[32]

On some missions, at the discretion of the Superior, particular instructions were given to various groups or categories of the people, if this was not provided for in the general mission-plan under the heading of 'Men Only', 'Duties of Parents', and so on. The instruction to married people, for instance, was to treat of the sanctity of matrimony, the graces connected with the sacrament, and the duties that spring from it. The preacher was to explain according to the Catechism of the Council of Trent and never to enter into details of the 'actus conjugalis', nor 'to go to extreme limits by telling how far married people may go before they are guilty of a *formale pec mortale'*.[33] Similarly, although there was always to be a sermon on the sixth Commandment at every mission, stress was to be made on the need to consecrate one's body as a temple of the Holy Spirit; the temporal consequences, implications or details of vice were not to be enlarged upon. In fact, in the English Province, the particular instructions to married men and women were rarely given, and when they were, the fathers were accused of being too forthright in discussing sex.[34] In the main, any particular abuses or dangers were covered in the evening sermons for all, unless they were considered too delicate to be widely aired. On the whole, the missioners tried to avoid too obvious or heavy a treatment. Fenianism, for example, was never mentioned by name; if it were deemed to be a problem in a parish, appeal would be made to return to the supreme influence of the Church and, without specifying, to shun any ideology or organisation which detracted from this. If the mission were large, or the church insufficient to seat all who wished to attend, it became the practice to have a separate mission for men and women, running either concurrently or sequentially, and this was found to be particularly effective in dealing with abuses that were peculiar to either sex. At St Patrick's, Edinburgh in 1869, for example, where 'the evils among the men were drunkenness and frequenting secret societies [and] among the women drunkenness, neglect of the sacraments and shameful behaviour (procationes inhonestae)', separate missions resulted in an easier and more thorough completion of the work.[35]

The mission would end with the solemn planting of the

mission cross, preferably outside, to serve as a remainder of the time of grace. The cross would be carried in procession while the *Vexilla Regis* was sung, planted and blessed according to the *Manuale* and a sermon on the cross preached. The actual close of the mission included the recitation of the rosary for the grace of perseverance, and a sermon on the same subject, and concluded with the Papal Blessing, five *Paters* and *Aves* for the Pope's intention in order to gain a plenary indulgence, Benediction of the Blessed Sacrament and a *Te Deum*. The morning after, before the missioners departed, there would be a Requiem Mass and an instruction on the holy souls in Purgatory.

To those who availed themselves of the grace of a mission and co-operated with the missioners by attending assiduously all the exercises, morning and evening, there was the promise of 'a true conversion and a lasting conversion'.[36] The whole point of a mission was to convince people of the need to turn away from the bad habits of sin and to turn to God and, having convinced and moved them accordingly, to provide the means for living a new, God-centred life. Thus, any mission revolved around four basic themes, which served to facilitate its main objectives. These were to provide the motives for conversion; to deal with the obstacles to conversion; to suggest the intellectual, spiritual and emotional means of conversion; and, finally, to inculcate the determination and provide the means for perseverance in the penitent state. These themes were interwoven, but the basic thrust of the mission was to convert sinners by shaking them out of their complacency and instilling them with the fear of death and of eternal hell fire. The mission preachers, like all good revivalists, were pulpit artists, who painted picturesque scenes of sin, death, judgement and hell in order to impress upon their hearers the horrors of sin and its punishment. This depended, in the first instance, upon the preacher convincing his hearers that they should share his frame of reference; if they did not, it would have been impossible to work on that deep, inculcated sense of guilt, so deep and pervasive that Man is almost defined by it and becomes wholly evil and repulsive, out of which the preacher could offer release in the blood of the Lamb. By working through a few standard themes, which the missioner knew would evoke a response, he sought to manipulate the people, as much by his acting ability as by his rhetoric, so that the atmosphere became heavily charged with an infectious emotion. Thus, the immolated Victim of Calvary, his broken and bleeding heart, was pitted against the base ingratitude of sin-soaked Man. The full consequences of these juxtaposed images were spelt out in stories and suggestions so that the full enormity of the dichotomy between human sinfulness and divine pity, mixed with judgement, was appreciated by all. At the same time, the forgiving, wounded healer washes away guilt and brings release from the deserved damnation, so that in the moment of deepest guilt and anxiety, if not despair, there was the offer of a personal experience of God's saving grace, which issued in conversion.

The 'orgy of emotionalism', to which people were exposed during a mission,[37] stood in marked contrast with the low emotional key of normal worship and preaching, but was an intended and expected feature of the mission. At Carndonagh in 1858, a reporter noted that

> every sentence, every word, nay, every gesture seemed to produce the most amazing effect. The big gushing tear and loud sigh were followed by an universal outburst of feeling, and the vast assemblage was soon buried in a flood of tears as if mourning the death of some dear departed friend.[38]

The missioners at Douglas, Isle of Man in November 1859 were worried that 'there did not seem the same enthusiasm as we have met elsewhere', but their fears were allayed on the last evening when 'the pent-up spirit broke loose and the sobbing was universal and most moving'.[39] That emotional release was a sign that the mission had done its work, although the Redemptorists found that the Irish were much more demonstrative than the English, who gave little external manifestation of their sorrow. Even so, the reporter of an early mission in the Virginia Street area of London found a working man audibly sobbing two hours after the end of the mission, and remarked,

> I did not wonder at the women sobbing and crying this afternoon, but at the sermon this evening, when there was not even one woman present in the chapel, and it was crowded to suffocation, the whole of the men, young and old, borne along, as it were, on a resistless tide, burst forth into one long continual wail and lament during, but particularly towards the end of the Fathers' farewell address.[40]

The similarities between such communal celebrations and Protestant revivals are obvious, both stressing the need for individual conversion and salvation and offering an experience of saving grace; they were based on a thoroughly evangelical view of redemption as the bringing by Christ of the message and the dynamic of the Father's love for all men. But, unlike in Protestant revivals, conversion was not so narrowly defined in terms of the doctrine of justification by faith, or as a single, never-to-be-repeated event. On the Catholic model, conversion to Christ and to the Church were indistinguishable. The central image of the suffering Jesus was united with devotion to the Blessed Sacrament, seen as the epitome of divine condescension and love, by means of which Christ was present to and among his people. In place of the penitent's form and the altar-call used by Protestant revivalists, Catholic missions provided the sacraments as the means of grace. The penitent, when pricked in his heart by the dramatic preaching of a skilled orator, could soon after the sermon enter the confessional and recite his sins and receive forgiveness. Being thus in a state of grace, he could avail himself of the supreme gift of the Eucharist. A major concern of Catholic missions was to induct people into a sacramental piety, consolidated by a strong catechetical element that ensured that the appeal was to the head as well as the heart, designed to assure their perseverance by strengthening their resolutions and the control of the institutional Church over the lives of the faithful. Catholic missions were characterised by what one historian has dubbed 'sacramental evangelicalism';[41] the conversion-appeal, directed to every individual, was meant to lead him to re-invest himself decidedly within the sacramental life of the Church. Despite the superficial similarities between Catholic missions and Protestant revivals, in terms of preaching methods, controlled emotional excitement, and of human response to the proffered gift of salvation, the two phenomena were quite different. Inherent within Catholic revivalism was the consolidation of the converted within a closed cultural world to a degree and to an extent that Protestant revivals never achieved, and which goes some way to providing an answer to the resistance and resilience of Catholicism to the same pressures that undermined popular Protestantism in the last century, and which revivals did little to halt and reverse.[42]

What made for a successful mission were good sermons which managed to plant firmly the seeds of conversion and later to reap the harvest that had been sown. The language of the mission sermons was often extreme, deliberately provocative and, at times, unmitigatedly harsh. In stimulating their hearers to repentance, there was little equivocation or over-concern on the part of the missioners for the sensitivity of the people, for they firmly believed that in a mission God opened up the treasures of his mercy and poured down his graces upon all, whose eternal salvation (or damnation) depended upon their response; neglect of a mission was thus regarded as 'one of the surest signs of damnation'.[43] There was no room for genteel politeness, for from the beginning the mission was an onslaught on sin, almost as upon a tangible force, and every sermon was to be a successive blow in this campaign, until sin was defeated and virtue triumphed. Recalling Christ's words in the Apocalypse that he would vomit the careless out of his mouth, an English Redemptorist reminded his hearers that it was precisely to such as these that the mission was sent, 'that they may enter into themselves in all earnestness during this time of grace — that they may see their dangerous state — that they may make every effort to become better — and see the necessity, not only of avoiding evil, but of doing good, and living the life of a good, penitent

Catholic'.[44] In appealing to all those 'who at this time are fit only for the fires of Hell', the preacher outlined the narrow spiritual limits of the mission and suggested the remedy it was concerned to apply.

The opening and first few sermons of the mission were crucial to its success, since they set its tone and compelling urgency. In suggesting motives for conversion, the first essential was to convince the people of the importance of salvation, that this was not a matter of indifference or cursory attention, but that the eternal fate of the soul should be the dominant concern of everyone's life:

> You are Christians, you are Catholics, you know that you have a soul — one immortal, never-dying soul — and yet do your actions, does your life correspond in any way to your belief?[45]

The end of man, his eternal union with, or separation from, God depended upon the constant influence of spiritual considerations above all temporal interests, so that, whatever their individual circumstances, the main object in life of all Christians was 'to glorify God by obedience to His command-ments — by suffering for His honour — by sacrificing all our wishes to his glory — to despise and give up everything — every person — every pleasure that interferes with God's holy will'.[46] Into this uncompromising dedication to the primacy of religious values in people's lives was introduced the leitmotiv of the threat of hell, which ran throughout the early sermons, as it was suggested that carelessness with regard to this primacy 'is one of the chief reasons why thousands of people go to Hell'.[47] This threat was of tremendous psychological importance in producing those motives of fear, upon which the missioners worked, and without which they believed it would be impossible to unite people to God. They deliberately cultivated and played upon their hearers' conflicting emotions and insecurity in order to propel them towards conversion; the failure to take seriously the threat of hell was one of the greatest obstacles to that conversion. This could easily be overdone. The intention was to shock, not to frighten away or cause despair. This, however, was not always the result, as a missioner at Saffron Hill, Clerkenwell, London found in 1862. The morning after the evening sermon on hell, he visited a man who had been taken ill during the night:

> He found him very bad, and the unfortunate man declared to him that after the Sermon on Sacrilegious Confession he had approached the sacred tribunal with the intention of telling all, but had given away again to shame, and concealed a sin. On hearing the Sermon on Hell his remorse was so great and his terror such, that it was this, he declared, and nothing else, that had made him so ill. He did not then go to confession and when the priest, after a few hours, returned again to see him, he found him raving and quite out of his senses.[48]

At the same time, shock was closely allied with fascination. An Irish Redemptorist recalled that in his country 'the old Irish people, especially those who spoke Irish, loved strong sermons that filled them with the holy fear of God and gave them also sure hope of forgiveness'. Although he thought that the spread of English had a deleterious effect, he nevertheless opined that 'the more terrifying the sermon, the more the people loved it', and he remembered people in the 1870s and 1880s making such statements as 'I like a sermon that makes my hair stand … I want to be moved, only a strong sermon does this'.[49] Although the Redemptorists fast gained a reputation for their forceful preaching, it does not mean that they were crude or unsubtle orators. After a mission in Montrose in 1881, one man remarked to the preacher, 'God bless you, Father! You put it canny, but you gave the whole truth all the same — you didn't spare them a bit'.[50] Someone who attended an early Redemptorist mission in East London considered that 'the moral instruction was well got up' and that

> there was no exaggeration or overstraining. Figures of speech and peculiarities they must have struggled hard to omit or forget. That deep science of human nature in the present state of the world, in which their holy founder was so well versed, and the consistency of their lives with

what they teach, give the Fathers an immense power, which they use with a hearty good will for the salvation of souls and the glory of God.[51]

If the arousal of fear was an early priority in the battle for conversion, it was important that it should be linked to an early determination to abhor and avoid the one thing that made the threat of hell a reality, which was mortal sin. A preliminary, emotionally-charged sermon on this subject was pivotal; if the preacher could not induce an early detestation of mortal sin in his hearers, the fate of the mission hung heavily in the balance. Mortal sin — any grave action, word or thought which caused God to abandon the soul to its fate — was portrayed as a gross and unnatural contempt for one's Creator:

> Sometimes, young man, you put in the balance on one side God, the head and fountain of all beauty — eternal beauty itself — and on the other side you put a filthy pleasure, which lasts only for a moment — a miserable creature, a prey to rottenness and worms.[52]

In addition, it was evidence of the basest ingratitude, for it negated all that God had given to Man for his benefit and spiritual welfare, including his membership of the Church. In an interesting appeal to national pride and Catholic self-identity, Fr Petcherine reminded his hearers ('ye sons of Ireland') in St George's, Southwark

> what God has done for you, when He destined you to be born in the Catholic Church, to be born in a glorious country, which is the admiration of the ages, a country that for so many hundreds of years stands unrivalled in its firmness to God — oppressed, persecuted, hunted to death, and still adhering to the vow: I will die rather than change my faith.[53]

Petcherine did not actually equate mortal sin with infidelity to the Catholic Church, but he came very close to it, since a wilful and deliberate transgression of the law of God and of his Church was synonymous. An appeal to residual community loyalty was insufficient stimulus for many. The crux of the sermon on mortal sin was that it was an open rebellion against one's Saviour, the equation of Christ's crucifixion with the present, personal, sinful state of those who were listening:

> Jesus Christ was nailed to the cross, suffering three hours of agony, shedding His blood to the last drop, and by whose agency? Who put Jesus Christ to death? You, sinner, your sins put Him to death ... When you committed a mortal sin, you came forward and said, 'Now I will go and crucify Jesus Christ' ... He who called you His own beloved child, washed you with his own hands in the water of baptism, fed you with His own Sacred Blood flowing from His side.[54]

The effect of such words could be shattering. Fr Gibson recalled the man who was so moved by such a sermon that he shouted out, 'Stop! I'm the man — I've crucified the Lord'.[55] The danger, however, was that denunciation of sin by itself could induce mere hopelessness. Therefore, the sermon ended by introducing the possibility that there was a way out of the impasse. This was the function of the peroration, which was exhortatory and designed, not only to produce compunction, but also to suggest its alleviation. It is worth quoting at length the peroration of a member of the English Province at the end of his sermon on mortal sin:

> My dear brethren, all that I have been saying to you, I do not say to discourage you, nor do I do it to reproach you. But I have done it out of love for your souls, to deliver you from the blindness and [? ignorance] in which the devil tries to plunge all who fall into sin. To make known to you the evil, and the enormity of the crime which is committed by the man who sins mortally, and the terrifying consequences which it draws after it. Will you abstain from evil? Will you not confess and weep with real sincerity over the way in which you have outraged God during your past life? Oh! sinner — my brethren — your condition is far too sad and pitiful — no longer friendship with God — no peace — no right to Heaven!! And remember well, that if death comes

upon you when your conscience is defiled by mortal sin, on leaving this life you will find a God who is an all-powerful God, a just God, a just avenger of his outraged honour. You will hear all the Sacred Wounds of Jesus cry out for vengeance against you.

Come back then — God comes to you — He wishes to forgive all and blot out all the past ... During the mission God is holding out pardon to all — and for all. Pray God tonight you will come back to Him — Make known to Him your desire, your good will by prayer, by abstaining from evil.[56]

The sermon ended with a *feverino*, an act of contrition and commendation to the Saviour and to Mary, Refuge of Sinners, designed to wring out the last drop of wretchedness, which sometimes poured out in a flood of tears.[57]

If anyone were left in a state of complacency or as yet unpersuaded of the urgency of the call to conversion, the following sermons on death, judgement and eternity were designed to demolish lingering doubters or waverers. The preacher would take his hearers to the deathbed of the sinner, to bring home to them the awful reality, universality and nearness of death, and of the despair which accompanies the last moment of the dying sinner:

Death is terrible for the sinner. When at last the world which he has lived for can be no more, and he feels that he must be torn from all that his heart has loved, and to which his whole being clings, there must be the supremest agony. No matter, too, how he may have tried to put out the light that is within, it will flare up at times, and from the dark caverns of memory, deeds are revealed which he must account for, if beyond this life there is another.[58]

The transience and ephemeral nature of life on earth was contrasted with the eternal fate of the soul:

Do you think that the glutton, the drunkard, or the lustful man, who does nothing else throughout his life [but] satisfy and gratify his evil passions, will meet with the same fate as the chaste, the sober or the mortified man, who constantly denies himself for virtue's sake? Never! To believe or assert this would be as much as to deny the existence of God.[59]

Image was piled upon image, story upon story, to make the people think about death and how it is 'hanging over our heads like a sword by a thread — one moment is sufficient — the thread is cut through by the hand of God and we are amongst the dead'.[60] To be avoided at all costs was an unprepared death, when the sinner dies in the full burden of his sins and is rewarded accordingly at the general judgement. At this point, the mission-preacher began to touch upon particular sins:

> On which side will you be on the last day, I ask you, slothful, negligent Christian, who are absent from Mass on Sundays? ... Where will you be, thoughtless girl, who think of nothing but flirting, courting, and company-keeping? You, who spend hours in sinful amusements; you, who though before men appear to be a virgin, yet before God are rotten with impurity? Where will your place be if you carry on in this way?[61]

None of this was gratuitous; the inculcation of guilt, through the suggestiveness of the preacher, was designed to effect a determination to amend in his hearers. Saying that the angel of death had not yet issued his summons, Fr Frohn still heard a voice

> of a long-suffering, merciful God — a voice from the cross — a voice from the tabernacle — a voice from heaven, from the very heart of my Lord — If thou wilt enter eternal life, keep the commandments — If anyone will come after me ... Come to me all you that labour ... Listen! Set to work now — whilst you have time — now is the day of salvation — make your peace with God — fly into God's merciful arms — rest there.[62]

Condemnation of sin was matched by the exhortation to avoid

the fate of the damned, in the conviction that 'every time we see a priest and hear his advice, it may be the last call of God. There are some here who will not live to hear another mission'.[63]

Having used his oratorical skills to draw the people along the intended path towards conversion, the preacher now introduced an element of theatre in the act of reparation to the Blessed Sacrament. The act was a dramatic form of preaching about sacrilegious communion, which the sermon that preceded it analysed and suggested all present were guilty of; by contrasting the fickleness and ingratitude of Man with the magnanimity of God, it was hoped to underline those motives for conversion which the previous sermons had suggested. More than this, the act itself was a catharsis, allowing the pent-up emotions to be released. A witness of the event in Cork in 1854 believed that 'his must be a heart harder than stone which was not touched with the cries of thousands who were assembled, imploring mercy and forgiveness from the God of Mercy veiled under the sacramental species, for the injuries and insults offered to Him'.[64] The function of the *Amende Honorable* in firmly establishing that reconciliation with God at which the mission aimed was reinforced by the instruction that its place in the mission 'schema' could be altered, if circumstances suggested; in a long mission, if the people were slow to respond, it could be put back or a second solemn act of eucharistic exposition could be made. This was rarely found to be necessary, as the act's message usually went home, often eliciting a response that words alone could not achieve. The reparatory devotion had a secondary, but equally important, function. In linking and controlling penitential distress with liturgical form, the missioners helped to promote a spirituality which was exuberant and exotic after the Ultramontane model, but unequivocally eucharistic, and to encourage forms of devotional piety which depended upon firm attachment to the Church for its continued sustenance. Like the rosary devotion, this had an eye to the theme of perseverance, with which the mission ended. For the present, having suggested, if not exhausted, the motives for conversion, the mission proceeded to deal with the obstacles to conversion.

Already, of course, reference had been made to these obstacles, the habits and occasions of sin, which had to be thrown over before conversion could become a reality. A sermon on the delay of conversion showed that the mission was not concerned merely to excite feeling, to arouse people to a deeper spiritual awareness, but to repair the harmful effects of past sin and induce the resolution to shun the tempting occasions of sin in the future:

> Good, thorough conversion means to declare all your hidden sins ... to repair the scandals you have given ... to restore the good name you have ruined; to restore the money, the property you have taken away or unlawfully required. To be converted means to change one's heart, to detest, to destroy, to abandon mortal sin by true repentance.[65]

One or several sermons, depending on the length of the mission, followed on this theme and were central to the mission's aims. Starting from the premise that Man is naturally inclined to evil and, if exposed to danger, will fall into mortal sin,[66] the preacher no longer needed to dwell on the awfulness of sin, but to attack any undue attachment to those places or habits which led his hearers into sin, and to expose the dangers that lay all around in their social milieu, infected as it was by evil. Reference would be made to the insidious and potentially immoral influence in mills, factories, pits, shops, in lodging houses or for those in service, as well as in places of amusement, which enticed to excess and abandon. Public houses came in for particular condemnation and, as drunkenness became an ever-greater problem, this 'great social evil of the day', by which 'the image of the living God is destroyed in man's immortal soul', was given extended treatment.[67] Further occasions of sin were company-keeping, leading to 'the gratification of the bodily passions of men' and a corresponding drifting away from religious influence,[68] together with all forms of bad company, including membership

of any society and attendance at its meetings which encouraged one to drink, brawl or neglect one's religious duties and
family responsibilities. 'Reason and daily experience teach us',
Fr Frohn told his hearers, 'that to remain in the occasions of
sin, and to go into the occasions of sin, and to fall into sin
is one and the same thing'.[69] Everyone present at the
mission was urged to look at his or her life and identify the
occasions of sin so that they could be eliminated. Conversion
meant breaking with anything and everything which kept one
in sin or led one into it, and this was just as important as
making a good confession:

> The public house — the glass — the bottle are that eye
> and hand of which our Saviour speaks — cut it off — avoid
> it — It is better for you to go to heaven without them than
> giving in to them to be plunged into hell. Impure man
> and woman, that hand and eye of which Jesus speaks
> is your company-keeping — those visits — those
> immodest talks and acts — those houses and persons
> wherein and wherewith you destroy your soul — cut
> them off — break them all — cast it away — far away from
> you.[70]

It was in order to reinforce the urgent pleas of the missioners
that conversion must have practical consequences in personal
morality beyond good intentions that the great sermon on hell
was preached at this stage of the mission. Its purpose was quite
simply to terrify with fear in order to induce the determination
to avoid it: 'Let us look into hell that we may not go there
… The thought of such a place may be unpleasant,
nevertheless, it is very wholesome. The medicine may be
bitter, but it certainly cures'.[71] The graphic description of
hell's torments, of the fate awaiting all reprobate sinners, and
of the misery which divine vengeance inflicts upon them, was
the missioners' last rhetorical device to effect conversion and
appeal directly to the categories of sinner which the preceding
sermons had addressed:

> The sense of hearing which the sinner uses to offend God
> by listening to immodest conversation shall be tormented

in hell ... The glutton who offends his God by eating meat on Fridays and fasting days shall be tortured in hell by the most ravenous hunger. Oh! drunkard, you who now make such ill-use of the sense of taste given you by God, how will you bear that thirst of hell?[72]

The sermon on hell marked a watershed in the course of the mission. Modern incredulity at its contents, mixed with amusement at its exaggerated grossness, should not obscure or detract from a true appreciation of its importance in the mission 'schema'. It was the last direct call to conversion.[73] Henceforth, the mission took on a more gentle aspect as the means of conversion were introduced and, with them, the theme of perseverance.

Throughout the preceding sermons, constant reference had been made to the fact that God delighted, not in the death of the sinner, but in his repentance, and the mission itself was oft-remarked evidence of the mercy of God. If it was necessary to instil the fear of God into people in order to bring them to a speedy repentance, it was realised that fear was insufficient to ensure the permanence of conversion and was an unstable basis for a life of faith and holy action. From now on, the missioners sought to produce those affections of love, which would consolidate conversion; it was this that gave a more gentle and compassionate tone to the mission than heretofore. Solid and lasting conversion depended upon the missioner's ability, not only to induce a state of religious shock, but also upon making deep impressions on the religious consciousness of those who attended the mission so as to arouse spiritual longings and sensibilities, which could only be met by the habit or pattern of continuing church attendance and active involvement in all that was associated with this. Perseverance was considered as important to the mission-objective as conversion.[74] Within this context, a special sermon on the mercy of God or the love of Christ formed an introduction to the sermon and act of consecration to the Virgin. Throughout the mission, sometimes by means of an early sermon, Mary was extolled as the Refuge of Sinners. Now, specific encouragement was given to cultivate and maintain a high regard and proper devotion for the Mother of God, who 'takes care of all our temporal and spiritual welfare'.[75] No one who had recourse to her patronage and protection could be lost, since she is the keeper of the treasury of all divine grace, which her Son deigns to bestow upon men through her:

> When she was here on earth she gave His sacred humanity to our Lord; she shared in His sufferings and kept then the will of that great Son of God. He will dispense graces to you through her hands, and He can refuse no favour that she asks, for she is His Mother. Therefore, Mary is our most powerful advocate in heaven because she is the Mother of Jesus.[76]

All who devoted themselves to her service would find assistance to live a faithful, converted life:

> Fear not — cling to Mary — pray to her incessantly, and pray each time you are tempted — then each time you will be able to overcome — Pray to her the remainder of your life, and all the rest of your life you will not fall into sin. Pray to her, to assist you at the end of your life, in your last struggle and temptation.[77]

The act of consecration that followed, with the statue of the Virgin bedecked with flowers and candles, engendered an atmosphere of warm, comforting piety and of beauty, which contrasted sharply with the earlier, horrific word-paintings. At Cork in 1854, eighty girls, dressed in white, each holding a bouquet of flowers and a wax taper to offer to Mary, showed how 'devotion to the Mother of God is one of the most vital and fundamental characteristics of the Catholic religion, the sole mention of which is sufficient to arouse even the most sinful and indifferent, and animate them with the desire of reconciling themselves with God'.[78] As with the act of reparation, the missioners used a piece of theatre to channel emotion, to engage the people, and to suggest how their raised spiritual feelings could continue to be met. As newly-consecrated children of Mary, the people were encouraged to foster a Marian piety which would lead them to emulate all

171

her virtues and be constant in the renunciation of sin. In providing the means of conversion, the missioners had also given long-term suggestions for preserving the good resolutions made. Enduring love for God, it was taught, must be based on constant meditation upon the Passion of Christ, which had first resulted in conversion, upon the Glories of Mary, and on prayer, 'the strength of the Christian ... the channel of all graces ... the only way to preserve our spiritual life'.[79] Only by filling life with prayer as the means of conversing continually and familiarly with God (as the title of one of Alphonsus's treatises had it), could the penitent hope to live in virtue and grow in holiness:

> If you wish to preserve the fruits of the Mission, for the love of God pray, pray, pray; morning, noon and night ... As certainly as you pray, you will be saved, and so sure as you forget prayer, you will fall into sin and be lost in the end.[80]

Prayer was necessary in order to obtain grace, but a Catholic did not stand before God as an individual merely, but as a member of the Church, which God had established for the sanctification and salvation of his children. Therefore, prayer itself needed to be nourished by the frequent reception of the sacraments of Penance and the Eucharist, and should lead to a greater attention to one's duties and obligations as a member of the Church. Indeed, prayer was facilitated by the cultic artefacts of the Church, such as rosaries, scapulars, holy pictures (especially that of Our Lady of Perpetual Succour) and medals, which were blessed in abundance towards the close of the mission, and by religious literature. Preservation in prayer involved the newly-determined penitent ineluctably in a certain kind of piety, of which the special ceremonies of the mission had been visible demonstrations. This piety was both individualistic and sentimental, depending on the ritualised performance of certain acts to a degree that could appear mechanical, concerned with the gaining of indulgences, and the use of *objets de piété* that could appear magical. Yet it was subject to a wider fellowship and solidarity of practice.

St Alphonsus told his missioners, 'the advice that is to be left as a memento for the hearers is, chiefly, to frequent the sacraments, to make a meditation every day, as also visits to the Blessed Sacrament and the Blessed Virgin ... the family rosary ... an act of contrition every evening'.[81] The cultivation of the *vita devota* did more than attach its practitioners more closely to the Church, providing a unifying bond and affirming allegiance, for the extension of the rituals, artefacts and bondieuserie of the Church into the homes and daily lives of Catholics was intended to assist the development of a way of life that was wholly informed, inspired and defined by a given Catholic model and marked the Catholic out from his non-Catholic neighbour. To live a converted, God-centred life meant a Church-dominated life, a life in which holiness is institutionalised. As Fr Furniss reminded his young hearers:

> The Mother of God is your mother. The angels who watch round the throne of God watch round your soul. Then there are those seven most wonderful sacraments to fill your soul with good things. There are lights and graces coming down from heaven every moment into your soul, a great deal more than the light of the sun comes to your eyes. The very happiness which God has in heaven will be yours when you die. Many other things God has made for your soul — there are crosses, that you might remember that Jesus was crucified for you; beads, that you might speak to your dear Mother, Mary; holy water, to send away the devil from your soul; medals, that you might be blessed in the hour of your death; and scapulars, that, by the prayers of Mary, your soul might come soon out of Purgatory.[82]

To remain a loyal Catholic Christian meant immersing oneself ever deeper into the cultic life of the Church. The mission was meant, not just to revive faith, to lift people out of a sinful state by providing an initiation into a new and elevating realm of holiness, but also to create and confirm feelings of uniqueness, of spiritual superiority that spilled out of the walls of the church and the hearts of the faithful into their attitude and behaviour towards the society in which they lived. The children who attended a mission at St John's, Perth in 1869 were thus reported to have gone about the town singing the mission hymns and prayers in order to annoy the local Protestant majority.[83] The practical measures that were taken to isolate Catholics within their own cultural, religious and social world were the counterweight to the fostering of this piety. While based in Limerick between 1853 and 1855, Fr Furniss was director of the Confraternity of the Holy Family for girls, which he established and in which the children engaged in a plethora of pious activities. One result of these activities was that

> on returning from their meetings, some of the children, full of faith, would often join hands in a circle in front of the houses of some very bigoted Protestants, and, bowing towards their windows, would sing with the greatest animation, 'Daily, daily, sing to Mary', thus proving what zeal for our sweet Mother's honour had been planted in their brave hearts by this true son of St Alphonsus.[84]

This is one example of the intended effect of the commendation of the exercises of the devout life and of how they helped to seal the identity of Catholics with their Church and to ensure that it became the controlling interest in their lives against the world, the flesh, the devil and other Christians.

That being so, the close of the mission was almost a paternal affair, a triumphalist statement of the power of the Church in the lives of its members, the evocation of a centuries-old tradition which had withstood persecution and trials and which had now been affirmed and renewed. Fr Hall, having congratulated all who attended the mission and 'corresponded with its grace', opined that 'this had been a happy time for Jesus. How He has looked; how His heart in the tabernacle has beat with joy day after day, especially when He saw old sinners again in the old home of the Church, or coming to the Altar', and his final admonition was 'love your faith, be proud of it, love all it teaches you to love, Pope, priest, Church, etc.'[85] The abounding hope and sense of victory over the powers of evil lent a joyful confidence to the mission's end, which was itself an encouragement to perseverance.[86] The pride and renewed self-identity, which ideally marked the close of the mission, confirmed the isolationism of Catholics, since preservation in the good resolutions made during the mission meant the determination not to look out of the closed culture of Catholic faith, which promised to satisfy all their needs. Latent in the missioners' repeated admonitions that to persevere in grace meant the shunning of the occasions and places of sin, was the reinforcement of those attitudes and barriers which separated Catholics from non-Catholics and restricted social contact to the most incidental kind. As one Redemptorist observed, 'a young man of the lower class (classe inférieure) cannot profess the Catholic religion without renouncing the company of his own kind (sans renonçer à la frequentation de ses pareils)'.[87] The printed 'Remembrance of the Mission', given to all who had attended and meant to be signed by them, instructed every 'child of Jesus and Mary' to 'keep the good resolutions of the Mission, AVOID SIN AND ALL DANGEROUS OCCASIONS OF SIN; PRAY WITHOUT CEASING, GO FREQUENTLY TO CONFESSION AND HOLY COMMUNION. Be faithful to the Christian practices which have been recommended to you during the Mission'.[88]

If Catholics were to be contained within their own cultural milieu, the great mission sermons on the Eternal Truths had to be supplemented and reinforced by more detailed teaching and by suggestions as to the practical means of converting the motives and intentions aroused by the sermons into effective ways of living a converted, penitent life as a Catholic Christian. This was the function of the morning instructions, which Coffin described as 'perhaps the most important part of our missionary labours'.[89] A preliminary instruction on faith and good works introduced the idea that one must believe all that God teaches and do all that he commands, but that without grace neither of these aims could be achieved, nor could one hope for salvation. The end of the mission was 'to destroy sin in your soul and, by destroying it, to restore God's grace to it'.[90] Grace, of course, was mediated, so that it could only be received by those who availed themselves freely and fully of the light of God's truth which the mission revealed, and cooperated with it by fulfilling all that was there recommended. The instructions, taking their cue from the mission sermons, explored the three themes of penance, the commandments of God and of the Church, and perseverance. The instructions on penance outlined the theological rationale of the sacrament and its various parts, and suggested how one should prepare for it, especially for a general confession or to repair a sacrilegious confession. In addition, emphasis was laid on the penitent state, manifested in such things as fasting and bodily mortification and in the permanent determination to avoid sin and its occasions in the future. Penance was, of course, proportioned to the enlightened state of the penitent, so that the need for continual examination of conscience was stressed. This revolved around consideration of the commandments of God, the commandments of his Church and the duties of one's state in life. All of these were set out in detail in those instructions that coincided with the mission sermons on the obstacles to conversion and the occasions of sin, and which they helped to balance. Prohibition of meat on Fridays, condemnation of recourse to charms and superstition, as of unedifying or anti-religious literature and 'vulgar' novels, grave disapproval of allowing adolescent children to share the same bed and its immoral consequences, all took their place in those instructions with a host of other recommendations and prohibitions. In addition, to combat temptation and instil the right dispositions, there was teaching on the Daily Acts — morning and evening prayer, grace before meals, pious ejaculatory prayers throughout the day, and the like — and the encouragement of pious thoughts: the sight of the sea, for instance, should inspire thoughts of God's immensity; a rock the idea of Holy Church or the see of Peter; flowers called to mind the fragrance of heaven, a butterfly the resurrection of Christ; a dog, whose faithfulness to his master was occasioned by a piece of bread, should lead one to consider how much more one ought to be faithful to God in consideration of all that he has bestowed.[91] In practice, to live a penitent life meant to live a life that was defined by the Church, an 'approved' life, in which the company one kept, the books one read, the daily round of chores and leisure came under, and were to be subjected to, the careful scrutiny of the Church.

The way in which Catholics were meant to model their lives on a pattern of perfection, created for them by clerics, is illustrated in *The [Redemptorist] Mission Book,* a collection of instructions, prayers, meditations and pious exercises drawn chiefly from the writings of St Alphonsus, suitably adapted to contemporary conditions in Britain and Ireland.[92] Written as 'a powerful means to maintain all in the fear of mortal sin, the desire of a holy life and the practice of every virtue', its purpose was to enable those who attended Redemptorist missions 'to revive at any time the feelings excited by the sermons, and thus aid them to persevere in their good resolutions'.[93] The book served as a guide to a

> truly devout and Christian life, for besides the rules it gives for passing every day in a holy manner, it contains the best and most necessary instruction on the Duties of States of life, so that you may know how to order your whole life in such a way as to secure the salvation of your soul, as well as the souls of those who may be entrusted to your care.[94]

The Rule of Life in the book, although it needed to be adapted to an individual's particular state of life, nevertheless mapped out a day that was filled with pious exercises, spiritual reading, mortification of the body, constant examination of conscience, and repentance. Even at the end of the day, after night prayers, the reader was urged to be careful

> to remain always decently covered in bed, and preserve a modest posture ... Until you fall asleep occupy the mind with the subject of the morning's meditation or with a remembrance of death or some other pious thought.[95]

The duties and obligations of Catholics were similarly cloaked in piety under the overriding call to sanctity. Mothers during pregnancy, for instance, were told not to lift any heavy weight, not for their own ease, but because 'you are charged with the safe keeping of an immortal being whom God has created for eternal happiness'.[96]

The melding of doctrine, belief and practice, which the *Mission Book* exemplifies, made of the mission instructions concerned with perseverance a bewildering hotch-potch; explanation of the doctrine of the Mass was related to devotional piety and tied to practical hints on the decency of dress, the proper physical and spiritual dispositions necessary for the worthy reception of the sacraments, and suggested forms of thanksgiving and of practical devotion to the Virgin, the need and use of pious objects. All of this was intended to emphasise correct belief and practice and to assist Catholics in their lives as loyal sons and daughters of the Church.

Whatever the value of these instructions, the whole edifice of the mission depended, in the last resort, upon getting people to attend to their duty of confession and upon the influence for good that the confessor was able to exercise over them: 'If preaching must be earnest and instruction must be sound and practical', wrote an ex-Redemptorist, 'it is the confessor who has the last word in the mission: and he must be no "gobe-mouche" himself, but stand by those doctrines of approved theology which the Church has taught him'.[97] Confessions were begun to be heard after the first few days of the mission and were heard throughout the day from early morning until the evening discourse and afterwards if there were demand, although only men would be heard late at night. Similarly, only working people's confessions would be heard after working hours. The hearing of confessions was the first and chief duty of the missioners,[98] a work 'which has less show about it [than preaching], but is of greater consequence, and more for the glory of God'.[99] This apostolic obligation, which occupied all the spare time of the missioners, provided the opportunity of applying to each person the general lessons of the mission and of ensuring their firm conversion and resolution, which explains why the Redemptorists preferred to hear all the confessions themselves, although often the sheer weight of numbers obliged them to call in other priests to help.[100]

Uniformity, both in the manner of hearing confessions and in the advice given, was necessary to avoid the reputation of either easy absolution or undue rigorism, both of which could destroy the work of the mission. St Alphonsus's *Praxis Confessarii* was the Redemptorists' textbook, and this urged gentleness, patience and the ability to inspire confidence and calm so that the penitent was able to confess all without fear. The fathers were also bidden to give encouragement so that the penitent felt himself welcomed in the sacred tribunal, where he could unburden himself before one who understood and sympathised with the deep recesses of individual conscience.[101] This often meant encouraging people to make a general confession, and the confessor was urged to help the penitent make a thorough examination of conscience. The 'principal event' of a mission in Ballygawley, Co. Tyrone in 1883 was deemed by the missioners to have been 'the large number of good general confessions heard of those who so much needed them and never had the opportunity of making one before'.[102] And at Templederry, Co. Tipperary, in 1874 and 1879, the success of the mission was evidenced, not only by the regular attendance at all the exercises, but also by the large numbers who 'with great zeal almost besieged the most holy Tribunal and there with tears repaired [their] sacrilegious confessions'.[103] Spiritual direction must, perforce, have been scanty in view of the number of confessions heard by each missioner. Fr Gibson recalled hearing 1,143 confessions during one mission,[104] and at St Mary and St Michael, Commercial Road, East London, in 1857, it was recorded that he heard 685, while Fr Vaughan heard 740, Fr Leo 680, Fr Plunkett 567, Fr Bridgett 455, Fr [? Kelly] 531, Fr Coffin 526, and the secular priests the remaining 1,247.[105]

Being, for the most part, a 'secret work', little can be said about this important aspect of the mission, although one recorded incident illustrates both the force of the confessor and the down-to-earth methods he could employ to achieve his ends. Asked by the confessor if he were a member of a secret society, a penitent immediately left the confessional, whereupon the priest sprang after him, exclaiming, 'The devil will strike you at the door', got hold of the man and brought him back. 'I'll show you what it is to meet a Priest', he continued, and set about the man's head, after which 'he was completely changed and made his confession with every sign of true repentance'.[106]

When the missioners left a parish, it was with the intent of returning after an interval of some months to conduct a renewal or renovation, with the object of consolidating the fruit of the mission.[107] This practice was peculiar to the Redemptorists and few of the English and Scottish missions did not have a renewal, although in Ireland the clergy preferred retreats to sodalities.[108] Whenever possible, the renewal was preached by the same Redemptorists as the mission, of which it was seen as the continuation, rather than as a separate exercise.[109] The purpose of a renewal was 'to encourage and strengthen in their resolutions those who have persevered, to raise up those who have fallen, and to give those who have missed or neglected the mission a new opportunity of grace and reconciliation with God'.[110] Believing that there was 'no more efficacious means of perfecting and solidifying the work of a mission',[111] the Dundalk Chronicler reviewed the improvement in Kingstown, Co. Dublin since the mission the previous year (1881) and noted the added success of this second-wave assault on the citadels of sin: many made a fuller and better confession than at the mission; some great public sinners, whose perseverance had been despaired of at the mission, had remained faithful and came up to the renewal with signs of compunction; a great many who had not gone to the mission now came to the renewal; the confraternities, established at the mission, were doing well; drunkenness and company-keeping had declined, and all the prostitutes had either left or were forced out of town.[112] It was even held by some that renewals 'do more good than the missions themselves in moving the heart of the recalcitrant'.[113] At Walsall in 1863, for example, the number of those at the renewal who had ignored the mission made it 'equivalent to a second mission',[114] while at New Ross, Co. Wexford three years later, between two and three hundred men, who had evaded the mission, were now brought up to their duties, and the parish priest was amazed that five hundred men gave their names for confirmation, since he had recently been unable to persuade anyone.[115]

Renewals were the primary means of dealing with those who had either relapsed or lessened in their fervour since the mission, or who had escaped the net the first time round. This was all the more important where a disturbance after the mission had checked its good effects, as at Belfast in 1872, where strikes and riots had led to drunkenness, violation of the pledge made at the mission and a resurgence of Ribbonism, which the renewal sought to remedy.[116] At St Anne's, Blackley, Lancashire in 1861, it was recorded that 'the weak who had begun to totter were strengthened, the strong were yet more strengthened, and many whom we failed to gain in the Mission were gained in the Renewal'.[117] The success of the renewal could stand in marked contrast to the apparent failure of the mission. Thus, at Sutton, Co. Dublin, in 1859, 'the public drinking-houses, which could not be closed after the Mission on Sundays and Holydays, were now efficaciously shut up. Company-keepers, who did not give up their wicked habits, now surrendered cheerfully and publicly promised they would never again relapse'.[118] To his ecstatic description of a renewal in St Andrew's, Newcastle in 1880, the Kinnoull Chronicler added the resolution that 'after the happy conclusion of the exercises in the church of S. Andrew, I shall never despair of any place or people, even the lost', and he wrote of the renewal's 'great and truly miraculous fruit' as being

> a spirit of faith, the exaltation of the mind, a softening of piety, a sincere love of religion, a flaming heart exhibited in this same place where, but a short time ago, all seemed hard as rock, cold as ice, [a place] sunk in the depths of every kind of turpitude and wasting away through the spirit of growing infidelity (in profundo

omnigeneris turpitudinis demersi, et spiritu tumentis infidelitatis tabescentes).[119]

The renewal was of shorter duration than the mission — generally, one or two weeks in length — and although many of the same subjects were covered, there was less excitement than in the great mission sermons. The emphasis was also different. Although sin was denounced, and the reality of death and judgement again displayed for the benefit of those who had either relapsed or grown tepid since the mission, the joys and rewards of living the Christian life were more prominent than the miseries and terrors of divine punishment. The concentration upon God's condescension and Man's co-operation with divine grace in his aspiration to sanctity lent a milder, winning aspect to the renewal, and assisted the subtle suggestions of long-term perseverance. The overriding intention was to leave the people with an abiding sense of hope and conviction in their allegiance to, and dependence on, the Church and all that had been recommended to them for their sanctification. This was summed up in the theatrical *finale,* the renewal of baptismal vows, when the people, lighted candles in hand, promised again to renounce sin and reject evil and to believe in God and all that he provided for their salvation within the bosom of the Church.

The missionary methods and techniques of the Redemptorists did not substantially alter during the nineteenth century, nor did the objectives of the missions. How far those objectives were realised is the consideration to which we must now turn.

9

Missions:
their effectiveness

Writing in 1899, Fr Burke reviewed with satisfaction 'the missionary work of our Congregation in these countries during the last fifty years', and noted that it had been 'vast, growing, and, moreover, unmistakably and eminently successful':

> During our missions we commonly feel that we are living in a spiritual atmosphere which is heavily charged with the magnetism of Divine grace [and] we are frequent witnesses of veritable miracles of God's mercy, of mighty deeds of revolution, and transformation and reformation wrought by the power of God in the souls of the most hardened, degraded, hopeless sinners.[1]

Such an assessment, intended for public consumption, undoubtedly represents one view of the Redemptorists' missionary labours and contains elements of the truth. So does the cynical remark of an unnamed Redemptorist, who tackled the young Patrick Sampson during a retreat he was making in the Limerick house before he entered the novitiate in 1862: 'Our missions', said the Father, 'do good at the time, but afterwards the people fall away and some of them become worse than ever before'.[2] This opinion is all the more interesting in coming from the early years of the Redemptorist missions in Ireland, when many of the fathers were intoxicated with their apparent success and the contribution they were making to the Catholic revival, rather than from the closing years of the century, when, beset by obstacles on the missions and divisions within the Province, a certain jadedness had set in among the Institute.

The two assessments set up the contrast between the short-term effects of the missions. Any assessment inevitably

183

depends on the angle from which one views them. On the one hand, missions were an extraordinary grace, and the transitory nature of such would naturally lead to a dissipation of their immediate effects, unless action were taken at a parochial level to maintain them. On the other hand, that conversion which the missions sought to effect was meant to have lasting consequences in the life of the penitent. A variety of reactions on the part of those who were missionised could be expected between these two positions. 'Such is human frailty', wrote St Alphonsus realistically,

> that many sinners, after having recovered God's grace, again lost it. But were there no other good, it is at least certain that generally speaking during the mission bad habits and scandals disappear, blasphemies disappear, many restitutions are made, and many bad confessions are repaired … a good many sinners persevere in God's grace, and if others fall back, they nevertheless keep from mortal sins for several months; at least through the sermons heard on the missions they acquire a greater knowledge of God and a greater horror for sin … I hold it for certain that of all those who attend the sermons, if any one dies within a year after the mission, it can hardly be that he will be damned. The fruits of the mission last at least a year or two.[3]

The saint's optimism should not obscure the essential modesty of the claims he made for the missions, in their enthusiasm for which others could easily exaggerate. In trying to give an estimate of them, while noting particular instances of failure or spectacular success, one needs to remember this modesty of claim and assess them from that standard, rather than from any other. Indeed, each mission was a separate exercise and judged solely on its own merits. In South Wexford in 1893, for example, the great scandal before a Redemptorist mission was considered to be company-keeping, which was 'so fully recognised and established that there seems no way of checking it'. During the mission, many people were reported to have shown 'traces of conscience' and to have responded to the missioners' efforts 'with a show of enthusiasm'.[4] At most, it could be claimed that a recognised scandal was temporarily and partially checked; no other claim for the mission was made. At the same time, certain questions are raised in the mind of the historian, which, acknowledging the various caveats, he must try to answer.

The first noteworthy fact is that large numbers of Catholics were attracted to Redemptorist missions throughout the period. Between 1848 and 1882, for example, there were close on fifteen hundred missions and renewals, in the course of which 4,239,934 communions were given.[5] Since it was rare to receive Holy Communion more than once during the mission, we thus have some idea of the total number of attenders. Of course, many would have attended more than one, and possibly several, missions during this period, so that the actual number would be considerably lower, but it is an impressive figure, nonetheless. In Ireland, the attendance and enthusiastic response of thousands of Catholics was not restricted to the early years and was not uncommon in Britain. The closing sermon at a mission in St Mary and St Michael, Commercial Road, East London in 1857 attracted so large a number of people that it was said that St Paul's Cathedral would have been insufficient to accommodate them.[6] Catholics came in such numbers to the first Redemptorist mission in the diocese of Menevia and Newport, at Brigend in 1863, that the parish priest said that he had no idea there were so many in his parish.[7] Similarly, at Cobridge, in the Potteries, the priest admitted that the congregation attracted to the mission was 'in great part altogether new to him'.[8] Even in places where missions were given often, the response could still be overwhelming. At St Patrick's, Wigan in July 1875, the efforts of the missioners were reported to have met 'with unprecedented success':

> From the beginning it has been necessary to have additional services in the schoolroom for the benefit of those who could not find even standing-room in the church. Crowds surround the confessionals all day long, and a large number of juveniles of both sexes, and of the

working class, are being prepared by the good nuns, acting under the direction of the missioners, for their first communion.[9]

Two months later, 'a really glorious mission, probably the most successful one ever given in Liverpool', at St Anthony of Padua, resulted in ten thousand communions and 2,587 confirmations. On St Patrick's Day, four thousand people crowded into the church and two thousand had to be turned away and the doors locked.[10] As late as 1894, the Franciscan Fathers of West Gorton, Manchester exclaimed that 'they had never seen such crowds in their own church' as during the Redemptorist mission.[11]

These examples illustrate the eagerness with which a mission was greeted and the fascination that drew people to them. Confessing that he was 'never more edified in my whole lifetime' than by 'the apostolic zeal, eloquence and self-denial' of the Redemptorist missioners at Navan, Co. Meath, in 1874, the bishop marvelled at the way the people 'rushed into it with enthusiasm from the first day', and informed the Rector of Limerick that 'the Fathers of your order seem to have a peculiar attraction for the people of this Parish; they quite fascinated them'.[12] The cause of that fascination was both the content and manner of delivery of the mission sermons and instructions. The reporter of an early mission in Gorey, Co. Wexford considered that it was 'a cheering spectacle to behold a church, of spacious dimensions, filled to the very threshold night after night by a dense mass of people, listening with intensive interest to the thrilling truths of religion as they came clothed with fire from the burning lips of these zealous and energetic Missioners'.[13] It was recorded elsewhere that people came up to two hours in advance of the evening sermon in order to ensure a seat.[14]

If few parishes went to the same length as the parishioners of Kirkham, Lancashire, who in 1861 met the missioners with a band, playing 'Hail, Holy Mission, Hail!',[15] many displayed a similar eagerness in allowing nothing to detract from their attendance at the mission. At Dunloy, Co. Antrim in 1887, the people were said 'to have set everything else aside during these three weeks for the sake of their souls',[16] while at Kirkintilloch, near Glasgow, neither the inclement weather nor the distance from the chapel was able to deter the people from attending assiduously both the mission and renewal in 1869.[17] A witness of the mission at St Anne's, Ashton-under-Lyne, Lancashire in 1860 thought the enthusiasm of 'the working classes [who] hastened to early Mass, and, when they left their factories at night, rushed to church' worthy of note.[18] A children's mission in St Patrick's, Leeds in 1856 had elicited a similar marvel:

> When the shades of evening fell — when the clack of mill, and the whirl of machinery, and the ring of hammer were heard no longer, there came hurrying to the mission the sons and daughters of toil, the young men whose hands are horny and rough from hood, and hoe, and shovel, and pickaxe, whose faces are blackened and begrimmed with the smoke, the dust, and stench of mill, and mine, and foundry — the young women who manage and tend spindle, and bobbin, and reel, and mule, and genny, and band ... Hundreds who had often knelt before at the tribunal of Penance reviewed their past lives, deplored in the bitterness of their sobs their shortcomings, taking counsel with themselves, and others, as to the best means of avoiding the like errors for the time to come, whilst hundreds more prepared themselves for receiving, for the first time, the sacraments of Penance and the Eucharist.[19]

Even more impressive is the example of the Dundee men, who, in 1867, stopped work early in order to get to confession, and were rewarded with dismissal by their employer.[20] The mere incidence of a mission was sometimes sufficient stimulus for local hostilities to be overcome in a wave of religious enthusiasm, as at Maryborough (now Portlaoise) in the diocese of Kildare and Leighlin in 1882, when not only was a country meeting postponed *sine die* so as not to clash with the mission, but even 'the most advanced and most violent of the politicians', who were estranged from the parish priest over the recent political agitation, overcame their antipathy in their desire to avail themselves of the mission.[21]

Analysing such an enthusiastic response to a mission, the Kinnoull Chronicler considered that the people were 'tired of sin and longing for an opportunity to get out of it: when it came, they eagerly seized upon it and made their confession with tears'.[22] What is remarkable is the number of confessions that could be heard; at Mullingar, Co. Westmeath in 1867, for example, 11,354 confessions were heard during the mission by the Redemptorists, aided by the bishop and thirty secular priests.[23] This was exceptional, but so commonplace was it for very large numbers to make their confession that the reporter of a mission in 1879 at Altrincham, Cheshire could remark casually, 'it is almost needless to say that the confessionals were besieged by crowds of penitents from early morning until late at night'.[24] In part, this was due to the willingness of the Redemptorists to hear general confessions, and the chance this provided to repair the injuries of the past. At Kells, Co. Antrim in 1893, 'one of the best signs of how deep and effectual the mission did its work was the large number who requested to make a general confession, even when it was not necessary, but who still liked to do it on account of the contrition they felt'.[25] Sixteen years previously, at Dungannon, Co. Tyrone, the local priest had been surprised at the number who made their confession for the first time, many of them from outside of the parish, with the result that the missioners heard five thousand confessions, a lot of them 'badly-needed general confessions', out of an estimated Catholic population of three thousand.[26]

It is easy to be cynical, to question the depth of religious sentiment, to talk about 'mission Catholics', caught up in the euphoric atmosphere. Undoubtedly, there were many such, whose conversion was of a temporary, histrionic or ambiguous nature. Fr Vaughan was both impressed and amused by his experience in the confessionals in Ireland, where people often exclaimed, 'Well then, your Lordship!, an' it's all my own fault intirely [*sic*]. Glory be to God — I'm the biggest sinner ever knelt before your honour's Holiness'.[27] Many would have lapsed again within a few months of the mission, and the Redemptorists knew this. Analysis of both French Catholic and British Protestant revivals has confirmed that growth rates peaked after mission campaigns, but were not generally sustained beyond a year or so.[28] Unfortunately, there is not the same available statistical evidence to provide a similar analysis of Redemptorist missions in Britain or Ireland, and one is left to depend upon the impression gained, and upon the reasonable assumption that analysis would not fundamentally differ in its conclusion that the number drawn to a mission and converted by it would not be commensurate with the number who were living as penitent Catholics some months later. This will have to be borne in mind when we come to consider the missions' shortcomings. Equally, it points to the need for regular missions to catch the backsliders before they slid away into indifference. On the positive side, it should be stressed that by attracting people who may have been largely indifferent about their religion before the mission and reverted again some time after it, the missions did help to re-affirm their sense of Catholic identity, even if in the long-term they remained 'marginal' Catholics.

The question that needs to be asked is why people were repeatedly drawn to missions and responded so enthusiastical-ly to them. The simple, and ultimately the only convincing, explanation is the perceived value of their message and of the services the missioners rendered. A witness of a mission in St Nicholas and St Kevin, in 'one of the poorest parts of Dublin', recognised as its chief benefit the restitution of thousands to 'peace and their friendship with God'.[29] Fr Walworth recalled missions to the operatives in the cotton manufactories of Manchester and the pleasure he experienced in preaching 'hope and joy to pallid-faced girls, going to and fro with wearied steps and listless eyes'.[30] The Redemptorists did nothing to alleviate the sufferings of the poor, but set themselves to repair the spiritual and moral damage that sufferings brought with them. Through the missions, they sought to 'lift the people into a higher atmosphere and make them forget, for a time at least, the petty vexations of life'.[31]

Instead of the hand-to-mouth existence, drink and squalor, which was all too common for many who attended the missions, the Redemptorist preacher showed the eternal worth, dignity and value of the individual soul, and recalled his hearers to serious, responsible Christian living, possible to all whatever their circumstances, which in turn was to lead to a development of their social responsibility in personal and family life. A mission in St Chad's, Manchester in 1862 could thus be characterised as 'a great solace amid the troubles of short-time and its concomitants of scanty food and diminishing clothing among the many unemployed or partially-employed of this parish'. The zeal and eloquence of the Redemptorist missioners, continued the newspaper reporter, 'would be no news' to the readers of his account, 'but when in this ever-working day metropolis of labour, thousands of pale-faced sons and daughters of Holy Church were seen crowding, I might almost say crushing into church, it shows that the one thing necessary is not forgotten'.[32] Even the bringing of the sick to be cured by the missioners, as at Coatbridge, Glasgow in 1857, although suggestive of superstitious, folk elements in people's religion, nevertheless demonstrates how they saw the mission in a positive light, as something from which they might gain.[33]

People responded to missions then, because they gave to them hope, a renewed dignity and self-respect, provided meaning and purpose in otherwise leaden lives. During a mission in Clonmel, Co. Tipperary in July 1863, one parishioner was heard to remark that 'the acts of my lifetime all sink into insignificance compared with that which it is now my happiness to participate in'.[34] Extolling the 'almost superhuman and unremitting efforts of the truly zealous Redemptorist Fathers', an address presented by the parishioners of Clonmel after the mission recalled that 'a few short weeks since, we were strangers — bound, indeed, by a common link, but yet unknown to each other. Today we meet as friends':

> Of your labours in the vineyard of the Lord we would speak, if language would permit us to characterise them

as they deserve. From morning until night they have been pursued, earnestly, nobly, and, we trust, profitably. At the Altar, in the pulpit, in the tribunal of penance, they have been unceasing, and, as you have been good and faithful ministers — as you have rescued many from the abyss of sin, and placed them on the road to Heaven — as you have instilled the fear and love of the great and merciful God, and as you have thereby reconciled thousands to offended Omnipotence, so we earnestly hope and pray that you may each and all be long spared to promote among our countrymen the blessings you have conferred on the people of Clonmel.

The address ended with thanks 'from our heart of hearts' and the promise that 'for long years to come the Mission of the Redemptorist Fathers will be held in loving and prayerful recollection by the people of Clonmel'.[35]

Such a eulogy shows that through the missions the Redemptorists stimulated a latent spiritual longing, a hunger for the ameliorating Word of God, and implanted the desire to put it into practice. This, after all, was the primary objective of the missions, the standard against which their success or failure was judged.[36] So, at Templederry, Co. Tipperary in 1890, the success of the mission was shown by nothing more than 'the steady attendance under trying circumstances, the eagerness, and the good dispositions with which the people came to confession'.[37] At the most basic level, the missions provided an opportunity for many who had fallen away or were negligent of their religious duties to return to the practice of the faith; even if such a return were only temporary, it should not be undervalued. The missioners at St Cuthbert's, North Shields in 1859 spoke

> to many, to hundreds of poor straying sheep that had long (some for fifteen or sixteen years) ceased to listen to the voice of their divinely-appointed shepherd ... Men whose faith had become (notoriously so) debased with the arguments of the infidel, and poisoned with the vile, cheap literature of the day, have deserted their associates,

191

and once again returned to the foot of the cross, and renewed their former faith. Fathers of families, who had not crossed the door of the church for many years, and would have been excellent 'capital to point to' for the enemies of Holy Church, have once more taken their place in God's holy temple.

The 'irresistible appeals' to the 'fallen children of the Church' were reported to have 're-baptised' the whole congregation 'with a zeal for Holy Church'.[38] Not all missions were blessed with such signal success, but it remains true that in countless missions 'many a poor wanderer has been recalled to a sense of his unhappy state, and induced to seek a reconciliation with his God'.[39] Although the mission accounts are full of remarkable conversions, it is the less spectacular examples that are more strikingly authentic; at Mortlake, Surrey in 1885, for example, a man, who was moved to go to confession after an absence of thirteen years, wrote to the missioners, telling them of the effect of their words: 'Oh! holy gentlemen, I have listened to your words until I thought I must perforce cry out aloud in the church for mercy. I have listened to you until I have learned to hang on your glorious words with a deep-rooted intensity and love'.[40]

A feature of the early Bishop Eton mission reports is the recording of the number of 'outstanders' who attended each mission, that is, those who had failed to make their Easter duties for some time and were considered to have lapsed. These were often quite large — 725 at St Anne's, Blackburn and 1,200 at St John's, Salford in 1858, for example.[41] Missions did succeed in bringing up many to their duties, and into contact with the Church, either for the first time or after an absence of some years. At Weymouth, Dorset in 1881, only eighty Catholics had approached the sacraments at Easter; the mission, a few months later, managed to attract a further ninety, so that it was said that there were only fifty Catholics in the town who did not now attend.[42] More dramatically, only fifty-five of the five hundred Catholics in Abersychan, near Pontypool, went regularly to Mass before the mission in 1893, which raised the number to 430.[43] In both these small places, the mission successfully appealed to the negligent and managed to halt the drifting-away from the faith and the slide into complete indifference which it was feared such negligence betokened. In the early years of the mission, when the Catholic community was less well-defined in the cities and towns of Britain, this aspect of their work was crucial. At Saffron Hill, London, described as 'even in this Babylon, notorious for theft, drunkenness and sin of every description', there were in 1862 an estimated four thousand Catholics, 'the poorest of the poor, living in out-of-the-way courts, alleys, etc., nearly all ignorant of the first principles of their religion and their duties', who were, for the most part, completely beyond the Church's normal reach. During the mission, the church was 'crowded to excess', and the dispositions of the people were 'most consoling', so that 1,900 confessions were heard, including many who had not approached the sacraments for upwards of forty years.[44] This experience was not uncommon; at St Patrick's, Liverpool in 1871, 'innumerable sinners, exiles (exules) from the sacraments for many years — some 10, others 20, 30, 40, 50, 60 years — others who had never been to confession — others sunk in the mire of evil (in vitiorum coeno demensi) — so that until then their salvation seemed to be despaired of — flocked to return (turnatum affluebant)'.[45] As late as 1896, a mission to the hitherto-neglected Italian community in Edinburgh brought up to the sacraments 'many who had not heard the Word of God for twenty, thirty, or even forty years'.[46] Missions managed, not just to halt, but also to reverse the decline into heathendom, which the Catholic authorities feared would be the result of negligence. At Stella, Northumberland in 1859, the missioners found that 'Catholicism is fast ebbing away', but a few months after the mission, the priest wrote to say that it had done 'permanent good', and the renewal a year later revealed '600 communicants who seem really *solid* Catholics, on whose perseverance the Pastor may depend'.[47]

The missions, in drawing a large number of people, many of them having little or no previous contact with their local church, or after an absence of some years, and infecting them with a sense of religious excitement, thus helped to combat what the Archbishop of Westminster described in 1894 as 'the alarming defections from the Church'.[48] The dearth of the kind of detailed statistical evidence available to historians of Protestant denominations makes it impossible to quantify this aspect of the missions, although it is undoubtedly true, as contemporaries averred, that many thousands were saved for the faith because they were touched by a mission which called or re-called them to the practice of a faith from which they were slipping.[49] A newspaper report of the 1873 general mission in Bradford, in which the Redemptorists took a prominent part, noted that

> a large number, whose absence from Mass and the Sacraments had made it impossible up to the Mission to distinguish themselves from Protestants, declared themselves Catholics and were seen every night at the services, and waited till a late hour for their turn at the confessional. Many, too, who were punctual when they first came here, but who had ceased to be so in the midst of their Protestant neighbours, have shaken off their carelessness and are now full of fervour and zeal in the service of God. This mission has shown a strength of Catholicity that was never believed to exist.[50]

Whether old loyalties were rekindled or new ones evoked, the missions assisted in the work of constructing and consolidating strong, local Catholic communities. A symptom of this was the way that they were used to bring up to confirmation many adults who might otherwise not have been persuaded to approach the sacrament.[51] Such action confirmed yet more firmly the link between Catholics and their Church and tightened its hold upon them. Another symptom was the first communions of the children, which could be very large in numbers, especially during the days of Furniss's apostolate.[52] A prime motive of children's missions was to give the children a special opportunity of approaching the sacraments of penance and the eucharist as an introduction to the world of the Holy. Given, by means of the missions, what was intended to be an unforgettable demonstration of Catholic holiness, the children were made to identify with it as the first step in their full sacramental participation in it. The missions were thus considered to be the essential means of 'bringing up to their duty a large number of grown boys and girls who had never been to their duty and who would have ended by losing their faith altogether'.[53] Certainly, priests recorded a large increase in Mass attendances for several years after a children's mission.[54] Many of the children would subsequently lapse for one reason or another. What was important, however, was to have made 'most deep religious impressions on the minds of children, at an age when the mind is most susceptible to those impressions which last through life',[55] to have provided childhood memories and an initiation into the cultic life of the Church which could later be re-invoked, when opportunity afforded, and a return to God made possible. The impressions were meant to be lasting and the influence of the Church inescapable, ensuring the local Catholic communities' continued existence and sustained growth in succeeding generations.[56]

The relative success of missions, and of the Catholic Church generally, in forming vigorous local communities meant that Catholicism was more resistant to the secularising pressures that weakened popular, urban Protestantism in the nineteenth century. This is not to suggest that Catholicism was not adversely affected by the same pressures; undoubtedly it was, and, as we shall see in the next chapter, the work of the missions was seriously undermined by them. Equally, one should not ignore the real achievements of the missions and the contribution they made to the Catholic community, not only in attracting Catholics whose previous commitment was languid, but also in the ideological influence that they exerted and which issued in both the resolve and in practical measures to resist external influences and to maintain the integrity of the Faith. What so intrigued commentators was the ability of the Redemptorist missioners to stir, impress, affect, and thus mould, whole congregations of people, who were then persuaded to effect what had been recommended to them.[57]

This was often in the face of difficulties or obstacles that made the missioners' success all the more surprising and remarkable. The people of Dundee, for example, were discovered in 1867 to be 'very corrupt and immoral, and even the Catholics, by the evil example and conversation of their fellow-citizens, are more or less corrupted'.[58] The mission was a great success and the people responded eagerly. Likewise, at Donagh-moyne, Co. Monaghan in 1896 the missioners found that there had been no mission for thirty-three years, that the people were largely neglected by their priests and, consequently, that there was much ignorance in religious matters. Feuds with the priests had led to much hatred and an unforgiving spirit on both sides, while 'many thought that the Sixth Commandment forbade nothing except downright adultery and fornication', the duties of the married state were nearly unknown for want of instruction, and 'prevention of generation through fear of too large a family' was prevalent, as was 'allowing full-grown boys and girls to sleep together or with parents'. Here were a people represented to the missioners as 'very self-willed, determined, dogged and unbiddable', whom the Redemptorists managed to manipulate to their purposes, so that 'they drank in eagerly our every word, were to us as docile as children, and softened under kindness as snow in the sun. *This* made the Mission a delight. It was just the place and the people that St Alphonsus meant for us'.[59]

Docility among the people made it easier to move them, but the Redemptorists knew that only firm instruction in the principles of their faith would given any solidity to the work. It was a feature of many missions, particularly in Ireland, that elementary instruction in the Catholic faith had to be given continuously, even in the confessional.[60] This continued to be necessary in areas where the Redemptorists pioneered missions and encountered uninformed, and thus somewhat negligent, Catholics. At Montrose in 1881, the native Catholics were found to be 'mainly ignorant of their faith; nearly everyone, young and old, had to be taught individually the Four Great Truths', and at Brechin 'the younger members of the congregation were like unbroken colts with regard to the practice of their religion, especially confession'.[61] The result was that they were not sufficiently distinguishable from their worthy Protestant compatriots. Having instilled the principles of their religion, the missioners succeeded in evoking 'a Catholic spirit that was worthy of Ireland'. Elsewhere, the fathers' labours were seen as tending 'to unify the Catholic population', and the missions as 'greatly strengthening the Catholic spirit of the district' by asserting Catholic distinctiveness.[62] The strong catechetical element in the missions reinforced the sense of Catholic identity, which was a prelude to the community's self-segregation.

Having imbibed the Catholic spirit, and having emerged from the mission with a renewed pride and self-identity, the people were encouraged to effect its practical concomitants, to achieve that form of 'ghetto-Catholicism' that issued from the isolationist mentality and which served to retain those whom the mission had reclaimed. The destruction of adverse, and the encouragement of favourable, conditions that were conducive to the perseverance of the people was meant to contain Catholics in their own world as a bulwark against secular encroachment. The most obvious example of this was the removal of children from local Protestant day and Sunday schools and, after 1870, from the new board schools. This was a feature of Redemptorist missions from the start. The 'glorious' attendance of people from 'a scandalous Rookery called Jenny's Building' in the parish of St Mary, Kensington, West London in 1862 did not make the mission 'extremely blessed … almost beyond any of our London missions', so much as the fact that 'several Catholic children were rescued from the soupers' school, which threatens to be shut up'.[63] It was not uncommon for the number of such 'rescued' children to be recorded,[64] or for this to be seen as the primary fruit of the mission, as at Elswick, Northumberland in 1884, where 'all or nearly all withdrew their children from non-Catholic schools, the frequency of which was one of the abuses we had to contend with'.[65] The reverse effect of such removals was that a mission could fill the dwindling rolls of

Catholic schools, as happened at Stranraer in 1885.[66]

Parents who sent their children to Protestant schools in those districts where Catholic schools existed usually did so because they had themselves lapsed from the Church, probably as a result of mixed marriages, so that the removal of their children often marked their own return to the Church and the regularisation of their marriages. Thus, a mission in Mitchelstown, Co. Cork in 1868 was marked by the return 'of many to the faith and a good life who, on account of mixed marriages especially, from a long time ago had fallen away from [their] religion and the sacraments'.[67] In a sense, all who were 'rescued' and who returned to the Church were heavily in its debt. This was particularly the case for those whom the missioners snatched from the jaws of proselytism. At Ballybunion, Co. Kerry in 1860, for example, 'poverty and sickness had made great ravages in the parish and in the train of both came the proselytizing Parsons to buy the sick and famishing poor from the Faith of their Fathers'. Upwards of 150 had succumbed, although most confessed that even in the Protestant church they were 'afraid of God and secretly said their rosary beads. Some, however, though no longer keeping up their connection with the ministers of error, were not yet sacramentally reconciled to the Church'. The mission renewed morale and turned into a demonstration of the Catholic Church coming to the aid of her stricken and beleaguered children, and resulted in 5,600 communions, including those of a thousand adults, for whom this was their first communion.[68] Similarly, at Ballinasloe, Co. Galway in 1875, a Redemptorist mission brought back many Catholic tenants who had been forced to attend the Protestant chapel by their landlord.[69]

As means of revitalising the Catholic community and reaffirming the religious allegiance of those who were tempted to stray, the success of missions in combatting the problem of secret societies is no less impressive. Men were attached to secret societies because they were politically or socially aggrieved, or because they were drawn into them through friendship, so that it took not a little courage for men to break contact with their fellow members. At Newcastle in 1858, 140 members of the Hibernian Society left as a result of a mission, to be joined by a further 250 at the renewal some months later, 'even though the leaders of the society did all in their power to impede this success'.[70] Similarly, in 1860, six hundred Ribbonmen left the society at the Brooms, Co. Durham, considered 'the chief stronghold' in the diocese of Hexham.[71] The breaking of the loyalty and solidarity of a secret society was no easy matter, especially as the Redemptorists offered nothing but a spiritual solution to the problems that had given rise to the societies. At Lavey, Co. Cavan in 1881, nothing could be done to get the Ribbonmen to confession, not even the condemnation of their society by the bishop in person. Throughout the mission, they remained resistant to all appeals by the mission preachers, whose words nevertheless worked their charm, for on the last day of the mission the men were told to destroy their insignia and place them in the hands of the missioners via the parish priest's letter-box: 'That same night from every part of the parish the insignia of the society were sent to the priest's house, and the destruction of this society can be said to have been the first and greatest fruit of this mission'.[72] It was not the weaning-away of individual members, however great their number, but the destruction of societies at which the missions aimed, since their very existence posed a defiant threat to the Catholic Church which it could not countenance.[73] Thus, at Ashton-under-Lyne, a 'hotbed' of Hibernians, the breaking-up of the society was considered by an observer as 'the most remarkable feature' of the mission:

> On the last day of the Mission, the Rev. Fr Schneider announced, to the great joy of Ashton, that the society was defunct, the declaration required by the Bishops signed, the club dissolved, the box broken up, and the funds divided.[74]

The existence of a secret society created friction in a parish, since the priests were bound to oppose it, and was one possible reason for discord within the Catholic community. The missions stressed the essential unity of the Church, and were concerned to effect reconciliation and repair the scandals that arose out of parochial hostilities. Thus, a mission at Boston, Lincolnshire in 1885, 'succeeded in effecting ... the reconciliation of parties who had been at war for years'.[75] At Rathkeale, Co. Limerick in 1863, the parishioners were even in rebellion against the bishop, had occupied the chapel and refused to admit any but the priest of their choice. The mission resulted in their surrender and an address of submission and apology to the bishop.[76] Some years later, the Archbishop of Tuam was reconciled to the Congregation, which he had kept out of his diocese for the past twenty years, because a mission at Castlebar, Co. Mayo managed to bring peace to a difficult parish which was divided among its parishioners and against its priest.[77] The most spectacular example of the reconciliation of seemingly irreconcilable enemies was at Emly, Co. Tipperary in 1862, where the Archbishop of Cashel had long been trying to suppress the long-running and bloody faction-fights between the so-called 'Three-year-olds' and 'Four-year-olds', involving upwards of twenty thousand men. Towards the close of the mission, the people made a solemn promise before the archbishop to cease their fighting and never to use again the designations that had caused so much trouble.[78] So ingrained had been the hostility, and so great the wonder that the Redemptorists had effected a reconciliation, that it was widely reported in the Catholic press at home and abroad, and the Pope, to whom the information was relayed, expressed his pleasure.[79] Twenty years later, it was found that there had been no recurrence of the old hostility.[80]

The example of Emly illustrates how a mission, and the Redemptorists thought only one of their missions, could work on those who were resistant to the ordinary pleas of the clergy and the claims made upon them by the Church. Thus, the pastors at St Alban's, Blackburn in 1857, where two previous missions by the Rosminians in 1851 and 1855 had produced little fruit, were astonished 'at seeing so many they seldom or never saw in their chapel: several hardened or long-standing sinners, who had ever resisted the voice of God, at the time of the previous missions, came in now converted and determined to lead a different life, and the number who thus returned to the Church was not less than 600'.[81] It sometimes needed many assaults to break down resistance and defiance. Missions and retreats had been given *'ad infinitum'* over thirty years, several of them by the Redemptorists, in the parish of the Pro-Cathedral in Dublin, reported the Dundalk Chronicler in 1885, and had 'come to be considered as a course of exercises mainly, if not exclusively for the roughs, the absentees, and, in general, the spiritually destitute'. Whatever past failings, 'many who had been leading very bad lives for years and had resisted the [previous] missions, now came up with every mark of true repentance'.[82] The threats of the missioners and the consequences of obduracy were sufficient to move many hardened sinners, like the man at Saffron Hill, London, who on the last day of a mission in 1862, 'when hearing the Father declare that he could not bless, nor would God bless, those who had neither profited nor intended profiting by this means of salvation, was so struck with terror as to seize at once upon one of the priests and to insist on making his confession there and then'.[83] On the other hand, countless missions effected no more dramatic conversions than those of the people of Uddingstone, Lanarkshire in 1885, whose 'faith, which was dead, was stirred up and their hearts warmed to the Church, and the interest in the education of their children was renewed. They showed a great desire to check drink by joining the Temperance Society of the Holy Family'.[84]

The reduction in the incidence of drinking was probably the most obvious manifestation of the good effects of a mission. At Govan, near Glasgow in 1880, large-scale Saturday-night drinking had led to neglect of Sunday Mass prior to the mission, but during its course no drunkard was found, and the innkeepers were peeved at the loss of trade.[85] In Washington, Co. Durham, the police were surprised that only three men were locked up for drunkenness on pay-night during a mission in 1886, since the lock-up was usually full.[86] Such sobriety was, of course, intended to last. In Ireland, one way to ensure this was to reinforce the bishops' ban against the sale and consumption of strong liquor on Sundays and feast days. The renewal of this law was made at a mission in Wexford in 1868, and a few months later, a parish priest wrote to say that all seventy-five public houses were closed on the stipulated days.[87] In the same year, at Mullingar, Co. Westmeath, the bishop expressed amazement at the sobriety of the people some months after the mission, and the absence of drunkenness in the place, a view that was echoed by the local police. The renewal at Ballylanders, Co. Limerick in 1871 showed that all the men had kept the promise not to take strong drink and that no one had broken the episcopal ban, or reverted to their old hostilities, which miracles of grace were attributed to the family rosary, commended at the mission.[88] The testimony of magistrates and of the local press concerning the decline of drunkenness and its beneficial effects, directly attributable to missions, was recorded with satisfaction by the Redemptorist chroniclers, who were convinced that their work was an important element in the campaign against this social evil.[89]

From the Redemptorists' point of view, it was an equally wonderful sign of the power of the mission that at Ashton-under-Lyne in 1863 not one Catholic took part in a riot by aggrieved factory operatives during the mission, while at Sheffield in 1867, where the missioners noted that there were frequent brawls and murders, the taming influence of the mission was revealed some months later, when a spate of trades-union trouble resulted in a murder, but it was found that all the criminals were Protestants and that not one Catholic had been involved.[90]

Whether it is evidenced by the decline in drunkenness, the resolution of violent feuds, the repair of public scandals, the conversion of prostitutes,[91] or the restitution of stolen money,[92] missions were concerned to raise the moral climate in a parish by recalling people to spiritual values. 'Our parishioners', wrote a priest, 'are totally changed for the better, and have become, with the blessing of God, truly penitent … Our opinion is, that with the help of God, the mission brought a change for the better in the parish which will last as long as any of us live'.[93] Writing three weeks after a mission in his parish in 1879, a Derry priest told the missioners that

> numbers have since enrolled themselves in the Temperance Societies, hundreds are attending daily Mass who never did so before; moreover, the poor and badly clothed, who used to be ashamed to go out on Sundays, may now be seen in multitudes, bare-headed and bare-footed, hurrying to hear early Mass. In fact, in every way there is a manifest change for the better in the morals of the people.[94]

The renewal at St Peter's, Jersey in 1864 revealed that since the mission an average of 150 people had attended the daily, public recitation of the rosary, while at St Mary's, Liverpool as late as 1896, 'the steady perseverance with which many have kept their resolutions with regard to abstaining from drink is the most consoling evidence of the good effected by the recent mission and a safe criterion of the healthy state of morality in the Parish'.[95]

Of course, it was recognised that a single mission by itself did not necessarily result in an improved moral and spiritual tone. At Bury, Lancashire in 1873, the long neglect and spiritual destitution could not be remedied by one mission and renewal, and the following year, at St Patrick's, Edinburgh, the missioners considered that 'another mission is needed to raise the people from their spiritual lethargy, and another to expunge it'.[96] Yet it was hoped that a mission would help to 'change and renew the face' of a parish.[97] 'All who were good before this month', wrote a priest in Wexford, 'are become better, and all who were bad, with a solitary exception or two, are become good. I know some who permitted all the missions for the last fifteen years to pass by without the least effort for repentance were seen at communion during our last mission'.[98] The spiritual state of the Catholics in Wednesbury, Staffordshire in 1886, was 'the lowest possible, a well-nigh total, practical denial of the faith', but as a result of the mission, the Redemptorists believed that 'a real Hell was changed into a beautiful Paradise'.[99] Writing in April 1863, a month after a mission in his see-city, the Bishop of Waterford and Lismore believed that it 'has wrought the most wonderful effects. Crowds have besieged the confessionals since your departure and the priests have had more employment in that department than they ever remember to have had on their hands before'.[100] The priest at Stanley, Perthshire, told the missioners at the renewal in 1868 that he would never have believed the effects following a mission if he had not witnessed them himself; not only were divided factions now at peace, but the Catholic schools had more pupils than ever, and many more now came to weekday Mass.[101] At Paisley in 1877, the priest similarly boasted to the Redemptorists of the 'thronged, nay *invaded*' confessionals and, apparently without irony, that 'everyone [is] wearing a smile of charity'. Less loftily, the fact that the New Year's festival had passed off without drunkenness gave the priest confidence of the people's stability for a long time to come.[102]

The Redemptorists were not always as sanguine in their assessment of a particular mission, but they were ever-hopeful. Reviewing their recent labours in Dundalk in 1859, they noted that local newspapers stated that no drunkard had been seen in the town for months after the mission, and that twenty to thirty prostitutes had disappeared. It seemed that 'the whole appearance of the town changed. How long it may continue so, God alone can tell. But certain it is that the good people of Dundalk paid every attention to all the instructions and promised in every way to persevere in the flight of occasions [of sin], prayer, and, above all, the regular frequentation of the sacraments'.[103] Elsewhere, an observer enthused that 'a reformation has been effected',[104] and Archbishop Cullen believed, not only that 'the whole city will derive the greatest benefit' from a Redemptorist mission in the Pro-Cathedral in 1865, but also that it had saved the city from Fenian revolution.[105]

If these comments represent others' estimate of the benefits of their missions, the Redemptorists clearly recognised that the long-term remedy of those abuses, which the missions and renewal were supposed to have dealt a fatal, if not mortal, blow, depended upon the continuing restraint and influence for good which could be exercised over the people by their formation into confraternities. These could then help to maintain the fervour, and create that 'spirit of solid piety', which was deemed essential to the life and well-being of a parish.[106] Thus, at Cadrow, Glasgow in 1885, for example, the Confraternity of Our Lady of Perpetual Succour was established 'that by mutual example and the frequentation of the sacraments and moderation in drink they might encourage each other to persevere'.[107] Where sodalities already existed prior to a mission, they were encouraged and, if moribund, reformed, possibly through affiliation to the two Redemptorist Archconfraternities of the Holy Family and (after 1876) of Our Lady of Perpetual Succour, which then assumed responsibility for the welfare of the branch.[108] The establishment of confraternities was seen as a necessary concomitant of the mission apostolate: 'If any hopes are to be entertained for the perseverance of the people after a Mission, they will be found solely in these confraternities'.[109]

The object of a confraternity was quite simply to keep people up to the mark, inducing them 'to ponder often on their destiny and all their religious and social duties', by providing weekly devotional meetings and an opportunity for monthly communion.[110] Regular attendance at the meetings also opened up the possibility of systematic religious instruction. In a statement that is telling of the intention behind confraternities, a Redemptorist wrote that they did 'for the person living in the world what a religious Order does for the person living in the cloister', and he went on to tell how the rules

> keep the members to the practice of the duties essential to Christian life, as the weakness of the individual member is braced up by the aid of rules, by the watchfulness of the Director, and by the example of his associates; and human respect ... becomes a powerful incentive towards piety.[111]

At best, confraternities were meant to mould people into lay religious, to enclose them in a world of piety similar to that set out in *The Mission Book;* at the very least, 'it can never happen to [the members], as to so many others, that they forget or lose sight of their obligations as Catholics'.[112]

Membership of the confraternity was open to anyone who was leading a fairly decent Christian life which, in practice, after a mission, meant anyone who had been drawn to approach the sacraments. It was hoped, not only that it would provide a sense of solidarity, an *esprit de corps*, for the members, a rallying-point and practical structure for those who would aspire to lead a better Catholic life, but also that its existence would prove a strong counterweight to contrary social and religious forces and an effective agent for the preservation of Catholic domestic life and the sanctification of the whole parish: 'Worked effectively', promised Fr Geoghegan, 'it becomes a powerful agent for promoting piety among its members, for putting down vice, even such a great one as that of intemperance, and for edifying and sanctifying the parish generally; in fine, confraternities well-worked are the regenerators of society'.[113] Cardinal Manning fixed upon this regenerative capacity in an address he delivered to the newly-formed branch of a Confraternity of the Holy Family in 1875. He expressed the hope that Catholic men all over London would be organised in the Confraternity as a means of withstanding the onslaughts of the devil and stemming the tide of leakage from the Church, for

> it is meant as a training for every man, one by one. It is meant to be a training for the family, for the homes, for husband and wife, for father and mother, for son and daughter, for brother and sister. It is to make the homes of our people to be like the Holy House of Nazareth [where] there was prayer and praise, worship and adoration, and industry, and work and service one to another ... The life of the spirit of the Holy Family is intended to go all through the week, all through the day. ... It is intended that the members of the Holy Family are to be new men, and that in the spirit of a new life, they as husbands and fathers are to rule their households,

and if unmarried they must lead a life of holiness.[114]

The confraternity could thus be itself 'a missionary body', sanctifying its own members first of all, 'but, secondly, by the force of good example, by prayer, by persuasion, and various other means, influencing for good the lives of those outside the Confraternity'.[115]

What added to the appeal of confraternities was that they drew men and women into the organisational life of the Church, giving them a sense of sharing in that life, and providing scope for local, which meant largely working-class, initiative, producing mutual charity, out of which sometimes emerged such things as penny banks, burial or benefit clubs, lending libraries and various social activities and outings. Although the director of each confraternity was one of the local clergy, the burden of responsibility fell upon the prefects and sub-prefects of each section of about twenty-five persons, into which the confraternity was arranged. These officials were to ensure the exact and punctual attendance of the members of their section, to keep a list of their names, addresses and professions, as also those who absented themselves without reason. They were further enjoined to visit the sick of the section and they had to report to the director once a month.[116] The parish priest thus had a ready-to-hand instrument of evangelisation and of moral control over his parishioners, which some used to great effect.

The proven worth and expectant hope of confraternities was reflected by bishops throughout Ireland and Britain, who recorded the increase in the reception of the sacraments, the growth in piety, the resolution of domestic strife and the conversion of heretics, which resulted from their erection.[117] Writing in 1874, Fr Harbison proclaimed that 'His Eminence Cardinal Cullen, the Irish Provincial of the Jesuits, and several of the missionary staff of the Jesuits, and all the P[arish] P[riest]s of Dublin unanimously acknowledge that the confraternities are by far the best and most practical work for the Irish working class that has yet been tried in Ireland'.[118] From the Redemptorists' point of view, sodalities helped to keep people to their duties, at least during the interval between a mission and renewal, and added a heightened spiritual atmosphere to a parish, which was meant to lead to an improved moral tone and, in turn, to aid the work of the missions by making the people amenable. The missioners at Prestwich in 1892, for example, found that a Sodality of Mary, established during a previous mission some years before, had given 'a real religious tone to the parish by the piety and general good conduct of the members'.[119] The parish priest of SS Peter and Edward, Westminster, where seventy-four men had been enrolled in a Confraternity of the Holy Family established during a mission in 1860, reported four years later that 274 men were now on the roll, with a weekly attendance of between ninety and a hundred. The sight of so many men approaching the altar-rail each Sunday was, he wrote, an edification to strangers, and the confraternity was so great a help that 'I do not think I could effect any good in the place without it'.[120]

One might question if any confraternity was as successful as the Confraternities of the Holy Family for men and women in Elswick, Northumberland, which were said to have 'made the parish a parish of saints',[121] but they were important in aiding perseverance in the good resolutions made during a mission, in continuing spiritual formation after the pattern suggested by a mission, and in combatting the dangers to faith outlined by a mission. When the Redemptorists preached a mission at St John's Port, Glasgow in 1889, arrests for drunkenness numbered two thousand. The establishment of a branch of the League of the Cross, as a result of the mission, reduced that number to three hundred by the time the Redemptorists returned to preach the next mission in 1892.[122] This is but one example among many, and suggests that a detailed study of confraternities would throw much light upon the Catholic community. Such a study is beyond our present brief, but it is worth quoting the words of Fr Lambert, C.SS.R., preaching on the occasion of the silver jubilee of the Confraternity of the Holy Family, established during a Redemptorist mission in the Wexford church where he had been a curate. Lambert recalled that the Confraternity was found to checkmate the Free-masons ... Excessive drink — I say excessive drink — was abandoned — I do not say that drink altogether has been given up — but excessive drink by the members of the Confraternity of the Holy Family, who kept the rules, who attended all its meetings, and who went to monthly confession and Holy Communion — but the excessive drink was given up, work was better attended to, the wants of families better provided for, children sent to school and educated, scandals were given up, the duty of prayer was discharged, sacraments frequented, and Mass heard. ... Thanks to the Confraternity of the Holy Family the moral tone and religious feeling of the people have improved.[123]

The establishment and encouragement of confraternities, which the Redemptorists made during their missions, shows that they had a keen and clear eye to the long-term perseverance and good effects of their mission work. The memory of a good mission could itself leave a lasting impression upon people, as evidenced by two Redemptorists who, while visiting Cork in 1860, were delighted 'to see how vividly the people remembered the mission given there nearly six years ago, and how generally they dated the great improvement in all religious affairs in Cork to this beginning'.[124] It was common for the Redemptorists to note the continuing good effects of a previous mission in those places where they returned after an interval of some years; at St Mary's, Carlisle in 1894, for example, the missioners noted that the fruits of the 1879 mission were 'still distinctly visible' among the children: 'We may also say that our former missions have been the means of preserving the faith among the people generally'.[125] Even after an absence of twenty-five years, the fruits of the previous Redemptorist mission at New Ross, Co. Wexford were said to have remained.[126]

Among the blessings attached to a mission in Wexford in 1878, a reporter noted 'the hold it has taken in the minds and hearts of the parishioners', that 'its influence has been wide and deep [and] has encompassed the whole parish, and even many outside its boundaries, within its scope, and marked them with its grace ... it has added a new brilliancy and fervour to the steady glow of zeal for religion that characterises the parishes of Wexford'. This was all the more remarkable, because

> before it began there were some amongst us who thought, owing to the many missions given previously, the great number of Retreats to Holy Family Confraternities and other sodalities of men and women, and to the increased spiritual advantages derived from the many religious orders now residing in our favoured town, that a new general mission would be, if not absolutely a failure, at least, a dull, tame, common-place affair — at best, but a pretty fair gathering of Church-going devotees, to be served a re-hash of old viands on which they had feasted sumptuously in days gone by, but which no spiritual cooking could ever render palatable in our altered circumstances. Those few persons were soon undeceived.[127]

Even in the face of expected failure, missions could still work their old charm and regenerate slumbering faith, bringing the lapsed back into contact with the Church, alleviating those abuses that were destructive of spiritual influence, re-asserting moral values, and inspiring fresh zeal and fervour for the Catholic faith. Yet the assumptions of the Wexford reporter, although proved false, indicate another picture of Redemptorist missions, which clearly emerges in the last quarter of the century, and which must be set in the balance and weighed against the favourable picture that has been given here.

10

Missions:
their shortcomings

At the end of the day, Redemptorist missions were only as good as the parochial structures they were designed to serve. The sheer size of some parishes created an insuperable obstacle to the missioners' work. Kiltimagh, in the diocese of Achonry, for example, extended over an area of thirty miles in circumference, so that it was too far for the 'poor, starved, naked' people to come to the one chapel in which the 1882 mission was given. It was 'a most decided failure because the people did not hear the sermons and instructions. If 6 Fathers had been sent, one or two able to speak Irish, and if the Mission had been given in the 3 chapels of the parish that were 4 miles apart, then the missioners would not have laboured so much in vain'.[1] Although urban parishes were more concentrated geographically, some of them were still very large and contained so many souls that many of them, inevitably, escaped the missioners' net. Even when a mission was deemed a success, it was recognised that any permanent good could not be expected if the size of the parish made it unworkable.[2] The few local publicans who were reduced to near-bankruptcy by the 1886 mission in Bootle, Lancashire, were proof of its having some success, but 'whether any good done will be lasting is very doubtful indeed — the priests cannot meet the spiritual needs of so many'.[3]

If the missioners held out little hope of perseverance in a place where 'there is only one priest in a parish of 2500-3000 people',[4] there was no hope in a parish like that of the Pro-Cathedral in Dublin, where 48,000 souls were served by eight priests.[5] This was a recurring problem for both the Redemptorists and the secular clergy; the area of work was always greater than available manpower. As a result of recent experience in Glasgow, Fr Vaughan explained to Fr Douglas that 'the work can never be exhaustive without larger bodies of missionaries, which the priests are often unwilling or unable to receive and we unable to give. There are also in the cities great numbers who live such degraded, drunken lives that they cannot be got at except as individuals'.[6] This was demonstrated by a mission at St Patrick's, Liverpool in 1894, where 'the great drawback to the proper working of the Mission was the smallness, and especially the weakness, of the mission staff ... *Absolutely* speaking the Mission was not a success; *relatively* it *was*. The mission Fathers left nothing undone to make it a success, really working themselves to death, but there is a limit which human nature cannot pass. The Fathers arrived there but could get no farther'.[7]

A great deal depended upon the quality of the secular clergy and of their efforts to perpetuate and consolidate whatever the missioners achieved. In spite of all that they did to ensure the solidity of their work, the Redemptorists believed that they could 'never be held responsible for the perseverance of the people: that is very properly put on the shoulders of the parish priest, and on the good will of the people'.[8] Many priests were, of course, assiduous and did all in their power to maintain the spirit and results of the missions; the great spiritual improvement between the mission and the renewal at St Peter's, Belfast in 1894, for example, was attributed by the Redemptorists to the local priests, 'who have kept up a continued mission — hearing confessions daily, sometimes for long hours — preaching almost daily to one confraternity or another'.[9] But there were many places, like Drumcollogher, Co. Limerick, where 'besides the frequency of missions, nothing was done after them to keep up the piety of the people, who consequently grew callous'.[10] Even during the short space between a mission and a renewal, the lethargy of the local clergy could destroy any good that had been done. At Duntocher, Dumbartonshire in 1884, the missioners had found that 'a great many neglected the practice of their religion and hence they required a good rousing up and awakening

Community and students at Teignmouth, 1896.

to the truths of Faith and the necessity of salvation'. The mission attracted nearly all the local Catholics, confraternities were established, and the Redemptorists were able to content themselves, on their departure, that 'the faith is in the ascendant, and with a little zeal and attention, [Duntocher] could be made a model Parish in this County and become a centre of vocations to the Church and conventual life'.[11] Such hopes, however, were to be disappointed, and at the renewal it was found that 'nothing whatever had been done to keep up the fruits of the Mission in the Parish generally. We could do nothing to get the few Societies [i.e. sodalities] out of their torpid state, for there was no prospect of their being taken care of afterwards'.[12]

The heavy dependence of the missioners upon the local clergy is further seen in the example of Kilsyth, Stirlingshire. In 1880, the Redemptorists found that a combination of zealous priests, the family rosary and well-run confraternities had maintained the fruits of the 1870 mission. Here, it seemed, was a model of how a mission could lay solid foundations, on which others must build.[13] When the Redemptorists returned in 1891 and again in 1893, there was a much altered state. Although the people were described as 'good-hearted', they were 'spiritually neglected; a zealous priest could do much to repair the evils of the parish', considered to be excessive drinking and neglect of Mass. The object of the mission, the missioners discovered, 'appears to be to give the people an opportunity of going up to their Easter duties; they have not many opportunities of going to confession between the missions, and the tradition is not to go'.[14] When the missioners returned six years later, they found much ignorance among the people, 'for which they are not as accountable as those placed over them to instruct them. Poor, abandoned souls'. The thriving confraternities of 1880 had disappeared altogether, and none was now established, 'as it would have been labour and time thrown away, as nothing would have been done to keep it up'.[15] This is not an isolated example of the local clergy neutralising or destroying the missioners' work, nor of the Redemptorists refusing to establish confraternities in parishes where they feared sodalities would be neither well-run nor supported. A confraternity to combat secret societies was badly needed at St Mary's, Manchester in 1871, 'but experience has taught us (experentia compertum est) that unless the local priests devote themselves to the work for all the men, sodalities do not survive for long (non dui sustinere)'.[16]

The fortunes of confraternities, it must be said, tended to ebb and flow depending upon a complicated mixture of elements, including the enthusiasm of the people themselves and the existence of good lay officers.[17] Five hundred men were found to have fallen away within two years of the establishment of a branch of the Confraternity of the Holy Family in Middlesborough, for example, because of 'Fenianism, fluctuating population, lack of priests and a spirit of opposition against the pastor'.[18] The mission accounts are full of examples of confraternities that were established during a mission but which had declined in numbers, or fervour, or were found to be nearly dead, at the time of the next Redemptorist mission, and had failed to fulfil the hopes entertained for them at their erection. Yet the biggest noted factor working against them was the failure of priests to work them. At St Alexander's, Bootle, in 1876, the missioners considered of a confraternity established at an earlier mission that 'the effect of this confraternity is clearly marvellous (prodigiosus plane) [as can be seen] from its most well-regulated order to its check (supprimendam) on drunkenness to its promoting of the frequentation of the Sacraments'.[19] Twenty years later, they thought that the parish was 'over-cared for with a super-abundance of confraternities' that were 'not kept distinct enough to work properly'.[20] The Confraternity of the Holy Family and Sodality of Our Lady of Perpetual Succour, established in 1881 at St George's, York, were found at the mission of 1886 to be 'dead and buried, and it was considered useless now to try and resuscitate them'.[21] Even when a mission led to the revival of a confraternity, as at Eldon Street, Liverpool in 1892, where six hundred men joined, it was regarded as 'a flash in the pan', because the missioners had no confidence in the local pastors.[22] Following a mission at Ballinskelligs, Co. Kerry in 1895, an exasperated chronicler considered the obstruction and indolence of local clergy and tellingly exclaimed, 'May the Lord send to His vineyard Pastors and Priests according to His own Heart'.[23]

The Redemptorists had a responsibility for the branches of their archconfraternities and, whenever possible, preached the annual retreat that was supposed to be a feature of the confraternity calendar. Between 1873 and 1900, the Redemptorists preached 1,144 confraternity retreats, which became an increasingly important feature of their apostolate. The retreats lasted a week, culminating in the renewal of baptismal vows, and often partook 'of the nature of a mission, owing to the large number who attend them and receive the Holy Sacraments'.[24] They were religious demonstrations of great popularity and could be used to recruit new members, bolster the fervour, or, more commonly, to stir up a sodality.[25] In addition, it was possible for them to take on the character of 'a week's mission to the whole parish than a retreat to the Confraternity',[26] since 'many, who do not belong to [the sodality's] fold, take this opportunity of going to the pious exercises, and of making their peace with God'.[27] It was this aspect that so pleased parish priests and explains why, in Ireland at least, retreats to confraternities were preferred to renewals. The danger, however, which soon became a reality, was that some priests expected the annual retreat to compensate for their own lack of attention to the sodality. Thus, for example, despite annual retreats to the Confraternity of the Holy Family at St Mary's, Athlone from 1872 to 1883, it had 'wholly declined in fervour and regularity' and the vast majority of its members were purely nominal.[28] At SS Peter and Paul, Cork in 1885, the Redemptorists found the confraternity 'in a wretched state', and the retreat managed neither to bring it to life nor to add much fresh vigour to it: 'Though the Administrator, Canon Hegarty, seemed pleased with it and said that he had not seen the men attend anything like as well for years, the Fathers, who gave it, were not so blind as to see that far from being in any way a success, it was a *complete failure'.*[29] In both these cases, and in many others, the source of the problem was the priests' neglect.

Annual retreats needed to be supplemented with regular missions; at Longford town in 1894, for instance, 'the evils too common from Confraternity retreats of one week without a sufficient number of real missions at proper intervals between them, are very conspicuous'.[30] There was a two-fold problem; on the one hand, priests turned confraternity retreats into missions for the whole parish. The Dundalk Chronicler complained that 'these exercises to Sodalities, especially in Dublin, are called *Retreats,* but in reality are nothing but very hard, short missions. The members have no special seats reserved for them; and consequently who can know whether they attend or not?'.[31] The Redemptorists were not averse to the retreats being quasi-missions, provided that they did not lose their primary purpose of benefitting members of the sodality or take the place of proper, regular missions. This was the second aspect of the problem; the growth of confraternity retreats was at the expense of the missions. As early as 1874, the parish priest of Trim, Co. Meath expressed the opinion that confraternity retreats were more efficacious than missions, because the sodality members stood in the greatest need of the sacraments and, since non-members were not obtruded from the exercises, anyone else could come who chose.[32] Such a view-point came to be shared by many others, to the chagrin of the Redemptorists. Even those without confraternities came to adopt the idea of a week-long retreat or small mission every year: 'No doubt, it does a certain amount of good', admitted the Dundalk Chronicler of such an exercise in Bray, Co. Wicklow in 1883, 'and the people may be said to be above the spiritual average, but the time is too short for real mission work, and there is much superficiality about the whole thing'.[33]

The anxiety that such superficial work caused is seen in the report of the 1892 mission in St Nicholas's, Dublin. Since 1865, the Redemptorists had given seven missions and almost annual retreats in the church:

> If we judge of the success of the Mission by the whole
> adult population turning up, neither this nor the few last
> Missions could be called a success ... And certainly the
> coming up to confession during the day was very sparse
> compared with the thronging there used to be, as I
> remember in the Mission of 1871. This is sadly wonderful
> considering all the Missions we have given in this Parish
> and the annual retreats for over 20 years.

One might suggest various reasons for this lack of success,
but the chronicler believed that

> it would seem — in part at least — the result of our turning
> these same annual retreats into quasi-missions, until at
> last the people have grown so accustomed [to] them —
> destroyed Missions as it were — that they have learned
> to destroy a Mission themselves. Again, when they know
> they are having one of these big retreats or retreat-
> missions next year, they easily let slip the opportunity
> they have now.[34]

It is telling that the parish priest of Mallow, Co. Cork decided,
in 1893, to drop the annual retreat to his Confraternity of the
Sacred Heart, because 'not a few put off their confession from
one to another and even omit Easter Duty to wait for the
Retreat, if it happens to be given out of Easter Duty time'.[35]
A year later, a mission at Newcastle West, Co. Limerick was
treated with the same lack of attention with which the people
had come to regard the annual confraternity retreats, which
had themselves been turned into a kind of mission, 'i.e. lots
took no notice of it or treated it as they would the annual
retreat: hear one sermon, go to confession and never appear
again'.[36] The relief when the Redemptorists were able to give
a traditional mission, unencumbered with requests for, and
the disadvantages attendant upon, annual retreats, is evident
in the report of a mission in Inistioge, Co. Kilkenny some
months later than the Dublin mission, which 'came up to the
highest expectation of what a mission should be. The people
of the parish attended, and they alone, morning and evening.
What a difference between this Mission and those where

annual retreats are given to the people'.[37]

Whether retreats were requested in place of missions, or in addition to them, the result was that the traditional, Redemptorist missions, assaults on individual souls and a whole parish, suffered. The Provincial outlined the problem thus:

> Amongst us nowadays the parochial clergy would like ordinarily to have a few missioners for a short time; but they would like to renew these meagre missions (ces Missions maigres) too often — even each year — under the pretext of a retreat to a confraternity. One does everything to accommodate them (to hear the Easter confessions) and for the worldly fee (l'emolument temporel) that is drawn from the missions.

He concluded sadly that the local Redemptorist Rectors 'seem often more solicitous to give many missions than to give them well'.[38] Because the Redemptorists bowed to the pressure of parish priests, the missions changed in their character and, consequently, in their effectiveness. In a tone that spoke of the Redemptorists' own fatigue and frustration, it was recorded that 'in general, too many missions are given in London's suburbs, and they are too short and with too few hands to do effectual work'.[39] Too-frequent missions made the people weary and lacking in enthusiasm; they ceased to have their special value as an extraordinary grace. If this was one consequence of giving more, smaller missions, the secular clergy's solution was equally unwelcome to the Redemptorists and constituted a further obstacle to their mission work. The sight of large numbers, and the religious jamboree this made possible, was too enticing to be resisted, and parish priests opened up the missions to the surrounding parishes. This happened, at the insistence of the Bishop of Elphin, at Castlerea, Co. Roscommon in 1887, when the church was 'filled with but comers and goers for the day, who, when they had heard a few sermons, 3 generally, and their confession over, went home to let their friends come for the day'.[40] Bemoaning the fact that it was 'not a mission according to the system of our H[oly] F[ather] St Alphonsus', the chronicler opined that for those outside of the parish, it was merely a 'Big Station', and as such totally unsatisfactory. He had to admit that such missions evoked a spirit of enthusiasm and that judged from the bishop and clergy's point of view ('big, crushing, crowded attendances'), such missions were a great success, but not when 'judged by *our* mission standard, i.e. constant, regular attendance of the *people of the parish*'.[41]

What was so impairing about these missions was that they reflected, and in turn perpetuated, the idea of the mission as little more than a station, an opportunity to bring up (preferably large) numbers of people to the sacraments, in the reception of which they might be somewhat neglectful, but in the efficacy of which they had no doubt. At Curry, Co. Sligo in 1894, the parish priest refused to hear of the mission being more than a fortnight, for it was for many 'only a huge station … a hullabaloo mission', in which 'the people of the parish did not get fair play', because of its unrestricted nature.[42] This was also the effect of the quasi-missions or annual retreats; at Youghal, Co. Cork in 1891, for example, the missioners found that the annual retreats had led to the formation of the idea among both clergy and people that a mission was merely a big station.[43] Although the problems of annual retreats, unrestricted non-parochial and quasi-missions were most acute in Ireland, they were not restricted to that country, but vexed the Redemptorists who worked in Britain, especially in the north of England and in Scotland, where one of their number railed against ' "Hullaballu" [*sic*] missions which are given during Easter-time to get people to their Easter duty. They give less trouble to the priests of the parish than real missions and satisfy their consciences; but in very many cases they do harm to the parish, and certainly seriously injure the *real* missions which follow them. Would to Heaven they were abolished. God grant it!'.[44]

The Redemptorists were caught in a cleft stick, in some sense victims of their own earlier success. They were dependent upon the secular clergy for their apostolic work, and the clergy wanted shorter missions of a particular kind on a frequent basis. Although this was destructive of traditional missions, and the Redemptorists saw the effectiveness of their work dwindle, even though the bishops and priests never questioned the missions' continued usefulness, the Redemptorists had to accept the terms that were dictated to them, whatever their misgivings and disappointments. Perhaps they should have resisted, as some of them wanted.[45] Certainly, there was a nostalgic longing for missions 'on the old traditional Redemptorist lines', which seemed now to be almost entirely lacking.[46] Yet this deficiency had a demoralising effect upon the missioners, so that the Visitor of 1894 complained that

> not infrequently a mission nowadays means to go to a place, settle down there for a time, do a certain amount of work ... preach some sermons without fire or interest, hear those who care to come to us [to confession], and then go away satisfied ... this is all that can be expected ... But where are the missions which St Alphonsus called with good reason 'assaults'? Where is the fervour and pressure by which men are forced in from the highways and bye-ways?[47]

Another priest thought there was need to give missions according to the old Redemptorist standard 'rather than be multiplied beyond our strength. Thus the esteem for our missions, and the credit of the Congregation, would increase instead of diminishing and sinking down to the level of other untrained bodies'.[48]

What Magnier's remarks ignored was the well-nigh impossibility of coercing people. It was expected that folk would lapse or grow lax between the missions, but, once the call had been made, that they could be coaxed and cajoled into returning. This is what the missioners found at Workington, Cumbria in 1881, when the long gap between the present and last mission was given as the reason for the lapse of many, who now came up well.[49] Little, however, could be done where the people stubbornly refused to be drawn by missions, like the people of Orwell, Cambridgeshire in 1871, who were distinctly cool ('frigidi') about the mission from beginning to end.[50] Elsewhere, the delights of horse-racing, boating or a royal visit were more powerful than the attractions of a mission, or provided alternative entertainment.[51] Missions depended upon a contagious excitement, by which the reluctant were swept up and along in the enthusiasm of others. Where this was lacking, the mission was like a damp squib. Fr O'Laverty considered the mission in St Patrick's, Nottingham in 1891 the worst in which he had ever taken part, because 'the people of the parish took no interest in it and the congregations were made up of people from all over Nottingham'.[52] It was, of course, possible to castigate people as 'milk and water Catholics, having all sorts of doubts about Faith, and seeing no great difference between one Religion and another, neglecting Mass, eating meat on Fridays etc.', but the transformation of such into 'practical Catholics' was precisely the function of the mission.[53] It was a strange self-defence for the Limerick Chronicler to admit that although the preachers at Kilmihil, Co. Clare in 1887 were not stirring enough for the people, so that some of them did not profit much by the mission, nevertheless, the careless and negligent were all visited by the fathers and everything possible done for them, 'so that if a few did not avail themselves of the mission, it was their own fault'.[54] Perhaps, it was true of them, as of the people of St Joseph's, Derby in 1892, that they simply 'did not seem inclined to put themselves to much inconvenience for the sake of the Mission'.[55] If so, it had serious repercussions, and foreboded ill, for the work of the missions.

In Ireland it was the decline of missions in the face of retreats, but in the urban Catholic communities of Britain it was the decided failure of missions to animate many parishes, where previously they had experienced much success, that was a source of grief and hurt pride to the Redemptorists. This was all the more striking when they viewed the seemingly triumphant progress of their apostolic work in the 1850s, 1860s and 1870s, when optimism had accommodated such failures as they had encountered. In the last two decades of the century, the immensity of the task, and of the obstacles they faced, enervated the Redemptorists' will, though not their energies, and they became much more aware of both the shortcomings and limited nature of their missions.

It had been early recognised that the labours of the fathers were 'like a drop of water in the ocean'.[56] Many, whom they saw as standing in greatest need, simply did not answer the call of a mission.[57] At Barnard Castle, Co. Durham, for example, a mission in 1858 found that half the congregation had fallen away since the last mission six years previously. Although a hundred were recovered, 'many others escaped, some of whom never set foot in the chapel the whole time of the Mission'.[58] The realisation that the missions were not appealing to large numbers of nominal Catholics became more insistent as time wore on and their numbers increased. Thus, the simultaneous mission in 1886 at St Mary's, St Patrick's and St Alphonsus's, Middlesborough was not judged a success, because 'though the number of confessions is not small, though many great sinners were reclaimed, and many living in concubinage were separated or settled, yet some 6,000 must have made no mission'.[59] Three years later, a mission in Southwark, South London 'left half the population untouched'.[60] Such people, if undrawn by a mission, would remain largely untouched by the Church in the ordinary course of events, as the Redemptorists had found to their horror in a visitation of their own London parish in 1866.[61] The number of Catholics was progressively increasing, but so too were the number and percentage who did not practise their faith. J.A. Lesourd has calculated that by 1885, 12.8% of Catholics were total 'non-practitioners', a figure roughly the same as for Protestants. Of the remaining 87%, 47% were ' "sassoniers" ou catholiques sociologiques' (i.e. were baptised and married in the Church, had their children baptised and sent them to Catholic schools and made them follow the cult, but were very irregular at Mass and had few, if any, relations with the clergy), leaving 40% who were regulars, 35% of whom performed their Easter duties.[62] There were, of course, regional variations. In London, for instance, it is doubtful that church attendance among the nominally Catholic Irish population was ever much above 30%, although attendance rates of something like 60% may have been reached among the immigrants in Liverpool and the Lancashire towns in the 1860s. This means that Irish Catholic rates of Sunday church attendance were often below those of English Protestants, if higher than those for the English working class: 'An average ratio of 50% to 60% for the country as a whole represents, give or take temporary fluctuations, the broad limit of the Catholic restoration. It would seem that the upward trend reached a plateau during the 1880s, when Catholic concern over what was dubbed "leakage" became a matter of public debate within the country, and at that level, religious practice stuck there'.[63]

In spite of the 'immense good', the 'solid work', the rescuing of 'many souls from sin', the Redemptorists came increasingly to realise that 'when the number of those who attended and went to the sacraments are compared with the number of people', it was difficult to decide whether the missions were a success or not.[64] Even where the local clergy were greatly pleased with the results of a mission, the missioners were less sanguine. Thus, although the number of confessions at a mission in St Mary's, Glasgow in 1883 was greater than in any previous mission, the Redemptorists were doubtful of its success precisely because 'a great number of very neglectful people never turned up'.[65] The missioners at Croydon in 1899 found the mission, with which the priest was well pleased, 'miserable, since the majority of the poor did not come near it and visiting seemed to have no effect upon them'.[66] The depressing conclusion was that many were completely lost to the Faith, and the missions could not reclaim them. At Grimsby in 1890, for example, a thousand of the town's two thousand Catholics were left totally unimpressed by the mission and were deemed to have lapsed altogether.[67] Instead, the missions appealed only to those who were within the regular fold, as at Prestwich, near Manchester in 1892, where 'scarcely any of those lost to the Faith could be got up; but nearly all the rest came'.[68] The numbers who were lost

Limerick Juvenate in 1896, shortly before the division of the Province.

seemed alarmingly to be on the increase; at Warwick Street, London in 1887, the missioners found that 'infidelity is making rapid strides. Hundreds who attended the last mission are now scoffers at all religion. Very little is done to oppose the evil and little can be done under the present regime. We were unable to produce any impression or get up any enthusiasm'.[69]

Although depression of trade or the general misery of the people might be adduced for such a situation, or placed at the door of the secular clergy, it was remarked that 'obstinate indifference and want of faith' were more marked among the poor than hitherto, and at Islington, London in May 1888, the Italian and London-born Irish, who made up the parish, 'simply refused to attend'.[70] In parishes where regular missions had been given, the Redemptorists witnessed a marked decline. Missions had been given, for instance, in the parish of St Mary and St Michael, Commerical Road, East London every three years since 1855 by the Redemptorists or members of other orders. The 1885 Redemptorist mission doubled the Mass attendance, 'but, after all, 3,000 out of 10,000 cannot be considered a large proportion. Compared with our Mission of '77, we notice a decline of 1,000 in the confession-return'.[71] This general, overall decline can also be gauged from a simple statistical consideration. Between 1883 and 1900, the Redemptorists preached over seventeen hundred missions and renewals and 768 confraternity retreats, in which 4,282,788 communions were given, only a small increase in the number given during the fifteen hundred missions and renewals up to 1882.[72]

The problem of 'seepage' or 'leakage' was obvious not only to the Redemptorists, nor were they alone in trying to tackle it.[73] That thousands of Catholics were being lost to the Church was recognised by the hierarchies, and efforts were made to combat the loss by a variety of means. One of these was the organisation of large-scale general missions, that is a simultaneous mission, given by the religious of a particular or, more often, several orders, in all the churches of a place. The Bishop of Salford arranged such a mission in the twenty-five churches of Salford and Manchester in 1884, and informed those who took part that 'the great duty of the present time is to preserve, nourish and strengthen the Faith', and he mentioned that out of a Catholic population of 100,000, the last census had shown a Mass attendance of 40,838. He went on to urge the missioners to impress upon the people the necessity of a thoroughly Catholic education for the young as the joint work of Catholic homes and schools, the duty of hearing Mass on Sundays and holy days, and the regular use of spiritual reading to combat secularist trends.[74] Sixteen Redemptorists worked in four parishes. In the mission as a whole, there were 429 converts and 3,182 were 'reclaimed', so that about half the Catholic population of Salford and Manchester made their Easter duties as a result of the mission, thus raising slightly the normal Mass attendance. This was, by no means, insignificant and represents a certain fidelity to the Church and recognition of its claims and of the obligations involved in its membership. But the half who did not attend were found to be lost in 'indifference, materialism and secret societies'.[75]

Like the Catholic Church generally, the Redemptorists found themselves overwhelmed, not to say defeated, by the conditions in which they had to work in the cities and towns of Britain, where Catholics increasingly and, it seemed, irresistibly, shared the mores of their unchurched non-Catholic neighbours. Those conditions, analysed in an earlier chapter, formed the backcloth to their labours and proved more and more intractable. The missioners at St Helens, Lancashire in 1879 thought that the people were so indifferent that they could be separated from infidelity only with great difficulty, and they noted an almost total neglect of Mass and the sacraments and of their parental duties by both men and women, caused by habitual drunkenness, and resulting in shameful impurity. The result was that many could not be disposed to attend the mission, and out of a Catholic population of seventeen thousand, only three thousand made their confession and communion.[76]

At Seaham Harbour, near Newcastle in 1889, it was admitted

that 'candidly speaking there cannot be said to have been the slightest improvement in the morals of the people since the last mission'.[77] And at St John's Cathedral, Salford, where regular missions had been given by the Redemptorists, the last one only five years previously, it was realised in 1893 that 'the people nevertheless seem to sink rather than to rise'.[78] On that occasion, just over three thousand confessions were heard, the work being 'of the hardest kind, yet consoling'. Yet this stood in marked contrast to April 1862, when 'such crowds as were never before witnessed in any Catholic Church in England since the Reformation' had attended, with three thousand present every evening and 4,500 at the close of the mission. Over five thousand confessions had been heard and 7,600 communions given, and after the mission 'the daily increase of penitents and communicants' had shown 'the wonderful effects of the assiduous labours of the Missioners'.[79] Now the missioners found it ever more difficult to break through the barriers that hardened urban Catholics against any spiritual influence, and which repeated missions seemed incapable of overcoming. At St Alphonsus's, Glasgow in 1899, for instance, the spiritual state of the people was found to be 'below zero'.[80] Many other places were not much better; at Greenock in 1890, the spiritual state was described as 'very low, partly from neglect ... all classes much given to drink, especially the women, while prostitution was rife and quite undisguised'.[81] In the face of such problems, the Redemptorists occasionally gave way to despair. Thus, the 'ignorant, stupid and unruly' Irish, who largely made up the congregation in Dewsbury, West Yorkshire in 1885, 'had had more missions etc. — far too many — year after year — given by every kind of missioner', and yet the Redemptorist missioners still thought them 'the most degraded people to be found in England'.[82]

Even when some progress, some improvement, seemed to be made as a result of a mission, it proved all too short-lived. The parishioners of St Joseph's, Stockport in 1891 were found to be 'worse than savages, utterly lost, caring for nothing but drink. A fortnight after the last mission they took to drink and gave up going to Mass, and even during *this* mission, after going to confession and Holy Communion were found blind-drunk on Saturday and Sunday'.[83] That this represented a progressive decline from happier times is shown by the enthusiasm and the success of earlier missions in Stockport; in 1860, for example, the crowds were so great that they had to be split into two separate missions, one in the church and the other in the school.[84] A mission report of the same year stated that the fathers always found an excellent spirit in Manchester and in the other cotton manufacturing towns of Lancashire, and that the usual characteristics of such missions was 'hard work and success'.[85] Something of the decline can be seen in the case of St Mary's, Wigan. The Redemptorists gave missions here in 1852, 1860 and 1867 with gratifying results. In 1874, the missioners noted a change; there was no enthusiasm for the mission and some were found in total ignorance of their Christian obligations.[86] Regular missions continued to be given, roughly every four years, but, by 1894, the Redemptorists discerned among the people 'very little faith, and what faith there is left, is worse than no faith at all'.[87] The mission of that year left the parish in exactly the same state as it had found it.

One reaction to such disappointments was to accept the limitations that were imposed on their work and make the best of it, reflected in statements about the missions like 'as successful as any mission in the large centres of population in England can be expected to be'.[88] It was not just that the Redemptorists were conscious of a decline in the effectiveness of their work, in the ability of missions to appeal to many lapsed Catholics above adverse social conditions, but that even such work as they did, and such results as they achieved, held out little promise for the future. When an observer spoke of the 'complete and most wonderful reformation', which the mission had achieved among the people of St Patrick's, Bradford in 1874, who were described as 'of the lowest state of moral degradation ... the vast majority living in utter disregard of God and of the Church — confirmed drunkards, never hearing Mass — the girls living in shocking prostitution

— and the young men sunk deep in corruption', the missioners did not take 'so bright and cheerful a view, remembering that many missions before were attended by the same good results, but shortly after the people [were] no better, or rather a good deal worse than before'.[89] Regular missions over a long period seem to have made little lasting impression or to have halted and reversed the moral and religious decline. The missioners at St Nicholas's, Dublin in 1892 felt that to particularise the abuses of the people 'would be rather an extensive task'; drink 'and the vices that are its offspring', mainly. Although some of the parishioners were prepared for the mission, 'a great many cared little about it', and, although many 'heavy fish' were dragged in, the chronicler wryly allowed himself the rhetorical question as to 'how many more lie at the bottom of the deep?'.[90]

It has been argued that parish missions helped to create durable Catholic communities among the largely Irish-immigrant and predominantly working-class population of Britain. What must now be admitted is their failure over a prolonged period to help in the consolidation of a local Catholic identity that was stronger, more resilient, a more effective bulwark against the contrary social and moral forces which drew large numbers of nominal Catholics further away from their Church and limited the number to whom a successful call to pursue a better standard of religious practice could be made. This can, perhaps, best be appraised by looking at one parish, that of St Vincent de Paul, Liverpool. An early mission in 1858 was instrumental in forming the Catholic community in the area, bringing the mainly immigrant Irish population into contact for the first time with the Church in England, seen in the admission of nine hundred children to first communion.[91] When the Redemptorists returned in 1865, they found the parish 'a perfect Augean stable', in which boys and girls of fourteen and fifteen seemed naturally to progress, after the manner of their elders, into a state of habitual drunkenness. Nevertheless, as a result of the mission, 'a fever of repentance fell upon all', and out of a Catholic population of 6,500, over four thousand made their confession and communion.[92] By 1869, the effects of the former mission had begun to wane and the normal Sunday Mass attendance had dropped to 2,387; the mission of that year managed to raise it to 4,352.[93] It would seem that the Redemptorist missions were successful in drawing people to their duties at a time when they had begun to grow slack and in temporarily alleviating the depressed conditions in which many of the people were sunk.[94] Indeed, a retreat to the two branches of the Confraternity of the Holy Family in the following year, showed that they were keeping up well, and the missioners, 'with the greatest joy', proudly noted that the mission had effected 'a great reformation in the morals both of men and of women in the parish of St Vincent'.[95] Their optimism was a little precipitate, perhaps, since many of the sodalists were found to have been lost by the time of the retreat of the following year, although that may have been due to the exclusiveness of the parish priest, who declared 'I do not wish many sodalists, but good and fervent ones, however few'.[96] A children's mission in 1874 proved consoling, and succeeded in drawing many young people up to the age of eighteen, 'which rarely happens'.[97] So far, although there was a certain slipping-off between missions, they seemed to be keeping pace and coping with the increasing population and to be addressing the adverse social and moral climate. A mission and renewal in 1878/9 gave cause for concern, however, since the confraternities were found to have declined both in fervour and in number and to have produced none of the desired fruit.[98] Some attempt to revive them was made in a mission five years later, which a newspaper described as 'a signal success throughout ... no mission ever given in this church has been so largely attended ... The crush at the confessionals was such that the missionaries were obliged to prolong the mission some days beyond the ordinary time'.[99] The Redemptorists, however, were less enamoured and not fooled by appearances: 'Although many missions had been given in this and in the neighbouring parishes, the people cannot be said to be fervent and religious, but rather tepid and negligent'.[100] This was borne out in the bishop's *relatio* for 1887, which showed that out of a population of 5,017 Mass attendance was 2,391 and only 1,746 fulfilled the paschal precept.[101] Two years later, the figures were 2,347 and 1,460.[102] The following year, the missioners found the spiritual state 'at a very low ebb', and a great many people 'supremely indifferent', so that they 'never put in an appearance'. The fact that many, who might have been expected, never came to the mission muted any estimate of the good that had been done.[103] Nine years later, the outlook was, if anything, bleaker, and the mission made little impression on the parish; only a quarter of the Catholic population made their Easter duties and although the priests did much visiting, the mission attracted only 'the best people'.[104]

The analysis of a typical urban parish reveals the reduced scope of Redemptorist missions. Although progressively increasing in number, their character and nature had altered in accordance with changing circumstances and demands, which had a deteriorating effect upon them. They had ceased to be, as they had been in earlier years, large-scale evangelistic exercises of a special kind, drawing into the Church many who stood in its fringes or outside its boundaries, converting residual faith into firm habits of prayer, piety and practice. Instead, they had become means of stirring up the already converted, but negligent, those who were within the holiness group but of tepid sanctity. Outside that group, their appeal was limited.[105] Even a mission in the Redemptorist church at Clapham in 1891 was well-attended, but 'by those who were already regulars. It does not seem to have in any way reached the careless and indifferent'.[106] Indeed, as means of reaching such people, of reclaiming the lapsed, the missions had ceased to be of much use. At St Anne's, Spitalfields in 1886 it was observed that 'the chasm between the good and the bad is growing wider and wider', and that the congregation made up only a quarter of the baptised Catholics of the district. The mission did nothing to remedy this: 'Outside the circle of ordinary church-goers, we did very little'.[107]

It is impossible to define the 'good' and the 'bad' beyond

the notion of those baptised members of the Church who performed or failed to comply with its formal requirements. It does not mean that 'bad Catholics' were morally degenerate or even irreligious, although it would be surprising if some were not infected with the unconscious secularism of many of their working-class contemporaries. Given, however, the Catholic emphasis on liturgical participation and cultural set-apartness, those who remained only vaguely or marginally Catholic in varying degrees of loyalty were considered to be well on the road to that 'indifferentism' which betokened the abandonment of, and resistance to, all religious, spiritual and moral influence. It may also be true that the missions, in so far as they were dependent on existing parochial structures, appealed more to the 'respectable working class' and lower middle class, who were naturally drawn to parish organisations and events, and that the poorer, 'rough working class' Catholics were effectively excluded, not sharing in the virtues of respectability and sobriety.[108] Nevertheless, the fact remains that the Redemptorists were disappointed that the missions seemed increasingly less able to appeal to, and to attract, those whom they thought should be drawn to them, and that their apostolate was concerned with confirming the already-held faith of those who were less in need of their especial help.

Missions continued in succeeding generations to draw large crowds of Catholics, including many who had formerly lapsed and now evinced genuine signs of conversion, but they were concerned with a smaller percentage of the potential Catholic population than in the earlier years, and often resulted, as at the Cathedral in Nottingham in 1889, in little more than 'a slightly better attendance at Mass on Sundays'.[109] They had ceased also to have the controlling and moulding effect of earlier times, save in those places and among those people who were still pliable, such as the Catholics of Scarisbrick, Lancashire, whose great merit was that they were English, 'and really in habits (moribus) [are] nearly angels (fere Angeli)'. They were described as 'well compliant (bene morigenti) ... who rarely indulge in intemperance and, with very few exceptions, fulfil the paschal precept'.[110] At Nenagh, Co. Tipperary the large concentration of the middle classes meant that the missioners found 'nothing wanting', and at Burscough, Lancashire the people were so good that a mission was more 'a preservative than a cure'.[111] Gone were the days when missions could appeal to the natural, unsullied faith of ill-formed Catholics, who were 'malleable (tractabiles)' or 'most addicted to their religion'.[112] The docility, which had aided the early missioners in their work, was not to be so easily found in the great industrial centres of Britain.

Instead, the spirit of those early missions was to be found in such places as the Hebrides and the Western Isles of Scotland, where the Redemptorists pioneered Gaelic missions in the 1880s. Here they found a people who were uninstructed, who had never experienced such things as Benediction and who responded to the novelty of the missions in a way that cheered the missioners and recalled the days of the early English and Irish missions. On Benbecula, in 1881, the people walked four to six miles across the bogs, without road or path, to get to the evening service, and

> the attendance at the confessionals could not be better and there are a great many sent away when we stop hearing [them]; fighting and shoving to get in in the most orthodox style goes on most regularly outside the confessionals ... They are a delightful people to deal with: very simple and full of faith ... There has been a great run on the objects of devotion ... Most of the people have beads now. It is particularly pleasing to see the young men pressing forward so eager for confession.[113]

Fr MacDonald enthused that he had never seen such truly Redemptorist work as on Barra in 1884, an interesting comment from someone who had worked in the missions in Scotland and northern England for over ten years. The reason for his enthusiasm was that the people were full of faith and 'extremely docile to the Priest and obey him in everything, even in the distribution of the fishing grounds'. Public penance was still in force, and 'their piety is such that men — big, strong men — pray aloud in church and groan and sigh — just like "biddies", while the girls carry holy medals in their kiss', and all wore the scapular.[114] Moreover, 'they are the best fishermen and the boldest seamen in Scotland; and yet not a boat goes to sea without a bottle of holy water fastened to the stern and a blessed candle to the prow'.[115] In short, they were innocent, malleable and wholly Catholic, not steeped in a climate of immorality or indifference, as was the case with urban Catholics.

The freshness and vitality of such accounts stand in marked contrast to those of missions in the densely populated towns of Britain, where the missions benefitted only those who were disposed to avail themselves of the proffered grace and accepted the assumptions on which whey were based. This is not to say that they were not productive missions; undoubtedly, they were, like the 1886 general mission in Liverpool, as a result of which 'all kinds of big fish are coming into our nets: no end of concubines, unbaptised children; a great many young men and women are being prepared for the sacraments every night'.[116] In Ireland, there were still spectacular and heartening results and a continuing enthusiasm shown for the missions.[117] But among the urban Catholic communities of Britain, the picture was otherwise. The missions had reached saturation point and the emphasis had shifted from winning souls and building up and expanding strong, resilient Catholic communities, to preservation and maintenance of what already existed against further decline. This, perhaps, is what lay behind Livius's remark that in England at least the missions had 'almost run their day'.[118] Paradoxically, the Redemptorists had helped to form and construct those communities to such an extent that now all their resources were exhausted and their energies contained, in the effort to keep them intact, to prevent further dissipation. The wonder is, perhaps, not that these communities were not larger, but that they were as large as they were and that the Catholic subculture was as firm and lively as it was. Part of the reason for this is to be found in the mission work of the

235

Redemptorists. At the end of a long survey, it is not their partial retreat in the face of overwhelming odds that is the cause of surprise but their real achievements and the distinctive, though not necessarily easily distinguishable, contribution that they made to the kind of Catholicism that survived in Great Britain and Ireland down to the Second Vatican Council.

Notes

Chapter 1

1. *Dublin Review,* 6 (1839), 406-34, pp. 429-30.
2. C. Leetham, *Luigi Gentili: A Sower for the Second Spring* (London, 1965), p. 100.
3. Besides the Rosminians and Passionists were the Oratorians (1847), the Marists (1850) and the Capuchins (1852). The Jesuits were already present in England.
4. Fr de Held in A.M. Tannoia, *The Life of St Alphonso Maria de Liguori,* edited and translated by F.W. Faber, The Saints and Servants of God, 5 vols (London, 1848-9), IV (1849), p. xvii.
5. Redemptorist Fathers, Provincial Archives of the London Province [hereafter, ALP], 'Provincial Chronicles, 1843-1853' [hereafter, PC], p. 18.
6. Leetham, *Luigi Gentili,* p. 120.
7. Scottish Catholic Archives [hereafter, SCA], Oban Letters, Kyle to Scott, 25 July 1842.
8. ALP, Buggenoms MS, p. 16.
9. Ibid., p. 19 (French original).
10. Ibid., p. 24 (French original).
11. Redemptorist Fathers, General Archives, Rome [hereafter, AGR], XII, C84, de Held to Ripoli, 30 July 1843. In September of the following year, the Redemptorists were offered the mission of Southport in Lancashire, AGR, 'Chronica Provinciae et Collegiorum Belgicae', II, 123. It may have been the Vicar Apostolic of the Lancashire District who appealed to de Held in 1843.
12. AGR, XII, C86, Ripoli to de Held, 6 September 1843 (Copy).
13. In 1841, Ripoli refused to accept Passerat's nomination of de Held as Provincial of Belgium, which had to be obtained direct from the Congregation of Bishops and Regulars.
14. AGR, XII, C87 & 88, de Held to Ripoli, 23 September & 2 October 1843. Ripoli also wrote to Passerat to protest against the Vicar General's tendency to allow new foundations, AGR, XII, B9, Ripoli to Passerat, 6 October 1843.
15. John Vincent Gandolphi (1818-1902) was a silk merchant and papal count. Nephew and heir of Thomas Charles Hornyold, of the distinguished recusant family, he assumed the name of Hornyold in 1859, in compliance with the terms of his uncle's will. He first encountered the Redemptorists in 1842, when he made a retreat in their house at Tournai. He determined to build the first church in England in honour of St Alphonsus and to have it staffed by Redemptorists, AGR, 'Chronica Provinciae et Collegiorum Belgicae', II, 70.
16. Redemptorist Fathers, Bishop Eton, Domestic Archives [hereafter, ADBE], 'Domestic and Mission Chronicles, Hanley Castle and Bishop Eton' [hereafter, CD/ALBE], I, sub anno 1849 (no page references).

17. C.A. Walworth, 'Reminiscences of a Catholic Crisis in England Fifty Years Ago', *Catholic World*, 69 (1899), 396-406, 549-59, 662-73, 812-23, p. 699.
18. ALP, PC, pp. 89-92.
19. M. de Meulemeester, C.SS.R., *Le Père Frédéric v. Held, premier provincial de Belgique* (Jette, 1911), pp. 203-4.
20. According to ALP, PC, p.131, there were 212 Catholics in Clapham, 188 in Stockwell and Brixton, and twenty-eight in Mitcham and Tooting by the end of 1849. The foundation stone of the church was laid on 2 August 1849. In use from October of the following year, it was solemnly opened in May 1851 and consecrated on 13 October 1852 by Cardinal Wiseman. Fuller details in the Domestic Archives, Clapham [hereafter, ADC], D28.
21. *The Catholic Directory and Annual Register* (London, 1853), p. 30.
22. Details of all these events in ALP, PC, pp. 225-30 and ADC, E1.
23. C.H. Collette, *Romanism in England: The Redemptorist Fathers in St Mary's Convent, Park Road, Clapham* (London, 1850), p. 116.
24. AGR, 'Chronica Provinciae et Collegiorum Belgicae', II, 380.
25. 'I Liguorini trovano molti novizi inglesi e promettono assai per l'Inghilterra', Archives of the Sacred Congregation 'de Propaganda Fide' [hereafter, APF], Scritture riferite nei congressi [hereafter, SC], Anglia, vol. 12 (1848-51), fo. 1002r., Faber to Propaganda, 6 June 1851.
26. C. Ryder, C.SS.R., *Life of T.E. Bridgett, C.SS.R.* (London, 1906), p. 22.
27. ALP, Db69, Coffin to Newman, 3 October 1850 (Copy).
28. Archives of the Archbishop of Westminster [hereafter AAW], 3/26.73, de Held to Wiseman, 14 October 1848, explains these as the reasons for the abandonment, and expresses the desire of the Congregation to work amicably with the episcopate. De Held wrote a virtually identical letter on the same day to Ullathorne, Archives of the Archbishop of Birmingham [hereafter, AAB], B1267.
29. ALP, Buggenoms MS, p. 54.
30. ALP, Cb42b, Heilig to Lans, 26 February 1848.
31. ALP, PC, pp. 172-4 contains details of the mission. *The Catholic Directory and Annual Register* (London, 1850), p. 51 mentions that twenty converts were made in the course of 1849 by Fr Ludwig.
32. ADC, F30, de Held to Wiseman, 6 June 1850 (Copy) & F42, de Held to Grant, 7 June 1859 (Copy). The chapel was in St Thomas the Apostle Lane, Cannon Street.
33. ALP, Db11, de Held to Wiseman, 24 May 1849 (Copy). Details of the Redemptorists' work can be found in PC, pp. 134-7. When they gave up the chapel in 1853, it was placed under a secular priest. When it was removed to Whitechapel in 1863, it was taken over by the Oblates of Mary Immaculate.
34. ALP, Db13, de Held to Wareing, 18 January 1851 (Copy).
35. ALP, PC, p. 241.
36. E. Hosp, C.SS.R., 'First Redemptorist Missions in Ireland according to Father Joseph Prost's diaries', *Spicilegium Historicum Congregationis Sanctissimi Redemptoris*, 8 (1960), 453-85, p 471.
37. Walworth, 'Reminiscences of a Catholic Crisis', p. 406.

38. ADC, Db12, de Held to [? Dechamps], 10 January 1851 (Copy).
39. ALP, Db16, Ullathorne to de Held, 23 July 1851; copy in AAB, B2228.
40. AAB, B4555, de Held to Ullathorne, 26 July 1851; copy in ALP, Db17.
41. CD/ALBE, III (1861), 329.
42. AGR, XLVII, 6, Coffin to Douglas, 6 June 1872.
43. ALP, PC, p. 383n.
44. AAW, 1/2.921, de Held to Wiseman, 24 November 1849.
45. W. Ward, *The Life and Times of Cardinal Wiseman,* 2 vols (London, 1897), II, 115-23.
46. Walworth, 'Reminiscences of a Catholic Crisis', p. 406.
47. Smetana to de Held, 17 December 1852, quoted in C. Dilgskron, C.SS.R., *P. Friedrich von Held: Ein Beitrag zur Geschichte der Kongregation des allerheiligsten Erlösers* (Vienna, 1909), p. 270.
48. ADC, Db63, Dechamps to Wiseman, 5 & 15 October (Copies in French). Dechamps sent copies of these letters, with an accompanying letter, to Ullathorne, AAB, B2577, B2582 & B2583. De Held had written to Wiseman on 31 August 1851, attempting to vindicate the Congregation and his own actions in this matter, AAW, R.79.88.
49. Dilgskron, *P. Friedrich von Held,* p. 268.
50. Ibid., p. 257.
51. ALP, Db104, MS 'Mémoires sur la Vie de Mngr Robert Coffin, C.SS.R., Évêque de Southwark, par le R.P. Lubienski' [hereafter, Lubienski, 'Mémoires'], p. 100.
52. ALP, PC, p. 180 (Latin original).
53. Ibid., p. 181.
54. ADC, 'Chronica Domestica' [hereafter, CDC], I, 16.
55. C.A. Walworth, 'Reminiscences of a Catholic Crisis in England Fifty Years Ago', *Catholic World,* 70 (1899/1900), 59-69, 239-52, 412-19, 506-13, p. 60.
56. ALP, PC, pp. 278-80.
57. Ibid., p. 252: 'Atque ad illos Sti Patricki filios, firmos in fide, et paupertate adversisque pressos de salute aeterna periditantes, ad illos dico, animos utique derelictos Congregati evangelizandum vocati sunt'.
58. ALP, Lubienski, 'Mémoires', p. 91. It was, however, a policy that needed some justification by the Provincial Chronicler, who argued that not only did the Congregation not prosper in England until work was begun in Ireland, nor were there sufficient English vocations, but that concentration on work among the Irish assisted, rather than detracted from, the conversion of Britain, since the sanctified Irish, when they emigrated, carried the faith to the English and Scots (PC, pp. 252-3).
59. T.P. Cunningham, 'Church Reorganisation', in *A History of Irish Catholicism,* edited by P. Corish, 6 vols (Dublin, 1967-71), 5/7 (1970), especially at p. 31. Like the Redemptorists, other missionary orders witnessed an initially overwhelming response; the early Rosminian missions were described by One of the Missioners, *Missions in Ireland* (Dublin, 1855), who concluded that thousands had been saved from the clutches of the proselytisers, or prevented from yielding to their

temptations, as a result of the Jesuit, Vincentian, Redemptorist and Rosminian missions, and that many Catholics had thereby been reclaimed (p. 317).

60. CD/ALBE, I, sub anno 1850.

61. E. Hosp, 'First Redemptorist Missions in Ireland', pp. 465-6. Cullen's wishes were partly fulfilled, and three years later, on 25 May 1854, he reported to Rome that 'i Gesuiti, i Domenicani, i Carmelitani calzuti e più ancora i preti della missione di S. Vincenzo e i Padri redentoristi di S. Alfonso fanno bene immenso, e danno grandissima edificazione', unlike the litigious Franciscans, Capuchins, Augustinians and Calced Carmelites, although he hoped, little by little, for a change among them also, APF, Scritture riferite nelle Congregazioni Particolari [hereafter, CP], vol. 158 (1851-60), fo. 234v.

62. ALP, PC, p. 390 (French original).

63. ALP, Miscellanea, 'Scraps of Information' contains a note about the clerical opposition. The bishop, however, was 'enchanted to have the Redemptorists in Limerick', and the people came at 4.45 a.m. to ring the bell for Mass, AGR, XLVII, 2, de Buggenoms to Douglas, 13 January 1854.

64. Full details in *Fifty Years at Mount St Alphonsus, Limerick* (Limerick, 1903), pp. 1-19.

65. Redemptorist Fathers, Clonard, Belfast, Domestic Archives [hereafter, ADB], MS 'Fr Sampson's Reminiscences', 2 vols, II, 42.

66. Redemptorist Fathers, Limerick, Domestic Archives [hereafter, ADL], 'Chronica Domestica et Labores Apostolici' [hereafter, CD/ALL], I (1859), 77. Sampson, 'Reminiscences', I, 45, recalled how, as a young man, he waited for hours in the Redemptorist church to make his confession, only to lose his place in the queue to another young man, who pushed him aside with the excuse, 'Let me in; I think I have more need than you; I am in a hurry'.

67. *Fifty Years at Mount St Alphonsus, Limerick*, p. 40.

68. AGR, Provincia Angliae [hereafter, Pr.An.], I$_1$, 'Mémoire du P. Bernard sur la Congrégation en Angleterre et en Irlande', 1855.

Chapter 2

1. Of the twelve missions in 1852, there were six each in Ireland and England. In the following year, eight missions were given in Ireland and only three in England. This pattern was repeated for some years to come.

2. ALP, PC, 319n. records of Petcherine that 'nihil boni faciendum in Anglia ipsi videbatur, ab eo tempore quo primam in Hibernia peregrinationem fecit'.

3. ALP, Lubienski, 'Mémoires', p. 94.

4. AGR, XLVII, A2, de Buggenoms to Douglas, 24 September 1855 & 29 September 1854.

5. Hosp, 'First Redemptorist Missions in Ireland', *passim*. Prost recalled one street in Limerick, inhabited entirely by Catholics, not one of whom went to church (p. 458).

6. *Tablet,* 10 September 1853, p. 582.
7. AGR, Pr.An., XI₁ (Pecherin), Swinkels to Pecherin, 14 May 1861.
8. ALP, Bb [unnumbered], Douglas to MacDonald, 11 June 1885 and AGR, XLVII, A2, de Buggenoms to Douglas, 10 June 1856.
9. ALP, PC, pp. 285-6 for the general features of the following account.
10. Ibid., p. 387. The previous year at Enniskillen, Co. Fermanagh, the crowds were so great that the clergy had wondered where they came from (p. 325).
11. Hosp, 'First Redemptorist Missions in Ireland', p. 481. Large crowds did not please everyone; CD/ALL, I, 50-1 mentions that the Bishop of Ossory complained of the numbers who attended a mission in Kilkenny Cathedral in 1858, and hoped that the greater part would fall off. He was particularly upset by the dust and dirt, which the 'uncouth crowd' brought onto the benches, and, having reprimanded the people for their excessive zeal, restricted the times when the cathedral was open.
12. *Tablet,* 26 June 1858, p. 403.
13. Ibid., 1 November 1856, p. 693. The reporter concluded that 'the mission would require ten or twelve Redemptorists to perfect the work that is created by four'.
14. ADC, D25, *A Printed Account of the Mission in the South Parish Chapel, Cork,* privately printed (Cork, 1854), p. 6.
15. Hosp, 'First Redemptorist Missions in Ireland', p. 481 and CD/ALL, I, 10 & 21.
16. Hosp, 'First Redemptorist Missions in Ireland', p. 476.
17. *Tablet,* 21 June 1856, p. 389.
18. ALP, MS 'Fr Lans's Diary', Miscellaneous Notes and MS 'Reminiscences of Life of a Redemptorist from August 1851—August 1881' by John Gibson, C.SS.R. [hereafter, Gibson, 'Reminiscences'], p. 109.
19. ALP, PC, pp. 327 & 394.
20. Ibid., p. 283 (Latin original).
21. CD/ALL, I (1859), 76.
22. AGR, Pr.An., IId, [?] to Douglas, Ascension 1854.
23. Ibid., I1c, Coffin to Mauron, 26 December 1855: 'On nous demande toujours des Missions, la seule chose qui nous manque c'est un nombre suffisant des Pères "Missionnaires"'.
24. ADBE, D17 and ALP, Cb13, letters dated 6 February and 12 October 1853.
25. ALP, Gibson, 'Reminiscences', p. 45.
26. AGR, Provinciae Hollandicae, I (1861), Swinkels to Mauron, 16 May 1861.
27. AGR, XLVII, A1, Prost to Douglas, 1 August 1855:
    My true motive for returning to Austria was the puzzle and the hurry with which we were driven about without any rest from one place to another, from one mission to another. I remonstrated against it repeatedly ... but without any success ... I am convinced if they go on in the same haste and hurry with the mission work in England and Ireland ... the consequences will be bitter ones.

28. ALP, Bb [unnumbered], Douglas to Coffin, 6 November 1859.
29. ADL, 'Recess Book', sub anno 1859.
30. AGR, XLVII, B1, Coffin to Douglas, 10 November 1859.
31. CD/ALL, I (1859), p. 73.
32. AGR, Pr.An., I1d, Van der Aa to Mauron, 11 October 1860.
33. ADL, C41, Mauron to Plunkett, 3 September 1861.
34. *Tablet*, 3 June 1854, p. 343.
35. CD/ALL, I, 22.
36. *Tablet*, 12 January 1856, p. 27.
37. *Freeman's Journal*, 8 December 1862; cf. *Munster News*, same date: 'What district of Ireland is not now conscious of the presence and services of the Redemptorist Fathers? In what Province has not their devotion and holiness had influence and effect?'.
38. AGR, XLVII, A6, Reyners to Douglas, 10 March 1855.
39. ALP, PC, p. 267.
40. ALP, Lubienski, 'Mémoires', p. 94.
41. Quoted in L.H. Lees, *Exiles of Erin: Irish Migrants in Victorian London* (Manchester, 1979), p. 173.
42. R. Swift and S.W. Gilley (editors), *The Irish in the Victorian City* (London, 1985) is the best, recent study of the Irish in Britain.
43. S.W. Gilley, 'Supernaturalised Culture: Catholic attitudes and Latin Lands, 1840-60', in *The Materials, Sources and Methods of Ecclesiastical History*, edited by D. Baker, Studies in Church History, 11 (Oxford, 1975), pp. 309-23 (pp. 310 & 318).
44. AGR, Pr.An., I1d, undated fragment of a letter in French [late 1861?], Van der Aa to Mauron.
45. AAB, B1986, Newman to Ullathorne, 17 September 1850. The Redemptorists did, however, acquire Coffin out of the negotiations.
46. ALP, Cb41.1, Heilig to Lans, 2 November 1850.
47. AAB, B3216, Shrewsbury to Ullathorne, 16 October 1854, in which the Earl said he would be 'delighted' with the Redemptorists, and B3374, Reyners to Ullathorne, 8 January 1855, in which the negative response of the Roman authorities was communicated to the bishop.
48. ADBE, 'Secretary's Book', III. A full list of Redemptorists, who worked in the Province in the last century, will be found in *English and Welsh Priests. 1801-1914*, edited by Charles Fitzgerald-Lombard (Downside Abbey, forthcoming).
49. ALP, Lubienski, 'Mémoires', p. 141. PC, pp. 186-7 makes similar comments, although the Chronicler felt that the blame was that of the parents, who, filled with ambition for their sons in the world of commerce, cultivated in them a distaste for the idea of a religious vocation, and a corresponding desire to be involved in commerce; to this end, parents deliberately undermined their sons' Latin studies. Interestingly, Gentili made similar observations, Leetham, *Luigi Gentili*, p. 236.
50. See above, p. 15.
51. ALP, Gibson, 'Reminiscences', p. 90.
52. AGR, XLVII, Ap 101, Riddell to H.D. Coleman, 18 July 1886 (Copy).
53. CDC, I (1862), 101 records the example of a student at the English

College, Rome, who joined the Congregation after a retreat there by Coffin. Frs Burke, O'Laverty and Harbison were among the number of secular priests drawn to the Congregation by its mission work.

54. Redemptorist Fathers, Dundalk, Domestic Archives [hereafter, ADDk], [?] to Fr Leo, 13 February 1879. Redemptorist missions did, of course, inspire many who never joined the Congregation; for example, James Cullen attended one of their missions at New Ross in 1854 and was inspired with 'the desire of saving souls, the passion of my life', quoted in L. McKenna, *The Life and Work of the Rev. James Aloysius Cullen, S.J.* (London, 1924), p. 14.

55. AGR, Pr.An., VII$_2$, 'Mémoire confidential sur l'histoire des premieres fondations en Angleterre et en Irlande, par P. Buggenoms, avec notes du P. Douglas', 1865, p. 33.

56. Social disparity should not be overstressed, and it is based upon the impression gained from reading necrologies rather than from any direct evidence. More detailed statistical analysis of the social background of Redemptorist recruitment cannot be provided from existing records.

57. ALP, Lubienski, 'Mémoires', p. 85.

58. AGR, XLVII, A6, Reyners to Douglas, 10 March 1855. Reyners wrote that before he would accept an Irish priest into the novitiate, he would examine him ten times.

59. AGR, Pr.An., Ild, Van der Aa to Mauron, 11 October 1860.

60. The first Scottish mission had been given in Airdrie in 1856.

61. ALP, Bb15 & 16, decrees of erection and appointment, 24 May 1865. There were twenty-nine priests, five priest-students, four clerical novices, twelve lay brothers and five novice lay brothers in the new Province.

62. Of his ambition, de Buggenoms, 'Mémoire confidentiel', p. 46, recalled that Coffin had wanted to be Vice-Provincial in 1855, as well as Rector of Clapham, and that to further his own cause he caused his name to be printed above that of de Buggenoms, whom he considered his chief rival, in the *Catholic Directory* for 1856.

63. Quoted in A. Sampers, C.SS.R., 'Wladimir Sergejewitsch Pecherin (1807-1885): Sein Austritt aus der Kongregation des allerheiligsten Erlösers, 1861', *Spicilegium Historicum Congregationis Sanctissimi Redemptoris*, 21/1 (1973), 165-97, pp. 195-6.

64. AGR, Pr.An., I$_2$, Coffin to Mauron, 18 January 1872. Whenever he received a letter from Rome, 'he kissed it and placed it on his head, thereby submitting his will entirely to his Superior even before he knew his desire', Redemptorist Fathers, Dublin, Provincial Archives [hereafter, ADP], MS 'Notes for "Historia Provinciae Hiberniae"', p. 9.

65. AGR, XLVII, B2, Coffin to Douglas, 21 March 1868.

66. ALP, Ba130, Mauron to Coffin, 16 June 1874 (French original).

67. E.S. Purcell, *Life of Cardinal Manning, Archbishop of Westminister*, 2 vols (London, 1896), II, 215.

68. W. Ward, *The Life of John Henry Cardinal Newman*, 2 vols (London, 1897), II, 127 & 142, and V.A. McClelland, *Cardinal Manning: His Public*

Life and Influence, 1865-1892 (London, 1962), p. 97. The text of Coffin's address to the Fourth Provincial Synod of Westminister (1873) on the subject of prohibiting Catholics from attending the two older universities, can be found in ALP, Ea17. Coffin's politicking was very much underhand, for his obituary in *The Times*, 7 April 1885, could state that 'Dr Coffin was a man of very ascetic habits and never took an active part in the theological or political controversies of the time'.

69. APF, SC, Anglia, vol. 16 (1861-3), fo. 785r (Italian original).

70. After Manning, Newman, Faber and Fr Ignatius, probably no one received more Oxford converts than Coffin, and no one retained the guidance and direction of so large a proportion of his converts afterwards; according to the *Tablet*, 18 April 1885, p. 623, Coffin had a reputation as 'a parson slayer'.

71. ALP, Lubienski, 'Mémoires', p. 126.

72. *Tablet*, 11 April 1885, p. 583. Referring to his translation of St Alphonsus's works, his labours as a preacher and missionary, his clergy retreats, and his provincialate of the Redemptorists, the obituary concluded that 'he performed a quiet, solid and enduring work which will be felt for many generations'.

73. *The Directory of the Missions in the English Province of the Congregation of the Most Holy Redeemer*, privately printed (London, 1877), p. 5.

74. AGR, Pr.An., I₂., report of Coffin, 12 June 1866.

75. ALP, 'Chronicles of the English Province' [hereafter, CEP], II, 87.

76. ALP, Ef2 for a full account of the foundation; a detailed description of the monastery appeared in the *Catholic Directory for the Clergy and Laity in Scotland* (Glasgow, 1869), p. 85. Completed in 1870, the solemn opening of the church caused a spate of anti-Catholic feeling in the local newspapers.

77. ADP, 'Diary of Fr Somers', p. 9.

78. See below, pp. 90-1.

79. *Tablet*, 11 September 1869, p. 475; cf. *Tablet*, 3 September 1870, p. 305, following a Redemptorist mission in Iverness, where 'the blessings … are happily no longer confined to the southern parts of the kingdom'.

80. AGR, Pr.An., I₂, Coffin to Mauron, 25 August 1866 and XLVII, B2, Coffin to Douglas, 19 June 1866.

81. He was reverting to an idea he had entertained as long ago as 1860 in establishing a house in or near Plymouth, AGR, Pr.An., IId, Van der Aa to Mauron, 5 September 1860, in which he complains about Coffin's idea.

82. ALP, Domestic Archives, Teignmouth [hereafter, ADT], BJaB7, Vaughan to Coffin, 8 July 1875. Coffin told Mauron that it would be difficult to find a bishop 'si bien disposé et qui voudra nous admettre sans aucun condition onereuse et sans se mêler de nos affaires', AGR, Pr.An., I₂., 27 August 1875.

83. ALP, 'Chronica Domestica domus CSSR ad St Joseph apud Teignmouth', p. 2. Vaughan told Mauron, 'J'ai certainement éprouvé une grande joie de voir arrivés dans mon diocèse une Congrégation pour laquelle depuis bien des années j'avais concu une profonde

éstime et un religieux respect', AGR, Pr.An., I$_2$, 5 January 1876.

84. Full details in ALP, Dg1-3. In 1880, the option to purchase the lease was not taken up, and the community moved to a nearby house, which could be extended. In 1884, the house was raised to a full 'collegium'.

85. ALP, CEP, II, 290.

86. ADP, 'Notes for "Historia Provinciae Hiberniae" ', p. 65.

87. ALP, ADT, 'Liber Secretarii, B', pp. 45-58.

88. AGR, Pr.An., III$_6$, Bennett to Mauron, 23 August 1890.

89. ALP, Ba148.151, Ulrich to Bennett, 24 September 1890 (French original).

90. ALP, Ba143, Mauron to Coffin, 7 September 1875.

91. ALP, Bb [unnumbered], Douglas to Coffin, 18 May 1876.

92. Of the fifty-nine priests in the Province in 1880, for example, thirty were Irish, twelve were English, and there were three Scots; the remaining fourteen were from the Continent.

93. AGR, Pr.An., I1d, Trevelyan to Mauron, 15 December 1857.

94. Ibid., same to same, 11 January & 11 February 1858, and rough copy of Douglas's reply.

95. AGR, Pr.An., IX$_2$ (Johnson), Johnson to Mauron, 21 September 1865 and ALP, Ba115, Mauron to Coffin, 26 April 1873.

96. ALP, Ba116 & 117, 23 May & 2 July 1873.

97. ALP, Lubienski, 'Mémoires', p. 287.

98. AGR, Pr.An., I$_2$, Coffin to Mauron, 18 August & 30 September 1873 and ADDk, McGettigan's official document of permission to settle in the diocese, 25 September 1873.

99. See below, pp. 73-4.

100. The *Ulster Examiner*, 30 September 1879, for example, concluded its report of a mission in Lisburn with the statement that 'the fathers of the Redemptorist Order are well known for their piety, zeal and humility in preaching the truths of the Gospel. Their names are now almost a household word throughout the Catholic world'.

101. *Freeman's Journal*, 29 August 1881.

102. S.J. Boland, 'Edmund Vaughan, C.SS.R., and the beginnings of the Congregation of the Most Holy Redeemer in Australia', *Spicilegium Historicum Congregationis Sanctissimi Redemptoris*, 25/1 (1977), 250-71 contains full details.

103. APF, Lettere e Decreti della Sacra Congregazione e Biglietti di Monsignor Segretario [hereafter, LDB], vol. 378 (1882), fo. 187r., Iacobini to Coffin, 12 April 1882.

104. APF, Acta Sacrae Congregationis [hereafter, Acta], vol. 250 (1882), fos 10-22, at fo. 20v.; cf. AAW, Roman letters, vol. 2, p. 65.

105. *Echo*, 18 April 1882.

106. AGR, XLVII, C1, MacDonald to Douglas, 26 August 1882.

107. ALP, Lubienski, 'Mémoires', p. 352.

108. *Tablet*, 15 April 1882, p. 565.

Chapter 3

1. AGR, Pr.An., II$_4$, unsigned, undated memorial in French.
2. AGR, XLVII, C1, MacDonald to Douglas, 26 August 1882.
3. APF, Acta, vol. 250 (1882), fos 10-22, at fo. 21r.
4. AGR, PR.An., VII$_{12}$, Geoghegan to Raus, April 1896: 'nulla foret utilitas alicui scribendi — circa vel contra illum [i.e. Coffin] Villae Casertae — tantum ponderis ejus solo verbo, ibi creditum fuisse'.
5. AGR, XLVII, F1, Bridgett to Douglas, 5 November 1885.
6. AGR, Pr.An., II$_4$, contains letters from various fathers with these strictures; for example, A. Barry to Mauron, 24 May 1882:
   L'Évêque-elu de Southwark pendant les 23 ans de son Provincialat a traité ses favorites admirablement bien et ceux qui n'étaient pas bien mal. Les pères qui lui montraient la servilité s'arrangeant avec toutes ses fantasies et ne trouvant rien à redire dans sa vie confortable et peu-rédemptoriste et qui surtout paraissaient le traiter comme s'il était le Supérieur-Général étaient ses amis et étaient considérés par lui les seuls dignes de ses faveurs.
7. Many of Coffin's letters to Mauron contain references to his illness — he suffered badly from sciatica — which often confined him to bed and prevented him from maintaining the full rigours of a Redemptorist's life. George Corbishley, however, thought that Coffin was something of a hypochondriac, AGR, Pr.An., II$_4$, Corbishley to Mauron, 15 March 1874.
8. A point made by Swinkels, when the accusation was first made, AGR, Pr.An., IIa, Swinkels to Mauron, 3 July 1860.
9. Ibid., 1$_2$, Coffin to Mauron, 18 January 1872 (French original).
10. Ibid., same to same, 11 April 1874 (French original).
11. AGR, XLVII, B1, Coffin to Douglas, 24 January 1860.
12. AGR, Pr.An., IIc, Coffin to Mauron, 29 July 1861 (French original).
13. Ibid., IId, Theunis to Mauron, 2 July 1860.
14. Ibid., I$_2$, Coffin to Mauron, 18 July 1865, 30 April 1871 and 26 April 1877.
15. Ibid., Coffin to Mauron, 1 June 1875.
16. Ibid., II$_3$, same to same, 26 June 1881.
17. Ibid., VII$_{12}$, Geoghegan to Raus, April 1896, complained that Coffin was one of those Oxford converts 'qui venerunt ad Ecclesiam persuasum sibi habentibus quod debent ibi regere'. This English quality of liking to govern was noticed by Van der Aa, who noted that in England Rectors acted like Provincials and Provincial Superiors [i.e. Coffin] like Rectors Major, AGR, Pr. An., IId, Van der Aa to Mauron, 27 October, 1860.
18. Ibid., Plunkett to Mauron, 25 August 1861.
19. ADP, MS 'Notes for "Historia Provinciae Hiberniae"' p. 71.
20. It was a Dutchman who found one of the early Irish subjects to have 'a strong spirit which rules him', AGR, Pr.An., IIa, Swinkels to Mauron, 3 July 1860; cf. ibid., IId, Van der Aa to Mauron, 11 October 1860, who noted that the English and Irish priests would not suffer each other.
21. AGR, Pr.An., IId, Plunkett to Douglas, 29 May 1859.

22. Ibid., II$_3$, Coffin to Mauron, 26 June 1881 (French original).
23. Ibid., I$_2$, same to same, 10 February 1868.
24. Ibid., II$_3$, same to same, 26 January 1879 (French original).
25. Ibid.,I$_2$ same to same, 30 April 1871 and XLVII, B3, Coffin to Douglas, 31 May 1876, concerning Frs Stevens and Vaughan.
26. ADBE, D71, Coffin to students, 18 March 1869.
27. AGR, Pr.An., II$_4$, unsigned, undated memorial (French original).
28. In 1885 he was considered for the vacant Scottish primacy, which went to his brother Angus, formerly Bishop of Argyll and the Isles; on this occasion, Mauron pleaded the necessity of him remaining Provincial, APF, LDB, vol. 381 (1885), fo. 415r. MacDonald described his elevation to Aberdeen as 'a death warrant', SCA, D3, MacDonald to Archbishop Smith, 31 August 1890. In October of the previous year, Archbishop Eyre had written to Smith, urging MacDonald's candidature, 'not only on account of his suitability, but also on account of the difficulty of selecting another', SCA, D2, 9 October 1889.
29. AGR, Pr.An., II$_4$, MacDonald to Mauron, 9 May 1885 (French original). His letters to the Rector Major are much less fulsome and detailed, and more business-like, than those of Coffin.
30. ALP, Ba148.116, Mauron to MacDonald, 5 February 1889 (French original); cf., ALP, Ba147.60, same to same, August 1886, 'Vraiment la bénédiction de Dieu est manifeste dans nos travaux apostoliques'.
31. *Tablet,* 21 April 1888, p. 642.
32. Mauron had made the request to Coffin in 1878, but he replied that it was impossible at the present time, AGR, Pr.An., II$_3$, Coffin to Mauron, 13 May 1878.
33. ALP, Cb39, circular letter, 20 September 1884.
34. ALP, Bb32a, undated letter of Rector Major. The prospectus, ALP, Eb15, appealed to parents of boys aged twelve to fourteen, who agreed not to stand in the way of their sons' vocation, to pay £30 p.a. for their education (a few bursaries were available), and not to expect them to come home during the vacations, save in the case of serious illness, nor to visit them without the permission of the Superior. Orphans, children from poor homes, unhealthy or physically-deformed boys, or those with 'obvious faults of character' were ineligible for consideration.
35. AGR, Pr.An., III$_5$, MacDonald to Mauron, 11 October 1887 (French original).
36. ALP, ADT, BJaE36, for example, gives the story of Richard Cagney who died as a novice in 1895 at the age of sixteen. He dictated a letter to his parents on his deathbed in which he said he was happy to be a member of the Congregation and thankful for the opportunity afforded him in the Juvenate to acquire his vocation.
37. AGR, XLVII, C1, MacDonald to Douglas, 28 September 1885, bemoaned the impossibility of obtaining English recruits; the poorer classes in England provided no vocations, while the better class, even in Ireland, did not like to send their boys because of the prohibition to return home during the holidays.
38. AGR, Pr.An., III$_5$, MacDonald to Mauron, 20 September 1889: 'Le

P. Maître remarque que l'esprit de nationalisme Irlandais est trop fort dans notre Province'.

39. AGR, XLVII, C1, MacDonald to Douglas, 17 January 1888: 'I think we are getting more fervent and more interior, more solicitous for the "better part". I used to be very much afraid that we were drifting away too much into the exterior life, to the neglect of the interior'.

40. AGR, Pr.An., III$_5$, MacDonald to Mauron, 11 March 1890 (French original).

41. Ibid., same to same, 17 September 1887 (French original). In 1885, Bennett's name had been included with MacDonald's on the *terna* of the Scottish bishops for the vacant primatial see. In 1887 and 1890, he was considered for Dunkeld.

42. ALP, Ba150.9, Mauron to Bennett, 31 March 1891 (French original).

43. AGR, Pr.An., III$_6$, Bennett to Ulrich, 12 August 1891, for example, in which the Provincial defended the students' theatrical productions against complaints made about them and stated that not all theatricals were, *ipso facto*, profane.

44. AGR, Pr.An., VI$_1$, 'Varia postulata pro divisione ad Capitulum Generale, 1894'.

45. Ibid., V$_3$, 'Visitatio Extraordinaria, 1894'; for more details, see below, pp. 114-5.

46. ADBE, C149, circular letter, 7 November 1894.

47. AGR, Pr.An., III$_7$ Vaughan to Magnier, 22 March 1895, and Magnier to Vaughan, undated (Copy).

48. ADP, bundle of letters relating to foundations.

49. Ibid., Dr Henry to Fr Somers, 18 November 1895.

50. ADB, 'Chronica Domestica', I, 4; cf. ALP, AK2, MS 'Short History of the House of the M.H. Redeemer, Clonard, Belfast'. Fuller details in P. O'Donnell, C.SS.R., *Clonard Church and Monastery* (Muckamore, no date), pp. 7-15.

51. AGR, Pr.An., III$_7$, Bennett to Magnier, 10 September 1896 & 18 September 1897, in which he told Magnier that a division was 'absolutely necessary and the sooner effected the better'.

52. ALP, Bb43, 'Actus conventus extraordinarius', 15-17 September 1897.

53. Ibid., notes in Vaughan's handwriting.

54. AGR, Pr.An., III$_7$, Bennett to Magnier, 10 September 1896.

55. AGR, XLVII, D4, Bennett to Douglas, 14 June 1896.

56. ADB, 'Chronica Domestica', I, 17.

57. ALP, Bb44, decree of erection, 1 April 1898. The greater strength of the Irish Province and the predominantly Irish flavour of the Institute in Australia made sensible the dependence of the houses there on Ireland, rather than on England.

58. ALP, Bal51.83, Magnier to Bennett, 23 November 1900. The phrase was used by one of the priests of the Province, who argued that 'a new sphere of activity is required' for the English Redemptorists.

59. ALP, Bal51.93, same to same, 19 May 1901.

60. Quoted in S. Raponi, C.SS.R., *I Redentoristi oggi e domani* (Rome, 1982), p. 64.

Chapter 4

1. See above, pp. 14-17.
2. APF, SC, Anglia, vol. 22 (1881), fos 817-22, at fo. 817. The previous year Mauron had told Coffin that 'il est certain que son Éminence et les Évêques d'Angleterre ont une estime de plus en plus grande envers la Congrégation', and that 'parmi tous les Ordres religieux, notre Congrégation est la plus unie aux Évêques', ALP, Ba200 & 201, letters dated 4 & 17 July 1880. Six years later, Mauron reported similar sentiments to MacDonald as regards the Irish bishops, ALP, Ba206, 3 December 1886.
3. Writing to Robert Cornthwaite, for instance, with whom he was on intimate terms, Coffin signed himself, 'your affectionate servant and friend', Archives of the Bishop of Leeds, Cornthwaite letters, 13 January 1868.
4. Negotiating with Bishop Strain for a Redemptorist establishment in the east of Scotland, Coffin wrote, 'I need hardly assure your Lordship of my desire that the Fathers should render to your Lordship's District all the services in their power', SCA, C10, p. 87, 1867.
5. ALP, Ba148.103 & 148.106, Mauron to MacDonald, 16 January & 25 March 1888.
6. ALP, Ba147.58, same to same, 1 March 1886 (French original).
7. ALP, Ba148.126a, same to same, 14 November 1889.
8. AGR, XLVII, B1, Coffin to Douglas, 28 January 1861.
9. AGR, Pr.An., I1c, Coffin to Mauron, 14 September 1864 (French original).
10. In 1868, Manning proposed either Coffin or Bridgett as bishop of the Western District of Scotland to counteract the possibility of Errington's appointment. Mauron pleaded with Simeoni, the Secretary of Propaganda, that 'la perdita dell'uno o dell'altro sarebbe un danno positivo all'opera delle missioni, che dipende dal P. Coffin comme Provinciale, ed in Irlanda immediatamente dal P. Bridgett comme Rettore di casa', AGR, Pr.An., I$_2$, copy of letter dated 12 September 1868.
11. CDC, I, 89.
12. Redemptorist Fathers, Kinnoull, Perth, Domestic Archives [hereafter, ADK], 'Chronica Missionum' [hereafter, ALK], III (1885), 74.
13. Lancashire Record Office [hereafter, LRO], Archives of the Roman Catholic Archdiocese of Liverpool [hereafter, RCLv], 5/4/184, Goss to Doyle, 17 October 1861 and 5/3/260, Goss to Bridges, 12 November 1859.
14. LRO, RCLv, 'Relatio Status Animarum Diocesis Liverpolitanae, 1882', p. 14. The phrase occurs again in the 'Relatio Status, 1893', in APF, Rubrica, vol. 24 (1893), 102/59-106, fo. 72r.
15. AGR, Pr.An., I1c, Coffin to Mauron, 25 July 1864 (French original).
16. Ibid., I1d, [?] to Douglas, Ascension 1854, said that the bishop had boasted of the Redemptorists to the other bishops assembled in Dublin for an episcopal meeting that 'he will get the Fathers again even if he had to write to Rome'.

17. APF, LDB, vol. 353 (1862), fo. 276r. and Archives of the Archbishop of Southwark [hereafter, AAS], Box 41, Mauron to Grant, 10 May 1862; APF, LDB, vol. 354 (1863), fo. 40r; vol. 356 (1865), fo. 718v; SC, Anglia, vol.17 (1864-6), fo. 499r. and AGR, Pr.An., VII₁, Secretary of Propaganda to Mauron, 13 March 1865; APF, LDB, vol. 359 (1868), fo. 356v; SC, Anglia, vol.18 (1867-70), fo. 656r.; SC, Irlanda, vol. 44 (1889-90), fos 729v. & 860r.

18. CD/ALL, 1 (1859), 68 & (1868), 308.

19. LRO, RCLv, 5/6/1, Goss's secretary to Gibson, 29 November 1855, and CD ALBE, II, 16.

20. LRO, RCLv, 5/1, Goss to Fr Leo, Feast of St Thomas Cantuar, [29 December] 1855.

21. AGR, Pr.An., I₂, Coffin to Mauron, 30 April 1871 (French original).

22. ALP, Bb [unnumbered], Douglas to Coffin, 20 February 1879.

23. ALP, Gibson, 'Reminiscences', p. 45, for example, records how Bishop Briggs of Beverley asked to be shown proof of the Redemptorists' wide powers in indulgencing medals and crosses.

24. ALP, Bc2, Smetana to Reyners, 19 February 1853.

25. An *Expositio succincta privilegiorum* had been published in Wittem in 1847, but was replaced by the *Elenchus facultatum et gratiarum spiritualium, CSSR* (Monaco, 1860). It was not until 1864 that the Redemptorists' exempt status, on par with the regular orders, was fully and finally recognised by Rome. Until that time, they were cautious of anything that might jeopardise or compromise their claim to exemption from episcopal jurisdiction. Full details of their exemption and privileges are to be found in J. Pejska, C.SS.R., *Jus Sacrum Congregationis Sanctissimi Redemptoris* (Brno, Moravia, 1910) and *Documenta authentica facultatum et gratiarum spiritualium CSSR* (Ratisbon, 1903).

26. *Decreta Quatuor Conciliorum Provincialium Westmonstariensium, 1852-1873* (London, n.d.), p. 35, sections 1 & 2.

27. Ibid., pp. 92-4, at p. 92.

28. ALP, PC, 348.

29. APF, SC, Anglia, vol. 13 (1852-4) fos 736-9 for the protest letter of the Superiors of the Jesuits, Dominicans, Redemptorists and Passionists.

30. ALP, PC, 348 and APF, SC, Anglia, vol. 13 (1852-4), fo. 675.

31. APF, LDB, vol. 349 (1858), fo. 503r.

32. AAS, Box 41, appended note by Grant to a letter from Mauron, 25 March 1859.

33. Ibid., Grant to Coffin, 28 October 1858 (Copy).

34. ADC, F7, decree dated 25 October 1859. The wording had been suggested by the Prefect of Propaganda in a letter to Grant, 13 September 1859, a copy of which, together with copies of the rest of the correspondence between Mauron, the bishop and Propaganda, can be found in AGR, Pr.An., XII₁. The Clapham fathers never questioned the bishop's right of visitation, his control of the elementary schools, or his division of the mission, all of which were contentious issues in the conflict of 1874-81, precipitated by the Jesuits

in Manchester. The Redemptorists were concerned merely to establish the peculiar title under which they held the Clapham mission and which placed them in a different position canonically with regard to the bishop from other religious who served missions.

35. ALP, Ba 126, Mauron to Coffin, 10 June 1881.
36. ALP, EF1, dated 19 May 1868 (Latin original).
37. ALP, CEP, II, 369, and AAS, Box 41, Bishop's secretary to Bennett, 26 February 1892.
38. ALP, PC, pp. 343-4.
39. ALP, Ec18, Douglas to Coffin, 23 March 1861.
40. CDC, II, 91.
41. ALP, Eg5, Vaughan to Coffin, 3 September 1878 (Copy) and Coffin to Vaughan, September 1878 (Copy). On 3 July 1878, Coffin had written to the Rector of Teignmouth (Corbishley) to say that if a request was made, the Rector was to refuse on the grounds that they did not have the cure of souls, but not to involve him as 'it is better that I should keep in the background in such matters as these as long as possible'. Also, ALP, ADT, BJaB10, Ryder to the Bishop's Secretary, 2 July 1895 (Copy), and the bishop's apologetic reply, 5 July 1895.
42. APF, SC, Irlanda, vol. 34 (1861-4), fo. 665r.; Coffin to the Secretary of Propaganda, claiming exemption; ibid., fo. 691r. for Cullen's response, 28 April 1863.
43. APF, LDB, vol. 354 (1863), fo. 271r., Coffin to Propaganda, 6 June 1863. AGR, Pr.An., I1c, Coffin to Douglas, 9 May 1862, said that in Ireland these theological conferences were the scene of many disagreeable collisions between bishops and clergy, and that it was best to avoid them.
44. ALP, Bc4, Raus to Bourne, 2 February 1899, for example, where the relevant privileges of exemption were cited to excuse the Redemptorists' refusal to attend.
45. ADL, E2, Douglas to Plunkett, 12 October 1861.
46. AGR, Pr.An., I1c, Coffin to Douglas, 9 May 1862.
47. ADL, E4, Douglas to Plunkett, 3 June 1862.
48. AGR, Pr.An., I1c, Coffin to Plunkett, 24 October 1862 (Copy).
49. Ibid., Coffin to Mauron, 12 May & 27 June 1863, and on 28 November he reported that the bishop regarded the fathers as 'ses propres Missionnaires diocésains'; further details in CD/ALL, I, 117 & 143.
50. ALP, Ba121, Mauron to Coffin, 19 November 1863.
51. AGR, XLVII, B2, Coffin to Douglas, 19 June 1866.
52. AAW, 3/29.78, de Buggenoms to Wiseman, 2 December 1851.
53. See above, p. 63. Similarly, Dominic Barberi, 'Ricordi Lasciati ai Nostri Giovani Missionari d' Inghilterra', p. 16 counselled against visits to local bishops after a mission for fear that the priests and people might suspect the missioners of being informers. I am grateful to Fr Paul Francis, C.P., for a xerox copy of Fr Conrad Charles' translation of the 'Ricordi', the original typescript translation of which is to be found in the Passionist Archives, London. Barberi's original is to be found in the Postulation Archives of the Passionist Fathers, Rome, Barberi MSS, VII, 3.

54. CDC, I, 81.
55. Quoted in CD/ALL, I, 66.
56. ALP, Ba151.46, Magnier to Bennett, 13 February 1899: 'The Bishop [of Southwark] seemed very satisfied with Fr Ryder [as the new Rector of Clapham] and said that the Priests do not complain of him as of his Predecessor [Fr Stevens] in the sense of drawing people'.
57. AGR, Pr.An., III$_7$, Bennett to Magnier, 10 September 1896, hints at this.
58. ALP, CEP, II, 63.
59. ALP, ADT, BJaB7, Vaughan to Coffin, 8 July 1875.
60. ADDk, McGettigan to Harbison, 7 July 1876.
61. ADDk, H1, McCann to Harbison, 3 September 1876.
62. ADDk, 'Chronica Domestica et Apostolici Labores' [hereafter, CD/ALDk,], I, 125.
63. ALP, Ba155 & 156, Mauron to Coffin, 27 July & 19 September 1876; AGR, XLVII, G8, Harbison to Douglas, 16 January 1883, mentions that little work was done by the fathers in Dundalk 'owing to the jealousy of the local clergy ... who fear that we will draw all or the greater part of the people to our chapel'.
64. CDC, 1, 50.
65. ALK, II, 101 (Latin original).
66. AGR, Pr.An., I$_2$, Coffin to Mauron, 14 February 1867 (French original).
67. CDC, I, 151 and CD/ALBE, IV, 18.
68. ALP, Bb [unnumbered], Douglas to Coffin, 22 February 1876. As a result of Vaughan's remarks in Rome, the Pope expressed himself well pleased with the Redemptorists' work, ALP, Ba149, Mauron to Coffin, 27 January 1876.
69. CD/ALBE, IV, 70.
70. Dr Murray, Administrator of the Pro-Cathedral, Dublin, quoted in CD/ALL, I (1865), 180; the *Tablet*, 26 June 1858, p. 403 noted that a Redemptorist mission in Carndonagh had 'inspired the priests of adjoining parishes to seek out the strayed sheep'. The parish priest of Wexford also remarked that 'priests are stimulated to emulate the example of the Redemptorists', ALP, E3b, letter dated 25 March 1868.
71. C.A. Walworth, 'Reminiscences of a Catholic Crisis in England Fifty Years Ago', p. 402.
72. ALP, Lubienski, 'Mémoires', p. 125 and CDC, I, 77; APF, CP, vol. 158 (1851-60), fo. 47r. noted of Maynooth 'in generale uno spirito avverso alla Santa Sede ed in particolare delle proposizioni non solo Gallicane, ma Febroniane, Giansenistiche e favorevoli allo scisma'. CD/ALL, I, 250 recorded that despite earlier opposition, by 1867 the authority of Alphonsus at the national seminary was paramount; this was mainly due to Edmund O'Reilly, a protégé of Cullen.
73. CD/ALBE, IV, 214.
74. ADBE, MS 'Notes for Clergy Retreats', III, 136.
75. Ibid., p. 137.
76. Alphonsus Maria de' Liguori, *The Selva, or a Collection of Matters for Sermons and Instructions for Ecclesiastical Retreats or for Private Spiritual*

Notes

Lectures, translated by a Catholic Clergyman (Dublin, 1844).
77. ALP, Cb35, Coffin to [? Crofts], 7 February 1880; Coffin was quoting Leo XIII's words to him.
78. Quoted in *Fifty Years at Mount St Alphonsus, Limerick*, p. 95.
79. CD/ALL, I, 86.
80. CD/ALBE, I, sub anno 1853.
81. ALP, Lubienski, 'Mémoires', p. 129. The *Codex Regularum et Constitutionum Congregationis SS. Redemptoris necnon Statutorum a Capitulis Generalibus annis 1764, 1855, 1894* [hereafter, *Codex*] (Rome, 1896), p. 59 told the Redemptorist preacher that 'benevolentiam, non odium audientium captabit'. Barberi, 'Ricordi', pp. 31-2 made similar observations and gave the same advice to the Passionists.
82. T.E. Bridgett, C.SS.R., *In Memoriam*, p. 10.
83. ALP, Lubienski, 'Mémoires', p. 129.

Chapter 5

1. *Circular Letters (Selected) of Redemptorist Generals* (Milwaukee, 1933), p. 46.
2. *Tablet*, 6 August 1853, p. 500. The other order was the Jesuits.
3. *Codex*, p. 141.
4. ALP, Ba152, circular letter of Raus, 6 January 1896. For a short exposition of Alphonsus's theological ideas, see my article, 'The Influence of St Alphonsus Liguori in Nineteenth-Century Britain', *Downside Review*, 101 (1983), 60-76.
5. ADL, C31, circular letter of Coffin, 2 September 1866. Cf. ADBE, 'Liber Secretarii', III (1867), 22:
   We recommend all to cultivate in their private devotions the spirituality and piety of our H.F. Alphonsus, and for this end to read frequently and habitually his writings, to make use of the Devotions generally practised in the Congñ as now given in the 'Manuale', and above all to study the Constitution, that our piety, spirituality and our practice of virtue may be really Redemptorist.
6. ADL, C32c, circular letter of Coffin, 4 December 1867.
7. Fr Burke, in *A Half Century's Jubilee in St Mary's, Clapham* (Southwark, 1899), p. 41.
8. *Codex*, p. 616.
9. Alphonsus Maria de' Liguori, *The True Redemptorist* (London, n.d.), p. 17.
10. *Circular Letters of St Alphonsus*, edited by C.J. Warren, C.SS.R. (Boston, Mass., 1912), p. 22, letter dated 8 August 1754.
11. T.L. Skinner, C.SS.R., *The Redemptorists in the West* (St Louis, 1932), p. 46.
12. ADBE, 'Liber Secretarii', III (1873), p. 35.
13. ALP, Cb23, circular letter of Coffin, 29 December 1867.
14. Ibid.
15. ADL, C37, Coffin to the Limerick community, 1 February 1869.
16. ALP, Cb23.
17. *Directory of the Missions*, p. 7.

253

18. Fr Passerat, quoted in Henri Girouille, C.SS.R., *Life of the Venerable Father Joseph Passerat*, translated by J.Carr (London, 1928), p. 59.
19. Fr Gibson, for instance, gave 262 missions and renewals in thirty years, Fr Bennett gave 164 in twenty-one years, Fr Johnson 192 in twenty-four years, Fr Van der Stickele 230 in thirty-three years, Fr Lans 186 in thirty-four years. Few, however, could rival Fr O'Laverty, who was involved in 496 missions and renewals over a fifty-three year period and was calculated to have helped over a million souls.
20. ALP, Cb41.1, Heilig to Lans, 2 November 1850.
21. *Codex*, p. 346.
22. ALP, MS 'Chronology of My Life by George Stebbing', p. 9.
23. ALP, Gibson, 'Reminiscences', p. 6.
24. *Regula Novitiorum Congregationis SS. Redemptoris* (Rome, 1856), p. 36.
25. ALP, retreat notes of Fr Livius.
26. ALP, MS 'Liber Novitiatus' [emphases his].
27. AGR, Pr.An., VIII, F, Coffin to Mauron, quoting Fr Stevens' report, 13 December 1865 (French original).
28. *Two Hundred Years with the Redemptorists* (Dublin, 1932), p. 22.
29. AGR, Pr.An., 11c, Coffin to Mauron, 3 June 1864 (French original).
30. ALP, Ba151.10, Magnier to Bennett, 25 April 1898.
31. ADDk, 'Order of examinations and list of theses for the annual examinations at Teignmouth, 1882, 1883 & 1885'.
32. ADL, MS 'Life Sketch of Fr Richard Crofts, C.SS.R.'. See my article, 'The Apostolate of the Pen in the English Province in the Nineteenth Century', *Spicilegium Historicum Congregationis Sanctissimi Redemptoris*, 35/1 (1987), 83-95 for a more detailed analysis of this area of the Redemptorists' work.
33. C.A. Walworth, 'Reminiscences of a Catholic Crisis in England Fifty Years Ago', *Catholic World*, 70 (1899/1900), 59-69, 239-52, 412-19, 506-13, p. 64.
34. ALP, Cb22, circular letter of Coffin, 1 March 1867.
35. F.W. Faber, *An Essay on Catholic Home Missions* (London, 1851), p. 31.
36. ADBE, C59, circular letter of Mauron, 25 June 1865.
37. *Codex*, p. 42.
38. CDC, II, sub anno 1872.
39. ADC, C36, instruction of Coffin, 8 October 1869.
40. ALP, Cb30, circular letter of Coffin, 6 January 1877.
41. ALP, Cb21, circular letter of Coffin, 24 June 1866.
42. ADC, C48, monition of Coffin, 27 December 1869.
43. ALP, Gibson, 'Reminiscences', p. 39.
44. ADB, 'Fr Sampson's Reminiscences', II, 132.
45. ALP, Cb22, circular letter of Coffin, 1 March 1867.
46. Gibson, for example, was giving a few mission sermons little more than a year after he began to undertake mission work, and was Superior of a mission within two years.
47. *Codex*, p. 595; cf. ALP, CN1, 'Notanda pro Secondo Novitatu', 12 October 1870.
48. ALP, Cb28, Coffin to [? Vaughan], 16 September 1870.
49. ALP, Eb10, MS 'Some remarks on the Second Novitiate to be held

at Bishop Eton, 1878'. CN3 contains Bridgett's notes on the 1883 novitiate for Fr Lassetter's benefit.

50. ADB, 'Fr Sampson's Reminiscences', II, 131. Cf. ADL, MS 'Life Sketch of Fr O'Laverty, C.SS.R.', who underwent the second novitiate in 1875, five years after his profession, and 'renewed his spirit of prayer and piety; he wrote many sermons and instructions and revived his theological studies'.
51. ADP, MS 'Diary of Fr Somers', p.1. It was not held again for some years, as MacDonald told Mauron in AGR, Pr.An., III$_5$, 14 January 1890.
52. ADL, 'Recess Book', p. 73 (1873).
53. AGR, Pr.An., III$_5$, MacDonald to Mauron, 10 August 1889 and ALP, Ba148.129, Ulrich to MacDonald, 15 August 1889.
54. ADL, 'Recess Book', p. 102 (1884).
55. AGR, Pr.An., II$_4$, MacDonald to Mauron, 6 December 1886.
56. ADL, 'Recess Book', p. 69 (1871).
57. ALP, Ba186, Mauron to Coffin, 29 July 1879, quoting from the priest's request for dispensation.
58. AGR, Pr.An., III$_7$, Vaughan to Raus, 9 February 1896.
59. AGR, Pr.An., XI (Urquhart), 'Matters of Counsel'. It was the custom for specially-composed songs and poems to be performed in the refectory on feast days.
60. CDC, I, 121.
61. *Tablet*, 22 May 1858, p. 324.
62. ALP, Gibson, 'Reminiscences', p. 51.
63. Hosp, 'First Redemptorist Missions in Ireland', p. 456.
64. *Tablet*, 26 December 1857, p. 821.
65. ALP, Gibson, 'Reminiscences', pp. 146-7.
66. AGR, Pr.An., II$_4$, Bennett to Mauron, 8 May 1884, reported that ten thousand copies had been sold and that demand far exceeded supply.
67. T. Livius, C.SS.R., *Our Lady of Perpetual Succour*, third edition (London, 1884), p. 200.
68. ALP, Lubienski, 'Mémoires', pp. 42 & 118.
69. ALP, Cb25, monition of Coffin, 9 June 1864.
70. ADC, C17, instruction of Coffin, 18 August 1870.
71. AGR, Pr.An., XI (Pecherin), Swinkels to Petcherine, 14 May 1861 (photocopy of original letter in French in private possession).

Chapter 6

1. ALP, 'Rough Chronicles'.
2. ADBE, 'Liber Benefactorum' (no page references).
3. *Perthshire Courier*, 2 July 1870.
4. ADP, MS 'Life of Fr Harbison', pp. 24 & 26.
5. ADL, MS 'Life Sketch of Fr Richard Crofts, C.SS.R.'
6. ADBE, 'Necrologium'. p. 52.
7. AGR, Pr.An., I$_2$, Urquhart to Coffin, 14 September 1876.
8. ADL, MS 'Sketch of the Life of Fr Edward O'Donnell, C.SS.R.'.
9. ADP, 'Diary of Fr Somers', p. 4.

10. ADB, 'Fr Sampson's Reminiscences', I, 132.
11. Full details in ADDk, MS 'Reminiscencs of Fr Hall, C.SS.R. by Fr Gibson, C.SS.R.', and ALP, file on Francis Hall for copies of Hall's letters.
12. M Magnier, *Father John Magnier and Fr John Mary Magnier, C.SS.R.* (privately printed, 1916), p. 11.
13. Ibid., p. 13.
14. Ibid., p. 25.
15. Ibid., p. 38.
16. Ibid., p. 30.
17. Ibid., p. 44.
18. CDC, II, 112 records of Fr Gleeson that he, and those like him, will receive the same reply from Christ at the Last Judgement as the foolish virgins.
19. ALP, CEP, II, 475, for example, tells of Fr Boland, who left the Congregation in 1895, apostasised 'and was publicly confirmed by the Protestant bishop of Liverpool. Drink was the cause of his ruin'.
20. ALP, CEP, II, 368 and AGR, Pr.An., III$_5$, MacDonald to Mauron, 14 June 1889, give the story of Fr Lejeune, a lecturer in theology at Teignmouth, who fathered a child by a local servant girl and was expelled from the Congregation.
21. ALP, CEP, II (1870), 124.
22. SCA, C10, p. 89, Coffin to Bishop Strain, 18 December 1867.
23. AGR, Pr.An., II$_4$, MacDonald to Mauron, 6 December 1886 and III$_5$, same to same, 12 January 1887 (French original).
24. AGR, Pr.An., V, 'Relationes Visitationum, 1880' (French original) and CDC, II, 128.
25. AGR, Pr.An., II$_4$, MacDonald to Mauron, 16 June 1883.
26. AGR, Pr.An., V, 'Relationes Visitationum, 1869'.
27. AGR, XLVII, E1-3, Lubienski to Douglas, 7 December 1880.
28. ALP, Ba162, Mauron to Coffin, 8 March 1877.
29. AGR, Pr.An., II$_3$, Coffin to Mauron, 28 March 1877 (French original).
30. T. Livius, C.SS.R., *Father Furniss and his Work for Children* (London, 1896), pp. 86 & 153.
31. AGR, Pr.An., I1a, Swinkels to Mauron, undated [late 1855?] (French original). Swinkels said that all the fathers complained against Furniss, who threatened to discredit the Congregation by admitting children of eight or nine to first communion without the consent of their parish priests.
32. Ibid., same to same, 8 August 1856 (French original). Swinkels reported the words of Furniss, whom he thought 'incorrigible'. He added that Furniss worked well and with success and that he hoped to keep him in the Congregation. Furniss regressed into an infantile stage for the last three years of his life, which, perhaps, explains some of his previous psychological oddity, and on 16 September 1865 wrote a pathetic letter to the Rector Major asking pardon for the faults of his life.
33. For more details, see E. MacWhite, 'Towards a biography of Father Vladimir S. Pecherin (1807-1885): a progress report and bibliography',

Proceedings of the Royal Irish Academy, 80, Section C, Number 7 (1980), 109-58.

34. Quoted in CDL, II, sub anno 1897.
35. AGR, XLVII, B3, Coffin to Douglas, 3 May 1875.
36. AGR, Pr.An., I₂, Coffin to the Rector of Limerick, 3 November 1876 (Copy). Coffin thought that Hall improved, but III₅, MacDonald to Mauron, 26 August 1889, mentions that Hall was still introducing politics and nationalism into his sermons.
37. AGR, Pr.An., I₂, Harbison to Coffin, 26 October 1876.
38. The archbishop did admit that the people liked his sermons: Ibid., Archbishop Leahy to Harbison, 28 October 1876.
39. ALP, Ba1.18, Mauron to Coffin, 5 July 1863.
40. ALP, CEP, I (1847), 34.
41. Ibid., II (1867), 86.
42. AGR, Pr.An., IV₈, Vaughan to Raus, 17 May 1899. Vaughan said that Ryder was restless-minded and too independent of action, as well as violent of speech.
43. ALP, Gibson, 'Reminiscences', p. 83.
44. ALP, CEP, II (1892), 415.
45. ALP, MS 'Biographical Sketch of Fr Gibson, C.SS.R.', p. 32.
46. AGR, Pr.An., V₃, 'Visitatio Extraordinaria, 1894' (Latin original).
47. AGR, XLVII, C1, MacDonald to Douglas, 27 May 1889.
48. ADBE, monition of Hëilig, 28 August 1849.
49. ADC, C36, monition of Coffin, 8 October 1869.
50. AGR, Pr.An., Ild, the novices to Coffin, 29 December 1861: 'La différence des contrées s'efface à nos yeux: tous enfants d'une seule et même famille, à laquelle nous nous attachons de coeur et d'âme, nous vivons en véritables frères dans l'union de la charité'.
51. ADK, Recess Book sub annis 1870 & 1872, for instance, told the fathers to avoid even the slightest appearance of nationality, both at home and on the missions, in their intercessions and in their relations with the secular clergy.
52. ADBE, D141, circular letter of Bennett, 14 July 1898.
53. AGR, Pr.An., II₄, MacDonald to Mauron, 14 July 1886.
54. ALP, MS 'Additional Notes on the Missions in the English Province, written by the Visitor of 1894'.
55. AGR, Pr.An., V₃, 'Visitatio Extraordinaria, 1894'.
56. AGR, XLVII, D4, Bennett to Douglas, 14 June 1896, mentions that many of the older fathers distrusted Magnier's judgement and that his visitation had not been sufficiently thorough.
57. AGR, Pr.An., VII₁₂, Geoghegan to Raus, 21 April 1896.
58. ALP, Ea24, response of the Second Consultor at Teignmouth to the 'Formula Systematis S.P.N. Alphonsi'.
59. AGR, Pr.An., VII₁₂, Geoghegan to Raus, 21 April 1896 (Latin original).
60. ALP, Ea24, documents addressed to Fr Vaughan on the 'Formula Systematis S.P.N. Alphonsi' (Latin original).
61. AGR, Pr.An., IV₈, Bennett to Magnier, 16 December 1898.
62. AGR, XLVII, H1 Livius to Douglas, undated fragment of letter.

63. ADB, 'Fr Sampson's Reminiscences', I, 88.
64. Quoted in CD/ALL, I, 57.
65. *Tablet*, 26 June 1858, p. 403.
66. Quoted in *Two Hundred Years with the Redemptorists* (Dublin, 1937), p. 37.
67. *Ulster Observer*, 6 December 1862.
68. *Cork Examiner*, 2 August 1878.
69. ALP, MS 'Memorial of Fr Laverty' and ADB, 'Fr Sampson's Reminiscences', II, 182-220.
70. *Ulster Examiner*, 30 September 1879.
71. *Limerick News*, quoted in CDL, II, sub anno 1878.
72. *Freeman's Journal*, 9 February 1886.
73. ADL, MS 'Life Sketch of Fr Francis Hall, C.SS.R.'.
74. AGR, Pr.An., I₂, Coffin to Mauron, 22 May 1874 (French original).
75. *Limerick Reporter*, 4 August 1876.
76. ADB, 'Fr Sampson's Reminiscences', I, 125.
77. ADP, 'Life of Fr Harbison', p. 102.
78. ADB, 'Fr Sampson's Reminiscences', I, 125.
79. *Morning News,* 11 October 1888.
80. ADB, 'Fr Sampson's Reminiscences', I, 152, referring to Fr Arnold Van Everdingen.
81. ALP, MS 'Life Sketch of Fr John Gibson, C.SS.R.'.
82. ALP, CEP, I (1860), 42.
83. ADB, 'Fr Sampson's Reminiscences', II, 154.
84. ALP, CEP, I (1853), 153.
85. ALP, 'Catalogus Defunctorum', p. 22.
86. CDC, II (1882), 220.
87. ADBE, 'Necrologium', p. 72.
88. CDC, II (1887), 268.
89. ADB, 'Fr Sampson's Reminiscences', I, 90.
90. ALP, CEP, II (1886), 324.
91. Full details in T. Livius, C.SS.R., *A Brief Memoir of the Rev. Father John Baptist Lans, C.SS.R.* (Liverpool, 1887).
92. ALP, CEP, II (1892), 412.
93. ALP, CEP, II, (1897), 495.

Chapter 7

1. For the origins and development of parochial missions, see M. van Delft, C.SS.R., *La Mission Paroissiale: pratique et théorie* (Paris, 1963), especially chapter 2.
2. J. Delumeau, *Catholicism between Luther and Voltaire: a new view of the Counter-Reformation* (London, 1977), pp. 189-94.
3. The Synod of Thurles (1851), the First Provincial Synod of Westminster (1852) and the Plenary Synod of the Scottish Bishops (1886) all required priests to have regular missions in their parishes.
4. See above, p. 32 & p. 242, note 43.
5. Thus, Manning reported to Propaganda in 1864 about Scotland that in Ireland [the poor Irish] are held to the fulfillment of their

religious duties by their parish priests, to whom they are bound
by inseparable ties. It is these ties which are the safeguard of their
faith, and where they are wanting, as in Edinburgh and Glasgow,
they lose themselves among Protestants and unbelievers. Without
parish priests or bishops, the hold which their religion has upon
them is not sufficiently firm.

Quoted in A. Bellesheim, *History of the Catholic Church of Scotland*,
translated by O. Hunter Blair, OSB, 4 vols (Edinburgh and London,
1887-90), IV, 301.

6. W.J. Amherst, 'Frederick Lucas', *Dublin Review*, Third Series, 16 (1886),
329-428, p. 403.

7. Archbishop Goodier, 'The Catholic Church and the Spiritual Life',
in *Catholic Emancipation, 1829 to 1929* (London, 1929), pp. 23-44 (pp.
39-40): 'After the schools, for to them and their army of teachers we
would give the first place, it is to these incessant missions and retreats
that we would ascribe the saving of the faith of thousands, in a time
of more subtle crisis than may at first appear'. Although canonical
parishes were not established in England until 1918, to avoid confusion
the term 'parish' has been used throughout instead of the more
technically-correct 'mission'.

8. APF, SC, Irlanda, vol. 38 (1878-80), fo. 910r., for example, records
of the diocese of Ferns that 'multae Missiones et sacri secessus,
fidelibus populis, vel sodalitatibus a religiosis hominibus v.g. Patribus
SS. Redemptoris vel aliis, tum etiam a Sacerdotibus dictis
Saecularibus, magno fructu et incremento religionis et pietatis
praedicati fuerunt'.

9. J. Magnier, C.SS.R., 'Parochial Missions', *Irish Ecclesiastical Record*,
Third Series, 16 (1896), 577-92, p. 577.

10. *Codex*, p. 37.

11. G.F. Drew, C.SS.R., *Bishop Eton and its Shrine* (St Helen's, 1951), p. 12.

12. LRO, RCLv, Miscellanea, mission leaflet for a Redemptorist mission
in St Clare's, Arundel Avenue, Sefton Park, dated 17 May 1891. The
printed leaflet has instructions that it should be fixed in the house,
so that all members of the family might see it. The formula was
standard; cf. ADC, D20, mission leaflet for St Mary's, Clapham,
February 1877.

13. Newspaper report from (?) *Dundalk Democrat*, in CD/ALDK, I, 8.

14. ADL, 'Apostolici Labores, Limerick' [hereafter, ALL], III, 206.
O'Keefe was parish priest of Callan who, dismissed by Cullen, took
his case to the secular courts.

15. Magnier, 'Parochial Missions', p. 597.

16. CD/ALBE, I, sub anno 1854.

17. AGR, Pr.An., VII$_1$, Van der Aa to [?], 15 March 1861.

18. ALL, III, 117-8.

19. ADC, 'Apostolici Labores, Clapham [hereafter, ALC], I, 50.

20. ADL, 'Chronica Domestica, Limerick' [hereafter, CDL], II (1886), 152,
quoting the *Wexford People*.

21. ADP, MS 'Notes for "Historia Provinciae Hiberniae" ', p. 41.

22. CD/ALBE, IV, 53.

23. ADBE, 'Apostolici Labores, Bishop Eton' [hereafter, ALBE], II, 209.
24. AGR, Pr.An., V₃, 'Visitatio Extraordinaria, 1894', report of Fr Moynahan (Latin original).
25. APF, Rubrica, vol. 93 (1896), fo. 102/566r., *relatio* of the diocese of Hexham (Latin original).
26. At Montrose in 1881, the Irish navvies were said by Fr Hull to be 'full of faith, without works, paid well, drank hard, fought vigorously and were the dread of respectable Montrose, where they had not contributed to give a good name to Catholicism. It was lucky they had migrated before the mission or we should have surely had bloodshed', ALP, Ef2, account dated 6 March 1881.
27. LRO, RCLv, 'Relatio Status, 1882', p. 16 (Latin original). ALBE, I (1873), 217 described it as 'vitium quod est radix prolifica omnium peccatorum et maxime incuriae de officiis sacrae nostrae religionis'.
28. ALK, I (1870), 82 (Latin original).
29. ALBE, I (1873), 211 mentions that at St Joseph's, Liverpool boys and girls of fourteen began to drink and soon became habitual drunkards. For the full implications of drink, see B. Harrison, *Drink and the Victorians* (London, 1971).
30. APF, SC, Anglia, vol. 27 (1887-8), fo. 494r.
31. CD/ALBE, V, 32.
32. ADDk, 'Apostolici Labores, Dundalk' [hereafter, ALDk], I, 89.
33. CD/ALBE, III, 16.
34. ADB, Sampson, 'Reminiscences', I, 89.
35. J.D. Mansi, *Sacrorum Conciliorum nova et amplissima collectio*, 53 vols (Florence, Paris, Arnhem and Leipzig, 1759-1927), vol.49 (Arnhem and Leipzig, 1923), p. 302 records the response of the Archbishop of Westminster, together with the Bishops of Hexham, Southwark and Beverley, to a questionnaire on certain matters of ecclesiastical discipline put to them by Propaganda in 1867, in which they said that in England mixed marriages were daily increasing and that they could not be prohibited without more serious evils resulting.
36. ALK, I (1870), 110.
37. ALK, II (1876), 155 ascribed all the problems in Carlisle to registry-office weddings, including the eating of fish on Fridays. ALBE, I (1877), 353 concerned Rainford in Lancashire, where 'ingens haec animarum ruina in decursu 90 annorum est per matrimonia mixta et contracta coram ministello necnon per educatione parvulorum in scholis haereticis'.
38. CD/ALBE, II (1856), 31 records that the religious indifference of the Protestant partners had this result among the large number of mixed marriages in Chorley, Lancashire.
39. APF, Rubrica, vol. 24 (1893), fo. 102/101r. Even so, O'Reilly thought that children of such marriages, even if called 'Catholic', were so merely in name and that 'conjuges Catholici etiam, etiamsi ante Matrimonium fuerint fideles ac devoti, in permultis casibus post Matrimonium facile incidunt in incuriam quoad Fidem aut Sacramenta'.
40. APF, SC, Scozia, vol. 8 (1879-85), fo. 807v (French original).

41. Ibid., fo. 808r.
42. ALBE, I, 13.
43. ALK, III, 225-6.
44. ALC, I (1885), 16.
45. ALDk, I (1885), 74.
46. APF, Rubrica, vol. 93 (1896), fo. 102/402r.: The report continued, Causa principalis est quod Catholici tam pauci sunt (unus inter mille), et propter paupertatem hic illic operam diurnam quaerentes vagantur, ita ut neque eorum filii sacerdotem cognascant nec a sacerdote cognascantur aut afficiantur, et hinc, sicut plebs circumdantur, cogitant et agant. Pudet eos vestimentis communibus extra domum apparere diebus dominicis, et aliis diebus in vitia praesertim et impudicitiam corrunt, qui fidem subvertunt.
47. A point made by the Bishop of Hexham, ibid., fo. 102/565r.
48. LRO, RCLv, Census, 1893-4. Out of a total baptised Catholic population of 196,614, 'we have barely 91,521 souls who are leading practical Catholic lives' (p. 6).
49. See my article, 'Juvenile Holiness: Catholic Revivalism among Children in Victorian Britain', *Journal of Ecclesiastical History*, 35 (1984), 220-38.
50. J. Furniss, C.SS.R., *The Sunday School* (Dublin, n.d.), p. 297.
51. Livius, *Father Furniss and his Work for Children*, p. 52.
52. APF, SC, Anglia, vol. 27 (1887-8), fo. 494r., *relatio* of the diocese of Liverpool.
53. ALK, I (1890), 39.
54. ALBE, II, 248; cf. ALBE, I (1869), 49, which mentions the difficulty of getting boys to the mission at St Anne's, Ashton-under-Lyne, Lancashire.
55. ALBE, I (1874), 210 (Latin original).
56. ALBE, II, 312.
57. ALBE, III (1893), 27.
58. CD/ALDk, I, 66.
59. AGR, XLVII, G8, Harbison to Douglas, 16 January 1883.
60. As Bishop Brownrigg of Ossory remarked to Archibishop Croke of Cashel on 11 December 1890, 'Parnell has a magic sway over the farmers and all with Fenian and democratic tendencies', M. Tierney, 'Dr Croke, the Irish Bishops and the Parnell Crisis, 18 November 1890 — 21 April 1891', *Collectanea Hibernica*, 11 (1968), 111-48, p. 122.
61. ALL, III, 238.
62. This success was in spite of some secret society men from another parish urging the parishioners of Tulla to boycott the mission because of some remarks allegedly made against secret societies in a previous Redemptorist mission, ALL, III, 64-6.
63. ALL, III, 97. Even here, however, the execution of two allegedly innocent men caused much excitement and put the mission in jeopardy.
64. ALL, III, 100.
65. APF, SC, Irlanda, vol. 44 (1889-90), fo. 836r (Latin original).

66. APF, Rubrica, vol. 69 (1895), fo. 104/229v.
67. ALDk, I (1892), 278 (Latin original).
68. ALDk, I (1893), 310 records that some Parnellites, including the editor of the *Meath Reporter,* refused to attend the mission in Kells, Co. Meath because they were at political variance with the clergy.
69. ALDk, I, 396-7.
70. M. Tierney, *Croke of Cashel* (Dublin, 1976), pp. 91-4. In 1878 he wrote to Cullen that
    where there is or has been for some years a bad or foolish or lazy or unsympathetic priest, the Fenian element has been on the ascendant; whereas in every parish well-worked, having confraternities and everything else as it ought to be, the Fenian element is feeble and non-existent.
71. ALL, III (1882), 62 records this as the problem of the people in O'Callaghan's Mills, Co. Clare.
72. Fully discussed by W.J. Lowe, 'Lancashire Fenianism, 1864-71', *Transactions of the Historical Society of Lancashire and Cheshire,* 126 (1977), 156-85.
73. AGR, XLVII, B2, Coffin to Douglas, 31 October 1869.
74. AGR, XLVII, G8, Harbison to Douglas, 16 January 1883.
75. ALL, I, 76.
76. APF, SC, Anglia, vol. 29 (1891-2), fo. 583r., *relatio* of the diocese of Shrewsbury (Italian original). The bishop evidenced strikes and Irish nationalism as proof of this revolutionary spirit.
77. APF, SC, Scozia, vol. 8 (1879-85), fo. 745v. mentions this.
78. AGR, Pr.An., II$_4$, MacDonald to Mauron, 30 November 1886.
79. ALBE, II, 287.
80. ALK, III, 157.
81. ALC, I, 172.
82. ALDk, I (1887), 145 [emphases original]. The Church had been opposed to wakes as potential sources of immorality since the 1780s. Patrick Kennedy, *The Banks of the Boro* (Dublin, 1867), p. 56, wrote of 'young men who became hardened in vice by attending wakes and young women who lost character thereby'.
83. ALDk, I, 247.
84. ALBE, II (1881), 141 (Latin original).
85. AGR, XLVII, D1, Vaughan to Douglas, 4 April 1879.
86. ALK, I (1868), 26 and II, (1874), 79 at St Andrew's Dundee and St Patrick's, Edinburgh; among the 'sea-weed' people of Kilmaly, Co. Clare in 1882, ALDk, I, 61; at St Mary, St Patrick and St Alphonsus's, Middlesborough in 1886, ALBE, II, 254; and at Cardiff in 1896, ALC, I, 200.
87. ADB, 'Fr Sampson's Reminiscences', II, 156. The purpose was, in part, to counteract the relief offered by Protestants; as late as 1881, 'souperism' was said to have injured the spirit and faith of the people in Ballingarry, Co. Tipperary, ALL, III, 45.
88. At Tulla in 1886 this was as much as half-a-crown for a seat and a shilling for those who stood, ALL, III, 184. This was in defiance of a decree of the Plenary Synod of Maynooth, which forbade collections

during missions for anything beyond the missioners' expenses, *Acta et Decreta Synodi Plenariae Episcoporum Hiberniae habitae apud Maynutia, anno MDCCCLXXV* (Dublin, 1877), pp. 70-1. The collections were often to pay off the debt on the building, as at Ashton-under-Lyne in 1857, CD/ALBE, II, 94.

89. As at Clonmany, Co. Donegal in 1881, ALDk, I, 45. For earlier examples, see CD/ALBE, I, sub annis 1852, 1853 and 1855.

90. ALK, III (1883), 18.

91. ALL, III, 356.

92. ALL, III, 363. In 1889 the missioners from Kinnoull discovered a parish where 'nothing is looked after but money, and what brings in money', and they wondered that a spark of faith remained in a parish ruled by such a pastor, ALK, III, 146. On the effect of missions being turned into money transactions, see J. Magnier, 'Parochial Missions', p. 590.

93. CD/ALBE, V (1867), 92 and ALL, II, 232.

94. ALBE, I (1872), 176 and CDC, I, 119.

95. At Lurgan, Co. Armagh in 1888, the interfering priest refused to let the Redemptorists hear confessions, with the result that the parish was 'far from being cleared out when we left ... nothing like a complete mission had been given', ALDk, I, 162. Other examples of interference are to be found in CDC, I (1857), 55, where Canon Brown of Birkenhead took to himself the management of the mission; at CD/ALBE, II (1857), 120, where the priest at Clayton Green, Lancashire, refused to allow the erection of the mission cross or Stations or the children to receive first communion; and at ALBE, II, (1888) 190, where the priest at St Paul's, West Derby closed the mission after the first week on account of 'some trifling inconvenience which the presence of the Fathers in his house caused'.

96. *Directory of the Missions*, p. 31.

97. One of the complaints against Petcherine was his vehement attack on Protestants. Barberi urged similar caution in his 'Ricordi', p. 4.

98. G. Maxwell, *St Alphonsus Liguori and the Redemptorists: their Immoral and False Teachings exposed by Quotations from their Writings* (Dublin, 1859), pp. 4-5: 'It is well known that these men have laboured to gain vast influence over the minds of our fellow-subjects both in England and Ireland'. This tirade was sparked off by the sight of the large wooden mission crosses in Ireland. CD/ALL, I (1855), 22 mentions how embittered Protestants were at the sight of pious Catholics bowing down before these crosses, and CD/ALBE, II (1855), 4 mentions that at Kingstown the Protestants 'were exceedingly alarmed and embittered at our proceedings, particularly at seeing so great a crowd of men and women lying down before the Cross'.

99. CD/ALL, I, 71.

100. CD/ALL, I, 86: 'The Protestant ministers, fearful of losing some of their flock, and perhaps a portion of the monies sent from England to all those who talk most and loudest against Popery and *for* the conversion of Ireland, made the strongest opposition'.

101. CD/ALBE, III, 214-5 & 223.

102. ADP, 'Life of Fr Harbison', p. 50.

103. CD/ALBE, III, 223 and ALP, Gibson, 'Reminiscences', p. 92.
104. ALL, II, 177; cf. ALK, II, 117 for a similar incident at Kinning Park, Glasgow in 1875.
105. ALL, III, 85.
106. ALK, I, 27 and ADC, E5, Sampson to MacDonald, 16 March 1885. Even so, sixty Protestants were reportedly converted in Belfast.
107. ADP, 'Diary of Fr Somers', p. 11.
108. ALP, ADT, 'Apostolici Labores, Teignmouth' [hereafter, ALT], p. 16 records that the large number of Methodists who attended a mission in Camborne, Cornwall in 1880 were led 'magis curiocitate quam desiderio veritatem Catholicam adiscendi', and there were no conversions. ALBE, II, 303 gives a similar incident at Poclington in Yorkshire in 1889.
109. CD/ALL, I, 60.
110. *Tablet,* 28 September 1872, p. 402.
111. *Tablet,* 23 February 1889, p. 313.
112. *Montrose, Arbroath and Brechin Review,* 25 January 1881.
113. ALK, I, 32. This was at Oakely, near Dunfermline, and nearly four hundred attended.
114. ALP, Ea24, documents from various houses addressed to Fr Vaughan regarding the 'Formula Systematis S.P.N. Alphonsi'.
115. AGR, Pr.An., VII, Van der Stickele to [?], 25 March 1859. A further extract from an anonymous letter informed the Roman authorities that 'il Parrocco [di North Shields] mi ha scritto doppo, che tutti questi monstrano una perseverenza ammirable'.
116. All tables are compiled from ALP, 'Elenchi Laborum Apostolorum'.
117. ALL, II (1874), 144 mentions the difficulty of gaining converts in the North.
118. The anonymous letter (note 115) mentioned that the children-converts were 'in gran parte figli di parenti che avevano contratto matrimoni misti e che non erano affatto battezatti, ovvero erano stati battizati nella chiesa protestante'.
119. ALK, II (1877), 201 records that many converts in Inverness, for example, had 'returned to their vomit' and were now apostates or semi-apostates.
120. *Fifty Years at Mount St Alphsonsus, Limerick,* p. 35.
121. *A Half Century's Jubilee in St Mary's, Clapham* (Southwark, 1899), p. 28.

Chapter 8

1. *Directory of the Missions,* p. 5.
2. See above, p. 126 for an example of the handbill. J. Magnier, 'Parochial Missions', p. 590 suggested that mention should be made of the mission from the pulpit for five or six weeks beforehand, and that the parish should be thoroughly visited.
3. *Tablet,* 15 April 1876, p. 500.
4. CD/ALBE, III (1858), 5.
5. ALBE, IV, 185. Even here, there could be problems; ALK, II (1878), 253 records that at St Godric's, Durham non-parishioners could obtain

tickets from the priest only on payment of a charge, which kept many of them away.

6. ALBE, II (1880), 132 (Latin original). ALK, II, 165 & 247 record that lack of preparation and publicity were destructive factors at Portsoy, Banffshire in 1876 and at St Mary's, Glasgow in 1878.

7. ADB, 'Fr Sampson's Reminiscences', II, 48.

8. *Tablet*, 26 June 1858, p. 404 records of the mission in Carndonagh that 'the name and prestige of the good Fathers had long preceded them. Their arrival was anxiously expected for months'.

9. See above, p. 19. On the basis of his experience, Walworth advised against such activity. Barberi dropped the Passionist practice of *svegliarini* in England because he saw visiting as a more practical means of bringing people to the mission, Father Herbert, *The Preachers of the Passion* (London, 1924), p. 54.

10. CD/ALBE, IV (1865), 199, concerning St Patrick's, Bradford.

11. ALP, Gibson, 'Reminiscences', p. 208.

12. ALDk, I (1893), 308 uses such language in relation to St Peter's, Belfast. ALK, II, 79 mentions the missioners making specific visits to the young women who sold fish in the city, whom the parish priest of St Patrick's, Edinburgh despaired of attracting to the mission in 1874.

13. CD/ALBE, III, 142, for instance, mentions that at Gateshead in December 1859, efforts were made to visit all the parishioners, who 'owing to their poverty or indifference seemed not enthusiastic with the mission'.

14. ALBE, III, 16.

15. As at Lancaster in 1865, CD/ALBE, IV, 178. *Tablet*, 31 March 1877, p. 403 mentions house-to-house visitation at a mission in St Mary and St Michael, Commercial Road, East London as resulting in many 'stragglers who had been indifferent to their religious duties' being brought 'back to the true fold'.

16. As at Keith, Banffshire in July 1894, where the missioners were prevented from visiting by the parish priest, ALK, III, 290.

17. AGR, Pr.An., V_3, 'Visitatio Extraordinaria, 1894'. The complainant called visiting 'the hardest work of the Mission and the most distracting', and he added that the need to be constantly changing out of the habit into trousers was a temptation not to do it!

18. ALBE, III, 75.

19. *Fifty Years at Mount St Alphonsus, Limerick*, p. 29.

20. *Tablet*, 26 June 1858, p. 403.

21. *Cork Examiner*, 2 August 1878.

22. ALL, III, 60.

23. Such stories occur frequently in the mission chronicles; for example, ALL, II (1870), 33 describes a wall falling on top of, and killing, a woman who refused to attend and (1872), 81, the death of a young drunkard who rejected the mission. The mission preacher could play heavily on such local incidents.

24. ALL, III, 60.

25. ALL, III, 120.

26. AGR, XLVII, D1, Vaughan to Douglas, February 1868, describing a

mission in Perth.
27. ALL, III, 280.
28. In 1875, an American Redemptorist, J.C. Wissell, produced a series of sermon outlines for missions, renewals and retreats, later expanded into three volumes. Although Wissell's work was undoubtedly read and was influential in the English Province, and gives the best available evidence of the course, intention and subject-matter of nineteenth-century Redemptorist missions, I have confined myself to surviving material from members of the English Province.
29. AGR, Pr.An., I1d, Prost to Douglas, 18 April 1853, was insistent that the rosary devotion was to be 'a meditation, a prayer and no sermon', and to last no more than twenty-five minutes.
30. *Directory of the Missions,* p. 19.
31. ALP, Ba147.8, Ulrich to MacDonald, 27 February 1883.
32. The 1883 order from Rome mentioned that nightly Benediction was in contravention of certain diocesan synodical decrees. If Benediction of the Blessed Sacrament could not be given, one using a crucifix was substituted.
33. ADBE, D[unnumbered], monition of Coffin, 1865.
34. ALP, Ea24, remarks of the Second Consultor at Teignmouth on the 'Formula Systematis S.P.N. Alphonsi'.
35. ALK, I, 44.
36. ADDk, MS 'Instruction Notes' of [? Fr Cyril Ryder], 'Invitation to the Mission', p. 2.
37. The term is used by J. Kent, *Holding the Fort: Studies in Victorian Revivalism* (London, 1978), p. 243.
38. *Tablet,* 26 June 1858, p. 403.
39. CD/ALBE, III, 130.
40. *Tablet,* 3 February 1855, p. 68.
41. J.P. Dolan, *Catholic Revivalism: The American Experience, 1830-1900* (Notre Dame, 1978), pp. xviii & 112.
42. There are, of course, many other factors to consider, which cannot be pursued here. The literature on Protestant revivalism (see bibliography entries under Carwardine, Colton, Kent, McLoughlin and Orr) shows that while they helped to form and perpetuate a strong Evangelical element in popular American religion, in England, in spite of the intensity of periodic campaigns, their success was limited and increasingly appealed to the lower middle classes.
43. ALP, MS sermon (anon.), 'Opening of the Mission'.
44. Ibid.
45. ALP, MS sermon preached in St Joseph's, West Hartlepool, Lent 1891 on 'The Great Dignity of Our Souls', p. 4.
46. Redemptorist Fathers, Dublin, Domestic Archives [hereafter, ADD], MS sermons of Fr Frohn, 'On the End of Man', p. 89.
47. Ibid., p. 84.
48. CDC, I, 94.
49. ADB, 'Fr Sampson's Reminiscences', II, 173.
50. ALP, Ef2, account dated 6 March 1881.
51. *Tablet,* 11 April 1857, p. 228.

52. V. Petcherine, 'Mortal Sin', a sermon preached in St George's, Southwark in 1848, published in E. Robillard and F. Milanta, *The Catholic Pulpit* (London, 1849), pp. 210-17 at p. 212.
53. Ibid., p. 214.
54. Ibid., pp. 215-6.
55. ALP, Gibson, 'Reminiscences', p. 72.
56. ALP, MS sermon (anon.), 'Mortal Sin'.
57. Hosp, 'First Redemptorist Missions in Ireland', p. 481 tells how, after Fr Bernard's sermon on this theme at Cork in 1854, the bishop, priest and all the people 'broke out into loud sobs'.
58. *A Half Century's Jubilee in St Mary's, Clapham*, pp. 32-3.
59. ADD, Frohn, 'On Eternity', pp. 60-1.
60. ALP, MS sermon (anon.), 'Death'.
61. ADD, MS sermons of Fr Urbany, 'General Judgment'. p. 458.
62. ADD, Frohn, 'On Eternity', p. 68.
63. ALP, 'Death'.
64. ADC, D25, *A Printed Account of the Mission in the S. Parish, Cork 7-30 October 1854* (Cork, 1854), pp. 4-5. CD/ALL, I, 13 records that at Athenry, Co. Galway in the same year, the people 'remained with their mouths wide-open, evidently not understanding what was going on'.
65. ADD, Urbany, 'On Delay of Conversion', p. 157.
66. ALP, MS sermon (anon.), 'Dangerous Occasions of Sin'.
67. ALP, MS sermon (anon.), 'The Great Social Evil of the Day — Drunkenness'.
68. ALP, 'Dangerous Occasions of Sin'.
69. ADD, Frohn, 'Occasions of Sin', p. 11.
70. Ibid., p. 14.
71. ALP, MS sermon preached in St Joseph's, West Hartlepool on 'The Terrors of Hell', p. 24.
72. Ibid., p. 25.
73. ALP, MS sermon (anon.), 'Hell':
    Will you sinners go on living for your bodies when you believe in Hell? Will you not return and do penance? Do not put off conversion — you may die any day and be cast into Hell, into that lake of fire. This is, perhaps, the last call — Repent — Confess. Do you think that Jesus Christ, who died for your salvation — who had waited so long — who now asks you - will reject you if you turn to Him? Oh! the Sacred Heart yearns for you.
74. *Codex*, p. 69.
75. ADD, Frohn, 'The Blessed Virgin Mary, Mother of God', p. 121.
76. Ibid., p. 121.
77. ALP, MS sermon preached in St Joseph's, West Hartlepool on 'The Blessed Virgin Mary', p. 30.
78. ADC, D25, *A Printed Account*, p. 5.
79. ALP, MS sermon (anon.), 'Necessity of Prayer'.
80. ALP, MS sermon preached in St Joseph's, West Hartlepool on 'Prayer'. pp. 21-2.
81. St Alphonsus, 'Exercises of the Mission', in *The Complete Works of St*

Alphonsus Maria de Liguori, Centenary Edition, translated and edited
by E. Grimm, C.SS.R., 24 vols (New York, Cincinnati, Chicago,
1886-96), vol. XV, *Preaching of God's Word* (1890), p. 236.
82. J. Furniss, *Almighty God* (Dublin, n.d.), p. 24.
83. ALK, I, 40.
84. Livius, *Father Furniss and his Work for Children,* p. 36.
85. ALP, MS sermon of Fr Hall, 'Perseverance'.
86. *Tablet,* 27 March 1858, p. 195 reported of Coffin's farewell sermon at
St Anne's Spitalfields, East London that
the eloquence and animation, with which he entreated the
congregation to endeavour to preserve the fruits of the mission,
by a life of perseverance, by their punctual attendance at church,
and the practice of their religious duties ... was affecting in the
extreme, and will be long remembered by all who had the
happiness of hearing him.
87. ALP, Buggenoms MS, p. 54.
88. ALL, Miscellaneous Papers, 'Remembrance of the Mission preached
by the Redemptorist Fathers at St Mary's Cathedral, Kilkenny, Lent
1893'; cf. *Directory of the Missions,* p. 45.
89. ALP, Cb23, circular letter of Coffin, 1 March 1867.
90. ADDk, MS 'Instruction Notes of [? Fr Cyril Ryder], 'Grace', p. 9.
91. Ibid., 'On Temptation and the Daily Acts', pp. 126-7.
92. Originally compiled by St Clement Hofbauer and translated from
German into English by Fr de Buggenoms, *The Mission Book* was
published in Dublin in 1855. Second and third editions appeared in
1857 and 1879, and a fourth edition, revised by Fr Krebs, in 1891.
93. Advertisement in the *Tablet,* 22 February 1856, p. 113.
94. *The Mission Book,* second edition (Dublin, 1857), p. 8.
95. Ibid., p. 512.
96. Ibid., p. 390.
97. C.A. Walworth, 'Reminiscences of a Catholic Crisis in England Fifty
Years Ago', p. 510. Cf. Magnier, 'Parochial Missions', p. 587: 'What
a missionary sows from the pulpit, he should reap in the confessional
... the action of the confessor is to be a confirmation of the teaching
of the preacher'.
98. *Codex,* p. 500: 'Quoniam per confessionem homines cum Deo in
gratiam redeunt, munus illas excipiendi in Missione primarium sit
ac praecipium, necesse est'.
99. *Directory of the Missions,* p. 6. Cf. St Alphonsus, quoted in Tannoia's
Life, II, 163: 'The preacher sows but the confessor gathers the harvest.
The confessional is the touchstone of the true labourer; he who loves
not the confessional, loves not souls, who receive there the application
of the blood of Jesus Christ, and the merits of his grace'.
100. CD/ALL, I, 76 comments upon the insistence of the Redemptorists
that they should hear only the confessions of the parishioners: 'No
doubt the Mission loses a part of its exterior *éclat* or glories, but the
sinners of the parish are *all* heard, which would be otherwise
impossible'.
101. ALP, Lubienski, 'Mémoires', p. 118 mentions that Coffin is supposed

268

to have possessed all these qualities.
102. ALDk, I, 10.
103. ALDk, II, 137 & III, 7.
104. ALP, Gibson, 'Reminiscences', p. 278.
105. CD/ALBE, II, 103.
106. ALP, Gibson, 'Reminiscences', p. 95.
107. *Codex*, p. 5 says that it should be after four or five months and that its purpose was 'fructus Missionis jam factae stabiliendi'.
108. AGR, Pr.An., V$_3$, 'Visitatio Extraordinaria, 1894'. ALL, II (1871), 67 mentions that the diocesan statutes of Ferns required missions every five years, which priests felt obviated the need for a renewal.
109. CD/ALBE, I, sub anno 1852, thus concludes the report of a mission in Derry with the words, 'May Almighty God preserve in [the people] the blessings granted, and may a second retreat soon confirm and complete the first, which left much unfinished'.
110. J. Magnier, C.SS.R., 'After a Mission', *Irish Ecclesiastical Record*, Third Series, 16 (1895), 894-904, p. 895. Cf. ALK, II (1873), 39, quoting a report from the *Ulster Examiner:*
    They have come [to Belfast], as is customary with the Order, to witness the results of their former exertions, to raise those who have fallen into the slough of indifference, and to strengthen the resolve of others who have preserved the effects of their teaching.
111. Magnier, 'After a Mission', p. 896.
112. CD/ALDk, I (1882), 109.
113. *Fifty Years at Mount St Alphonsus, Limerick*, p. 40. Cf. the *Tablet*, 31 January 1863, p. 71: 'It appears, as a rule, that the ''Renewals'' are found to be more fruitful in the conversion of sinners and in the reception of converts than the missions themselves'.
114. CDC, I, 99.
115. CD/ALL, I, 78.
116. ALL, II, 105. The chronicler thought that 'Ribbonismus feri tritus est, et quod ebrietati magna impedimenta posita sint'.
117. CD/ALBE, III, 310. Cf. ALK, III (1891), 214: 'The renewal gave us good hope that the good have been confirmed and the fallen have been raised up'.
118. CD/ALL, I, 69-70. The parish priest wrote three months later that the renewal had effected 'more visible, permanent good' than any other such work by religious.
119. ALK, II, 326.

Chapter 9

1. *A Half Century's Jubilee in St Mary's, Clapham*, p. 42.
2. ADB, 'Fr Sampson's Reminiscences', II, 65.
3. St Alphonsus, 'Letter to a Bishop', *Preaching of God's Word*, p. 85.
4. ALDk, I, 296-7.
5. ALP, Ba151.45.
6. *Tablet*, 11 April 1857, p. 227.
7. CDC, I, 102.

8. CDC, I, 103.
9. *Catholic Times*, 22 January 1875.
10. Ibid., 25 March 1875.
11. ALC, I, 159.
12. ALL, II, 152. Copy of letter, dated 9 November 1874.
13. *Tablet*, 21 June 1856.
14. ALK, II (1876), 157.
15. CD/ALBE, III, 276.
16. ALDk, I, 141.
17. ALK, I, 60 & 86. At the first mission in Inverness in 1875 (p. 123), many travelled four or five miles, and some as many as sixteen miles, to attend.
18. *Tablet*, 17 March 1860, p. 166.
19. *Tablet*, 13 December 1856, p. 789.
20. AGR, XLVII, D1, Vaughan to Douglas, 20 July 1867.
21. CD/ALDk, I, 100.
22. ALK, III (1889), 151-2.
23. CD/ALL, I, 276.
24. *Tablet*, 15 November 1879, p. 628.
25. ALDk, I, 311.
26. CD/ALDk, I, 17-8.
27. AGR, XLVII, D1, Vaughan to Douglas, 7 December 1871.
28. Christianne Marcilhacy, *Le Diocèse d'Orléans sous l'épiscopat de Mgr Dupanloup* (Paris, 1962), especially chapter 8, has shown that Easter communions rose after the missions but soon slumped again in the following years between missions. Richard Carwardine, *Transatlantic Revivalism: Popular Evangelicalism in Britain and America, 1790-1865* (Westport and London, 1978), notes the effects of James Caughey's revivalist campaign among Wesleyan Methodists in seven English towns and cities between 1842 and 1846, together with the increase in Nonconformist congregations in the Lancashire towns and the west of Scotland as a result of the 1859 campaign, but his graphs (pp. 114 & 194-5) show that in both cases increased growth was not sustained beyond a year or so.
29. *Freeman's Journal*, 28 December 1865.
30. C.A. Walworth, 'A Catholic Crisis in England Fifty Years Ago', p. 62.
31. *Two Hundred Years with the Redemptorists*, p. 107.
32. *Tablet*, 19 April 1861, pp. 245-6.
33. AGR, XLVII, A4, Lans to Douglas, 26 May 1857.
34. *Tablet*, 7 February 1863, p. 92.
35. CD/ALL, I, sub anno 1863; cf. above, p. 118, for another example from Kilkenny.
36. ALK, III (1892), 246: 'The whole fruit of the mission [at Campbeltown, Argyllshire] was the revival of faith in the whole district, and the hunger they showed to hear the Word of God and put it into practice'.
37. ALL, III, 267.
38. *Tablet*, 25 February 1859, p. 134.
39. *Tablet*, 27 March 1858, p. 195, report of a Redemptorist mission in St Anne's, Spitalfields, London.

40. ALC, I, 17. The *Tablet,* 17 March 1860, p. 166, said that the sermons 'nerved every heart, brought tears to every eye, and did [their] work of reclaiming many a prodigal child'.
41. CD/ALBE, III, 7 & 44.
42. ALP, ALT, p. 29.
43. ALC, I, inset between pp. 144-5; cf. ALBE, I (1868), 15, where a mission brought up three hundred of the 450 Catholics who had failed to make their Easter duty.
44. CDC, I, 92.
45. ALBE, I, 110.
46. ALK, III, 326.
47. CD/ALBE, III, 124, 140 & 188.
48. Quoted in CDC, III, sub anno 1894.
49. ADC, D25, *A Printed Account,* p. 6 said that it was impossible to know how many thousands had been converted from long habits of sin and total neglect of their religious duties, how many families had been restored to peace and domestic union, how many enemies had been set at rest, and how many were enlightened more perfectly in the way of salvation and stimulated to a more perfect Christian life: 'Not until the last day will it be known how blessed, how merciful were the fruits of the glorious and splendid mission'.
50. *Westminster Gazette,* 4 October 1873. The *Tablet,* 1 March 1862, p. 133 commented that as a result of the mission in St Patrick's, Liverpool

    one and all have reason to rejoice, but especially the Irish portion of St Patrick's congregation have reason to bless the Providence of God which, even in a wilderness of sin and impiety and irreligion, has checked the heart of the exile, and roused it from the effect of contamination to the warmth of Faith and the practice of its Divine Religion.
51. *Tablet,* 31 March 1877, p. 403, for example, records that the mission doubled the number of confirmands at Commercial Road, East London.
52. CD/ALBE, II, 64 records five hundred at Burnley in July 1859, when there were seven hundred confirmations; at St Patrick's, Liverpool in 1862, 1,400 boys and girls made their first communion, ibid., III, 123.
53. CD/ALBE, I, sub anno 1854.
54. Livius, *Father Furniss and his Work for Children,* pp. 170 & 120 mentions that one priest claimed a permanent sevenfold increase in Mass attendance in some parishes following Furniss's missions, and the parish priest of Barton-on-Irwell, where Furniss gave two missions in 1857 and 1859, who considered them

    eminently successful, not only in their effect upon the children, but also upon the adult parishioners. Their influence was felt for five years afterwards; and, for the two years on each occasion following the mission, the attendance at church and the frequentation of the sacraments was such as was never known before or since.
55. J. Furniss, *The Sunday School,* p. 282.
56. The children's missions often helped the adult missions that followed,

as at St Patrick's, Wigan in 1886, ALBE, II, 247. The sight of the children's communion was said to move many people, like the eighty-year-old man in Mullingar in 1867, who was prompted to make his own first communion, CD/ALL, I, 277.

57. *Tablet*, 29 September 1883, p. 512 and 22 December 1888, p. 1000, for example.
58. ALP, CEP, II, 92.
59. ALDk, I, loose notes, sub anno 1896.
60. CD/ALL, I, 81 records that at Ballybunion, Co. Kerry in 1860 'very plain instructions' were given and 'the principal mysteries of the faith, the Apostles' Creed and the essentials of the sacraments were repeated every day and frequently in the day'.
61. ALP, Ef2, account dated 6 March 1881.
62. *Tablet*, 10 November 1883, p. 752 and 31 March 1877, p. 43, referring to South Bank, Middlesborough and Commercial Road respectively.
63. CDC, I, 85.
64. ALK, III, 375, for example, records that sixty children were rescued from Protestant schools at St Thomas, Port Clarence-on-Tees in 1881.
65. ALK, III, 35; cf. CD/ALBE, IV, 126, where 'one of the many happy events' of a mission in St Mary's, Manchester in 1864 was 'the rescuing of numbers of children from heretical and proselytising day schools'.
66. ALK, III, 76.
67. ALL, II, 15-6 (Latin original).
68. CD/ALL I, 81.
69. ALL, II, 175.
70. CD/ALBE, III, 61 & 81. In the end, even the leaders were persuaded to relinquish membership and return to the Church.
71. CDC, I, 74.
72. CD/ALDk, I, 83 (Latin original).
73. If the society continued to exist, there was always the fear that the men would return. ALP, Gibson, 'Reminiscences', p. 77 mentions the relapse of several men in Sunderland in 1859.
74. *Tablet*, 17 March 1860, p. 166. A sick and burial club was started forthwith with the requisitioned funds.
75. ALC, I, 1.
76. ALP, CEP, II, 61; CD/ALL, I, 145; AGR, XLVII, 13, Plunkett to Douglas, 14 March 1864. The bishop petulantly refused to attend the mission to administer confirmation.
77. AGR, XLVII, G7, Edward O'Donnell to Douglas, 27 April 1875.
78. ALP, CEP, II, 56 and CD/ALL, I, 123. The factions had supposedly gained their names over a disagreement about the age of a bull.
79. *Battersby's (Irish) Catholic Directory* (Dublin, 1864), p. 214; *Tablet*, 6 December 1862; *Le Monde*, 13 November & 14 December 1862.
80. ALL, III (1883), 106. CD/ALDk, I, 36-7 describes how, at Lorrha, Co. Tipperary in 1878, the heads of the warring families were brought together by the missioners in the sacristy of the church and the breach healed.
81. CD/ALBE, II, 149.
82. ALDk, I, 64-6.

83. CDC, I, 93.
84. ALK, III, 125.
85. CD/ALDk, I, 60.
86. ALK, III, 94.
87. ALL, II, 3 and ADC, E3b, letter dated 25 March 1868.
88. ALL, II, 6 & 46.
89. Examples include CD/ALL, I, 305 and the *Limerick Reporter*, 28 January 1868, concerning a great mission in the Redemptorist church in Limerick; CD/ALBE, III, 271, concerning a mission in Blackhall, near Newcastle in 1861; *Limerick Reporter*, 17 October 1865, concerning a mission in Killadysert, Co. Clare.
90. CD/ALBE, IV, 75 and CDC, I, 161.
91. CD/ALL, I, 20 and ALL, II, 3 record the conversion of prostitutes.
92. *The Catholic Directory of Ireland* (Dublin, 1866), p. 353 records that at a Redemptorist mission the previous year in the Pro-Cathedral in Dublin, 'nearly £800 was received as restitution money and forwarded to the parties from whom it had been stolen'.
93. Quoted in *Fifty Years at Mount St Alphonsus, Limerick*, p. 38.
94. CD/ALDk, I, 54.
95. CDC, I, 113 and ALBE, III, 95.
96. ALBE, I, 203 and ALK, II, 79.
97. CD/ALBE, IV, 79-80 uses these terms about a mission in Oldham in 1863.
98. ADC, E3b, letter dated 25 March 1868.
99. ALBE, II, 231-2.
100. Letter dated 13 April 1863, quoted in CD/ALL, I, 128. A priest wrote further that Mass attendance had increased three-fold and that it was impossible to leave the confessionals before 10 o'clock at night (p. 129).
101. ALK, I, 34.
102. ALK, II, 226.
103. CD/ALL, I, 74-5.
104. *Tablet*, 1 March 1862, p. 133, report of a mission in St Patrick's, Liverpool. The *Limerick Reporter*, 17 January 1868, believed that a reformation had been effected in that town as a result of the recent mission.
105. Letter dated 11 April 1865, quoted in CD/ALL, I, 174.
106. J. Magnier, 'After a Mission', p. 879.
107. ALK, III, 71.
108. By 1893, for example, there were 193 affiliated branches of the Archconfraternity of the Holy Family in England and 123 in Ireland. Full details, history and description in M. de Meulemeester, C.SS.R., *L'Archiconfrérie de la Sainte-Famille: Une page d'histoire religieuse contemporaire, 1847-1947* (Louvain, 1946). AGR, Pr.An., V_3, mentions that the

> Holy Family is best for large places with active, zealous priests. In other places and cases it decays and dies. Our Lady of Perpetual Succour for quiet, country parishes, especially as a devotion for all, and a confraternity for women, but it often does well even for men. In small towns and country villages the Association of the Sacred Heart.

109. ALBE, III (1895), 69. The mission reports often mention that the Redemptorists looked to the confraternities for the fruits of the missions to be sustained.

110. J. Cantwell, 'Confraternities: their object and use', *Irish Ecclesiastical Record*, Third Series, 3 (1882), 560-3, p. 561.

111. J.A. Cleary, C.SS.R., *Confraternity Work and its Problems* (Dublin, 1932), p. 12. Cleary's work was based on the notes of Fr Bannon, C.SS.R., Director of the Confraternity of the Holy Family in Limerick from 1892 to 1898.

112. Ibid., p. 15.

113. M. Geoghegan, C.SS.R., 'Our Confraternities: How are they to be worked effectively?', *Irish Ecclesiastical Record*, Third Series, 14 (1893), 235-55, p. 253. Cf. Magnier, 'After a Mission', p. 904: 'A fervent confraternity is a perpetual preacher. Its members, by their good example, are a living exhortation'.

114. H.E. Manning, *An Address delivered on the occasion of the Consecration of the first members of the Confraternity of the Holy Family, recently erected, in the Church of St John, Duncan Terrace, Islington* (London, 1875), pp. 7, 11 & 14.

115. J.W. O'Byrne, C.SS.R., *History of the Wexford Men's Confraternity of the Holy Family* (Wexford, 1910). p. 19. In terms of sanctification and the promotion of holy living, confraternities were comparable with Methodist class meetings; encouragement and exhortation between meetings, the group-pressure to conform, the self-regulation and expulsion as a final threat, were important in both organisations. Confraternities, however, unlike class meetings, provided no scope for organised, inquisitorial lay discipline or teaching, both of which functions belonged solely to the priest, and which were factors leading to the eventual decline of the class system: see Robert Currie, *Methodism Divided: A Study of the Sociology of Ecumenicalism* (London, 1968), pp. 125-30.

116. *Manual of the Archconfraternity of the Holy Family of Jesus, Mary and Joseph* (London, 1854), p. 10.

117. APF, SC, Irlanda, vol. 38 (1878-80), fo. 932r.; Rubrica, vol. 24 (1893), fo. 103/203v.; Rubrica, vol. 93 (1896), fo. 102/402r.

118. AGR, XLVII, G8, Harbison to Douglas, 19 January 1874.

119. ALBE, III, 1.

120. ADC, E3a, letter dated 22 September 1864.

121. ALK, III (1889), 147.

122. ALK, III, 220.

123. O'Byrne, *History of the Wexford Men's Confraternity*, pp. 45-6.

124. CD/ALL, I, 79.

125. ALK, III, 53.

126. ALL, II (1878) 229.

127. *Wexford People*, 6 April 1878.

Chapter 10

1. CD/ALDk, I, 98-9.
2. ALL, II (1872), 80 mentions this as a debilitating factor at St Paul's, Arran Quay, Dublin, where the mission was only 'successus temporarius'.
3. ALBE, II, 256.
4. ALC, I (1898), 233.
5. ALDk, I (1885), 63.
6. AGR, XLVII, D1, Vaughan to Douglas, 9 October 1878.
7. ALBE, III, 59.
8. ADC, C25, instruction of Coffin, 26 March 1866.
9. ALDk, I, 321.
10. ALL, III (1888), 216, ALC, I, 250 records of Gravesend in 1899 that 'there is little hope of good remaining as long as the Pastor continues his work in a lifeless manner'. The missioners at St Cuthbert's, Durham in 1886 found that the priests had almost given up the parish; they were 'too refined and quiet for work among rough folk', ALK, III, 95.
11. ALK, III, 44-5.
12. Ibid., 69.
13. ALK, II, 320.
14. ALK, III, 259-60.
15. Ibid., 417-9.
16. ALBE, I, 151.
17. ALBE, II (1887), 264, for instance, records that at Preston the poor fortunes of the confraternity were caused by the want of good prefects.
18. ALBE, I (1870), 81.
19. ALBE, I, 319.
20. ALBE, II (1897), 122.
21. ALBE, II, 240.
22. Ibid., 374.
23. ALDk, I, 354.
24. ALP, CEP, II (1866), 85. For the text of a confraternity retreat, see T.E. Bridgett, C.SS.R., *A Retreat for Men* (Dublin, 1882).
25. ALDk, I, 8 records that the desire of both men and women to attend the annual retreat to the Sodalities of Temperance in a parish in 1883 induced them to take the pledge some weeks before in order to qualify for attendance at the retreat.
26. ALL, III (1882), 84, concerning Gort, Co. Galway.
27. O'Byrne, *History of the Wexford Men's Confraternity*, p. 18.
28. ALDk, I, 16. A year later (p. 43), it was recorded that the confraternity 'exercises a wonderful influence in preserving the spiritual life of a great number who were faithful to the Rules'.
29. ALDk, I, 92.
30. Ibid., 328.
31. ALDk, I (1886), 102; cf. report on Ballinasloe, Co. Galway (p. 120), where

> justice seems never to have been done to this Branch. The director did not really understand the working of it, and the Retreats that

were given each year partook of the nature of a small mission (the members not sitting in their sections, and no preference being given to them in any way), than retreats to the Holy Family.

32. ALL, II, 186.
33. ALDk, I, 4-5.
34. Ibid., 258.
35. Ibid., 291.
36. ALL, III, 394.
37. ALDk, I, 268.
38. AGR, Pr.An., III$_5$, Bennett to Mauron, 11 March 1890.
39. ALC, I (1893), 144.
40. ALDk, I, 150.
41. ALDk, I (1888), 172-3.
42. Ibid., 324.
43. ALL, III, 290.
44. ALK, III (1899), 400.
45. See above, p. 115.
46. ALDk, I (1896), 378.
47. ALP, MS 'Additional Notes on the Missions in the English Province, written by the Visitor of 1894'.
48. ALP, Ea24, response of the Second Consultor at Teignmouth to the 'Formula Systematis S.P.N. Alphonsi'.
49. ALK, II, 364. At the renewal, the missioners found 'omnia in melius mutata erant', and that those who had attended the mission exercises had persevered in their good resolutions (p. 394).
50. ALBE, I, 125; cf. ALK, III (1884), 43, which blandly states that the people of Wick did not want the mission.
51. ALC, I (1885), 9; (1895), 178; (1896) 197 and ALL, II (1868), 10; III (1895), 240.
52. ALC, I, 122.
53. ALBE, II, (1891), 348. This was at the Sacred Heart, Leicester, where only 180 of these 450 'milk and water' Catholics attended.
54. ALL, III, 199.
55. ALC, I, 218.
56. CD/ALBE, IV (1863), 90.
57. CD/ALBE, II (1857), 149.
58. CD/ALBE, III, 53-4.
59. ALBE, II, 254.
60. ALC, I, 85.
61. ADC, C18, Directions on Parish Visitation, 4 November 1866: unbaptized children abound on all sides; numbers have been found who did not know where the church was; in a word, there is an amount of spiritual desolation equal to that which we find in the most populous towns where we give missions.
62. J.A. Lesourd, *Sociologie du Catholicisme Anglais, 1767-1851* (Nancy, 1981), p. 153. He argues that the 1885 figures reflect the conditions in England in the years 1840-1855, when immigration caught the Church unawares, and that it never fully recovered. More detailed analysis is available in his six-volume doctoral thesis, 'Les Catholiques

dans la Société anglaise, 1765-1865' (University of Strasbourg, 1974).

63. G. Connolly, 'Irish and Catholic: Myth or Reality? Another sort of Irish and the Renewal of the Clerical Profession among Catholics in England, 1791-1918', in Swift, R. and Gilley, S.W. (editors), *The Irish in the Victorian City* (London, 1985), pp. 225-54, at p. 231.
64. ALK, III (1883), 19.
65. Ibid., 24; cf. CD/ALBE, V (1866), 41 for an early example, where the priests of SS Peter and Paul, Wolverhampton, 'wondered that the Fathers should expect more good than was actually done'.
66. ALC, I, 249.
67. Ibid., 102; at Bow, East London in the same year, 'many had almost or entirely lost their faith' (p. 98).
68. ALBE, III, 380.
69. ALC, I, 46.
70. Ibid., 73.
71. Ibid., 5.
72. Figures gleaned from ALP, *Elenchi Laborum Apostolorum*; see above, p. 185.
73. See bibliography entries under Britten, C.G., Curry, Milvart and Tynan, who calculated that a million persons had been lost to the Church in England over the previous fifty years.
74. ALP, Eb12, printed letter of the Bishop of Salford to the Provincials of religious orders, 24 January 1884. The number of men, in particular, who 'have lost the habit of hearing Mass on Sunday must be counted in thousands' (p. 2).
75. ALP, Eb12, printed letter of the Bishop of Salford to the Provincials of religious orders, 26 April 1884, p. 3. 61,556 fulfilled the paschal precept in Manchester and Salford, 54,199 of them during the mission. The census of that year showed a Mass attendance of 56,337. In the diocese as a whole, the figure was 109,583 out of an estimated Catholic population on 212,000, APF, SC (Anglia), vol. 26 (1885-6), fo. 756 r. & v.
76. ALBE, II, 68.
77. ALK, III, 156.
78. ALC, I, 143.
79. *Tablet*, 19 April 1862, p. 245.
80. ALK, III, 396.
81. ALC, I, 100.
82. ALBE, II, 385.
83. ALBE, III, 367.
84. CD/ALBE, II, 154; cf. *Tablet* 14 & 28 January 1860, pp. 20 & 53.
85. CD/ALBE, II, 152 & 181.
86. ALBE, I, 226.
87. ALBE, III, 52.
88. ALBE, II (1890), 328, concerning St Patrick's, Liverpool.
89. ALBE, I, 212-3.
90. ALDk, I, 256 & 259.
91. CD/ALBE, III, 13-6.
92. CD/ALBE, IV, 183-4.

93. ALBE, I, 32.
94. CD/ALBE, IV (1865), 213 expressed this belief.
95. ALBE, I (1870), 67 (Latin original).
96. Ibid., 127 (Latin original).
97. Ibid., 224 (Latin original).
98. Ibid., 32 & 57.
99. *Tablet*, 31 March 1883, pp. 510-11.
100. ALBE, II, 182 (Latin original).
101. APF, SC, Anglia, vol. 27 (1887-8), fo. 508r.
102. LRO, RCLv, 'Lent Return, 1889'.
103. ALBE, II, 342. APF, Rubrica, vol. 93 (1896) fo. 102/632r. shows that the population of the parish was between 4,718 and 6,077, that Mass attendance was 2,500 and that 1,545 fulfilled the paschal precept.
104. ALBE, III, 161.
105. Carwardine, *Transatlantic Revivalism*, p. 193 similarly notes that the American revivalists of 1859 drew the majority of their English converts 'from within the unregenerate but evangelically minded group of church adherents', especially the young, and that 'the socially outcast' were absent from the audiences.
106. ALC, I, 117.
107. Ibid., 32.
108. The terminology is suggested by Hugh McLeod, *Religion and the Working Class in Nineteenth-Century Britain* (London, 1984), pp. 38-9. It is impossible to know the extent to which 'indifferentism' represented lack of interest or genuine apathy. See David Hempton, ' "Popular Religion" 1800-1986', in T. Thomas (editor), *The British: Their Religious Beliefs and Practices, 1800-1986* (London and New York, 1988) pp.181-210.
109. ALBE, II, 318.
110. Ibid. (1873), 212 & (1882), 167.
111. ALL, II (1868), 9 and ALBE, III (1893), 17.
112. ALBE, I (1871), 107 & 70, referring to Little Crosby and Chorley in Lancashire (Latin original).
113. ALP, Db42, MacDonald to Coffin, March 1881.
114. AGR, XLVII, C1, MacDonald to Douglas, 21 August 1884.
115. AAS, Box 41, MacDonald to Coffin, 17 July 1884.
116. AGR, XLVII, C1, MacDonald to Douglas, 13 October 1886.
117. ALDk, I, 272, for example records that the 1892 mission at Monasterevan, Co. Kildare was 'a model one — a highly successful one in every sense of the word — overflowing attendances — crowded confessionals — constant work, more than enough to do — splendid dispositions for receiving the sacraments'.
118. See above, p. 117.

Appendix: Mission Plans

[Source: ADK, Miscellaneous Papers]

A. Two-Week Mission

	Morning	Evening
Sun	Early Masses. Invitation. High Mass. The End of Man or Opening.	General introduction to Rosary. Importance of Salvation.
Mon	Mass. The Way of Salvation, Necessity of Faith & Good Works.	Explanation of the Rosary. The Malice of Mortal Sin.
Tue	Mass. Grace — sanctifying and actual.	Explanation of the Rosary. Sacrilegious Confession.
Wed	Mass. General Confession — when and how.	Explanation of the Rosary. Death (in general or of negligent Christian).
Thu	Mass. Contrition and Firm Purpose.	Explanation of the Rosary. Reparation to the Blessed Sacrament.
Fri	Mass. Satisfaction.	Explanation of the Rosary. Particular Judgement.
Sat	Mass. Examination of Conscience.	Explanation of the Rosary. Sacramental Penance.
Sun	Early Masses. Renewed exhortation to attend. High Mass. Holy Mass.	Explanation of the Rosary. Delay of Conversion.
Mon	Mass. Sixth and Ninth Commandments — bad thoughts and temptations.	Explanation of the Rosary. Occasions of Sin.
Tue	Mass. Fraternal Charity and its opposite.	Explanation of the Rosary. Hell.

Wed	Mass. Good and Bad Books.	Explanation of the Rosary. Consecration to the BVM.
Thu	Mass. Practical devotion to the BVM.	Explanation of the Rosary. Prayer.
Fri	Mass. Daily Acts of a good Christian.	Explanation of the Rosary. Way of the Cross or Love of Our Lord Jesus Christ.
Sat	Mass. Rules on frequentation of the Sacraments, preparation and thanksgiving.	Perseverance. Instruction, blessing and investiture with scapular.
Sun	Early Masses. High Mass. Mission Cross or Frequentation of Sacraments.	Close and Papal Blessing.
Mon	Mass. Purgatory.	

B. Three-Week Mission

	Morning	Evening
Sun	Early Masses. Invitation. High Mass. End of Man or Opening.	General introduction to Rosary. Importance of Salvation.
Mon	Mass. Way of Salvation, Necessity of Faith & Good Works.	Explanation of the Rosary. Malice of Mortal Sin.
Tue	Mass. Grace — sanctifying and actual.	Explanation of the Rosary. Sacrilegious Confession.
Wed	Mass. General Confession — when and how.	Explanation of the Rosary. Death (in general or of negligent Christian).
Thu	Mass. Examination of Conscience.	Explanation of the Rosary. Reparation to the Blessed Sacrament.

280

Fri	Mass. Contrition.	Explanation of the Rosary. Particular Instructions.
Sat	Mass. Firm Purpose.	Explanation of the Rosary. Refuge of Sinners or Mercy of the BVM.
Sun	Early Masses. Exhortation to attend. High Mass. Consequences of Mortal Sin.	Explanation of the Rosary. Delay of Conversion.
Mon	Mass. Satisfaction.	Explanation of the Rosary. Drunkenness.
Tue	Mass. Integrity and Sincerity.	Explanation of the Rosary. Impurity.
Wed	Mass. First Commandment.	Explanation of the Rosary. Hell.
Thu	Mass. Second Commandment.	Explanation of the Rosary. Mercy of God.
Fri	Mass. Fourth Commandment.	Explanation of the Rosary. Way of the Cross.
Sat	Mass. Fifth Commandment.	Explanation of the Rosary. Sacrament of Penance - resumé.
Sun	Early Masses. Third Commandment. High Mass. The True Church.	Explanation of the Rosary. Occasions of Sin.
Mon	Mass. Sixth and Ninth Commandments — bad thoughts and words.	Explanation of the Rosary. Misery of Sin and Happiness of Virtue.
Tue	Mass. Seventh and Eighth Commandments.	Explanation of the Rosary. Consecration to BVM.
Wed	Mass. Practical devotion to the BVM.	Explanation of the Rosary. Prayer.
Thu	Mass. Daily Acts of the good Christian.	Explanation of the Rosary. Frequentation of the Sacraments.

Fri	Mass. Temptations.	Explanation of the Rosary. Love of Our Lord Jesus Christ.
Sat	Mass. Rule on frequentation of the Sacraments, preparation and thanksgiving.	Instruction, blessing and investiture with scapular, proper devotion to the BVM, Perseverance.
Sun	Early Masses. Danger of Relapse. High Mass. Heaven or Death of the Just or Blessing of Mission Cross.	Close and Papal Blessing.
Mon	Mass. Purgatory.	

C. Four-Week Mission

	Morning	Evening
Sun	Early Masses. Invitation. High Mass. Opening.	General introduction to Rosary. Importance of Salvation.
Mon	Mass. Grace.	Explanation of the Rosary. Mortal Sin.
Tue	Mass. Penance.	Explanation of the Rosary. Sacrament of Penance.
Wed	Mass. General Confession.	Explanation of the Rosary. Death.
Thu	Mass. Contrition.	Explanation of the Rosary. Particular Judgement.
Fri	Mass. Purpose.	Explanation of the Rosary. Reparation to the Blessed Sacrament.
Sat	Mass. Satisfaction.	Explanation of the Rosary. Instruction on the Scapular.

Sun	Early Masses. High Mass. Faith.	Explanation of the Rosary. Hell.
Mon	Mass. Commandments in general.	Explanation of the Rosary. Drunkenness.
Tue	Mass. First Commandment.	Explanation of the Rosary. Impurity.
Wed	Mass. Second Commandment.	Explanation of the Rosary. Duties of Parents.
Thu	Mass. Fifth Commandment.	Explanation of the Rosary. Duties of Children.
Fri	Mass. Seventh Commandment.	Explanation of the Rosary. Way of the Cross.
Sat	Mass. Eighth Commandment.	
Sun	Early Masses. High Mass. Charity Sermon.	Explanation of the Rosary. The Last Sin.
Mon	Mass. Particular Sins.	Explanation of the Rosary. Men Only.
Tue	Mass. Bad Words.	Explanation of the Rosary. Abuse of Mercy.
Wed	Mass. Good and Bad Reading.	Explanation of the Rosary. Prayer.
Thu	Mass. Crosses and objects of piety.	Explanation of the Rosary. Consecration to the BVM.
Fri	Mass. Rule of Life.	Explanation of the Rosary. Mercy of God.
Sat	Mass. Spirit of Prayer.	
Sun	Early Masses. High Mass.	Explanation of the Rosary. Eternity.
Mon	Mass. Presence of God.	Explanation of the Rosary. General Judgement.

Tue	Mass. Domestic Virtues.	Explanation of the Rosary. Men Only.
Wed	Mass. Sacraments in general.	Explanation of the Rosary. Scandal.
Thu	Mass. Devotion to the BVM.	Explanation of the Rosary. Occasions of Sin.
Fri	Mass. Devotion to the Passion.	Explanation of the Rosary. Love of God.
Sat	Mass. Devotion to the BVM.	
Sun	Early Masses. High Mass. Heaven.	Close and Papal Blessing.
Mon	Mass. Purgatory.	

Bibliography

Notes on Sources

A. REDEMPTORIST

The General Archives in Rome [AGR] are well-organised and catalogued, and are divided into two sections: *generalia* and *provincialia*. The *generalia* are sub-divided into *documenta historica, observentia,* and *privilegia*.

The documenta historica, which form the most extensive and important element of the first section, are divided into fifty-nine parts, of which parts nine to fifteen treat of the Transalpine Vicariate, parts seventeen and eighteen of the General Chapter of 1855 and the regime of Fr Mauron, and parts nineteen to fifty-four comprise matters relating to communities in existence prior to the Chapter of 1855, biographical documents, and data on the General Chapter of 1894. The *provincialia* are documents on each of the provinces and communities after 1855. Documents relating to the years after 1909, or anyone living in that year, are not available for inspection.

The Provincial Archives of the London Province [ALP] are situated in Clapham, London. The bulk of them were catalogued at the end of the last century, when a uniform system of division was introduced into the archives of the Province, both provincial and domestic. For the most part, documents were arranged chronologically under five headings: A, Decrees of the Holy See for a) the whole Congregation, b) the Province, and c)—k) each of the houses in the Province; B, Decrees of the Rector Major, subdivided as A; C, Decrees of the Provincial, with the subdivisions b)—k); D, Letters, subdivided as C; E, Miscellaneous, with the same subdivisions as C and D. The Provincial Archives were reorganised in the 1950s, when some documents relating to the Irish houses were transferred to the Irish Province; these have mostly sunk without trace.

The absence of a Provincial Archivist for some years has meant that the Provincial Archives are in a somewhat disorganised state; several documents have been removed and others have been misplaced, with the result that there are large lacunae and it is not always possible to locate documents mentioned in the, not altogether reliable, handwritten catalogue.

The domestic and mission chronicles of each of the houses have all survived, but the documents have, in varying degrees, been dispersed or lost in the course of time.

What has been written of the London Province is doubly true of the Dublin Province. Until recently, the Provincial and Domestic Archives have been badly neglected. The recent appointment of an assiduous and enthusiastic Provincial Archivist has reversed the decline.

Among printed sources, mention should be made of the following:

Codex Regularum et Constitutionum Congregationis SS. Redemptoris necnon Statutorum a Capitulis Generalibus annis 1764, 1855, 1894 (Rome, 1896).

Regula Novitiorum Congregationis SS. Redemptoris (Rome, 1856).

Documenta authentica facultatum et gratiarum spiritualium Congregationis Sanctissimi Redemptoris (Ratisbon, 1903).

Manuale Presbyterorum Congregationis Sanctissimi Redemptoris (London, 1866).

Catalogus Congregationis Sanctissimi Redemptoris (Monaco, 1852; Rome, 1856, 1857, 1859, 1863, 1867, 1869, 1876, 1884, 1887, 1890, 1895, 1898, 1900).

Litterae Circulares Rssmi Patris Nicolai Mauron (Rome 1896).

Litterae Circulares Rssmi Patris Mathiae Raus (Rome, 1908).

Circular Letters (Selected) of Redemptorist Generals (Milwaukee, 1933).

B. ECCLESIASTICAL ARCHIVES

Until recently, access to the papers of the Sacred Congregation 'de Propaganda Fide' was restricted to the years prior to 1892. The decision of Pope John Paul II to allow researchers access to all the papers relating to the pontificate of Leo XIII has meant that it was possible to see material relating to the final years of the century.

The amount of material relating to the Redemptorists in the Sacred Congregation's archives is very scanty and underlines the desire of the Redemptorists to work without drawing attention to themselves.

The same dearth of material is evident in the diocesan archives. The archives of the archdioceses of Westminster, Birmingham, Southwark and Liverpool, and of the dioceses of Plymouth, Hexham and Newcastle, Leeds and Dunkeld yielded little (and in some cases, no) joy to the Redemptorist historian. The following diocesan collections proved most useful:

Birmingham — various letters, as detailed in the Third Report, Series B.
Leeds — Briggs Papers, Cornthwaite Papers.
Liverpool — Letter books of Bishop Goss, other episcopal correspondence, Relationes Status, Lenten Returns, Miscellaneous Papers.
Southwark — Box 41 on St Mary's, Clapham, Coffin letters.
Westminster — Roman letters vol. 2, letters from individual correspondents.

The Scottish Catholic Archives proved useful for the old Northern and Southern Districts and for the archdiocese of St Andrews and Edinburgh until the end of the century. The Oban letters and other episcopal correspondence contained some things of interest. Access to the archives of the archdiocese of Glasgow, including the archives of the former Western District, where the Redemptorists conducted most of their missions, was not afforded me.

I did not consult the archives of the Irish bishops. The archives of Archbishop Croke have been catalogued in the *Collectanea Hibernica,* and the archives of his predecessor and of the bishops of Limerick have been searched in the past by Redemptorists for any information relating to their order.

C. NEWSPAPERS

Another source for Catholic history in the nineteenth century is the newspapers. The difficulty here is that, although in Ireland local newspapers gave wide coverage of Catholic events, the local press in Great Britain was dominated by Nonconformists who tended to ignore most Catholic events, save for polemical purposes. This, however, is not always the case, and there were local Catholic newspapers in Glasgow and Liverpool. The footnotes indicate when newspaper accounts are used as a source.

The most important Catholic weekly was the *Tablet*, which included reports from regional correspondents, and is of particular value in its accounts of the missions.

Printed Works

A. WORKS OF REFERENCE

Anson P.F., *The Religious Orders and Congregations of Great Britain and Ireland* (Worcester, 1949).

Battersby's Register for the Catholic World (Dublin 1846-57), which became *Battersby's Catholic Directory* (Dublin, 1858-64), which became *The Catholic Directory of Ireland* (Dublin 1865-9), which became *The Irish Catholic Directory* (Dublin, 1870-98).

Boase, F., *Modern English Biography*, 6 vols (Truro, 1892-1921).

Brady, W.M., *Annals of the Catholic Hierarchy in England and Scotland, A.D. 1658-1876* (London, 1883).

The Catholic Directory and Annual Register (London, 1843-1900).

The Catholic Directory for Clergy and Laity in Scotland, (Glasgow, 1867-1900).

Catholic Encyclopedia, 16 vols (London, 1907-14).

New Catholic Encyclopedia, 17 vols (New York, St Louis, San Francisco, Toronto, London, Sydney, 1966-1979).

Dictionary of Catholic Biography (London, 1962).

Dictionary of National Biography, 42 vols and 6 supplements (London, 1885-1912).

Dictionnaire de Théologie Catholique, 16 vols (Paris, 1915-72).

Dictionnaire d'histoire et du gèographique écclesiastique (Paris, 1909-).

Gillow, Joseph, *Bibliographical Dictionary of the English Catholics from the Breach with Rome in 1534 to the present time*, 5 vols (London, 1885-1903).

Gorman, W.G., *Converts to Rome* (London, 1910).

Hastings, J. (ed), *Dictionary of Religion and Ethics*, 13 vols (Edinburgh, 1908-26).

Steele, F.M., *Monastic and Religious Houses of Great Britain and Ireland* (London, 1903).

Viller, M. (ed.), *Dictionnaire de Spiritualité* (Paris, 1927-).

B. BOOKS AND PAMPHLETS

Acta et Decreta Synodi Plenariae Episcoporum Hiberniae habitae apud Maynutiam, anno MCCCCLXXV (Dublin 1877).

Anonymous (non-Redemptorist), *"Old Betty's Book" or "What every Christian must know", being the Dominicans' New Year Gift to the People of Tralee* (Kerry, 1857).

_____, *The Foundations of the Sisters of Notre Dame in England and Scotland from 1845 to 1895* (Liverpool, 1895).

Anonymous (Redemptorist), *Hymns for the Confraternity of the Holy Family* (London, 1854).

_____, *Manual of the Archconfraternity of the Holy Family* (London, 1854).

_____, *The Imitation of St Joseph*, translated from the French under the supervision of the Redemptorist Fathers (Dublin, 1854).

_____, *The Mission Book*, first edition (Dublin, 1855), second edition (Dublin, 1857), third edition (Dublin, 1879), fourth, revised edition (Dublin, 1891).

_____, *St Alphonsus proclaimed Doctor of the Church* (privately printed, 1871).

_____, *Meditations for the novena in honour of St Alphonsus* (privately printed, 1871).

_____, *Alphonsi Doctoris Officium: Novena and Little Office in honour of St Alphonsus de' Liguori, Doctor of the Universal Church* (London, 1872).

_____, *Directory of the Missions in the English Province of the Congregation of the Most Holy Redeemer* (privately printed, 1877).

_____, *Directory of the Archconfraternity of the Holy Family* (Dublin, 1878).

_____, *Directory of the Confraternity of Our Lady of Perpetual Succour* (Perth, 1884).

_____, *Manual of Our Lady of Perpetual Succour: Devotions taken principally from the Writings of St Alphonsus by a Redemptorist Father* (London, 1886).

_____, *History of the Limerick Holy Family* (Limerick, 1893).

_____, *A Half Century's Jubilee in St Mary's, Clapham* (Southwark, 1899).

_____, *A Son of St Alphonsus: Father Bernard Hafkenscheid* (Dublin, 1903).

_____, *Fifty Years at Mount St Alphonsus, Limerick* (Limerick, 1903).

_____, *Golden Jubilee of the Confraternity of the Holy Family* (Limerick, 1918).

_____, *St Mary's Clapham: The Parish and its History, 1852-1922* (Clapham, 1922).

_____, *The Redemptorists in Dundalk: Golden Jubilee Souvenir, 1876-1926* (Dundalk, 1926).

_____, *Souvenir of the Diamond Jubilee of the Confraternity of the Holy Family* (Limerick, 1928).

_____, *Two Hundred Years with the Redemptorists* (Dublin, 1932).

_____, *Golden Jubilee, Clonard* (Belfast, 1947).

_____, *St. Mary's, Clapham. 1848-1948* (Clapham, 1848).

_____, *Centenary of St Joseph's, Dundalk, 1876-1976* (Dundalk, 1976).

_____, *The Story of St Joseph's, Bishop's Stortford* (Bishop's Stortford, 1982).

_____, *Bishop Eton: Devotions for the Forty Hours* (Salford, no date).

_____, *Meditations for the novena in honour of St Joseph* (privately printed, no date).

_____, *Our Lady's Manual: Devotions for the Confraternity of Our Lady of Perpetual Succour* (Dublin, no date).

Anson, P.F., *The Catholic Church in Modern Scotland, 1560-1937* (London, 1937).

Anstruther, G.E, *A Hundred Years of Catholic Progress* (London, 1929).

Arnold, Thomas, *Passages in a Wandering Life* (London, 1900).

Aubert, Roger, *Le Pontificat de Pie IX* (Paris, 1958).

_____, *The Church in a Secularised Society* (London, 1978).

Aveling, J.C.H., *The Handle and the Axe: The Catholic Recusants in England from Reformation to Emancipation* (London, 1976).

Avery, Gillian, *Nineteenth-Century Children* (London, 1965).

Barry, Albert, C.SS.R., *Life of Blessed Margaret Mary Alacoque* (London, 1889).

_____, *Life of St Patrick* (Dublin, 1895).

_____, *Lives of Irish Saints* (Dublin, 1901).

_____, *Means of Enjoying a Holy and Happy Death*, a translation of M. Stoufflet, 'Moyens d'obtenir une douce et sainte mort' (Dublin, no date).

_____, *Holy Rosary*, a translation of J.M. Sarnelli, 'Le Glorie e Grandezze della divina Madre' (London, no date).

_____, *Life of St Joan of Arc* (Dublin, no date).

_____, *Life of St Mochoemog* (Dublin, no date).

Batho, E.C. and Dobrée, B., *The Victorians and After*, second edition (London, 1950).

Beames, Thomas, *The Rookeries of London*, second edition (London, 1852).

Beck, G.A. (editor), *The English Catholics, 1850-1950* (London, 1950).

Beckett, J.C., *The Making of Modern Ireland, 1603-1923* (London, 1966).

Bellesheim, A., *History of the Catholic Church of Scotland*, translated by O. Hunter Blair, OSB, 4 vols (Edinburgh and London, 1887-90).

Berthe, Austin, C.SS.R., *Life of St Alphonsus de' Liguori*, translated by H. Castle, C.SS.R., 2 vols (Dublin, 1905).

Besant, A., *On Eternal Torture* (London, 1874).

Best, G.F.A., *Mid-Victorian Britain, 1851-1875* (London, 1971).

Blakeney, R.P., *Awful Disclosures of the Iniquitous Principles taught by the Church of Rome; being Extracts translated from the Moral Theology of St Alphonsus Liguori* (London, 1846).

_____, *St Alphonsus Liguori; or, Extracts translated from the Moral Theology of the above Romish Saint, with remarks theron* (London, 1852).

Blanchard, John, *The Church in Contemporary Ireland* (Dublin and London, 1963).

Boland, S.J., *Faith of Our Fathers* (privately printed, Australia, 1982).

_____, *A Dictionary of the Redemptorists* (Rome, 1987).

Bolton, C.A., *Salford Diocese and its Catholic Past* (Manchester, 1950).

Bossy, John, *The English Catholic Community 1570-1850* (London, 1975).

Bourke, W.J., *The Life and Times of the Most Rev. John McHale* (New York, 1883).

Bowen, Desmond, *Souperism: Myth or Reality?* (Cork, 1970).

_____, *The Protestant Crusade in Ireland, 1800-1870* (Dublin and Montreal, 1978).

_____, *Paul Cardinal Cullen and the Shaping of Modern Irish Catholicism* (Dublin, 1983).

Brandhuber, G., C.SS.R. (editor), *Die Redemptoristen 1732-1932* (Bamberg, 1932).

Bridgett, T.E., C.SS.R., *The Ritual of the New Testament* (London, 1873).

_____, *Our Lady's Dowry* (London, 1875).

_____, *The Discipline of Drink* (London, 1876).

_____, *Sermons on the Sacraments by Th. Watson, last Catholic Bishop of Lincoln, with a preface and autobiographical notice of the author* (London, 1876).

_____, *The History of the Holy Eucharist in Great Britain*, 2 vols (London, 1881).

_____, *A Retreat for Men* (Dublin, 1882).

_____, *Historical Notes on Adare* (Dublin, 1885).

_____, *Life of Blessed John Fisher*, second edition (London, 1890).

————, *The True History of the Catholic Hierarchy deposed by Queen Elizabeth* (London, 1889).

————, *Blunders and Forgeries: Historical Essays* (London, 1890).

————, *Life and Writings of Sir Thomas More* (London, 1891).

————, *The Wisdom and Wit of Blessed Thomas More* (London, 1892).

————, *A Flag of Truce* (London, 1893).

————, *Lyra Hieratica* (London, 1896).

————, *The Art of Lying as practised by some writers of anti-catholic tracts* (London, 1898).

————, *Sonnets and Epigrams on Sacred Subjects* (London, 1898).

————, *Selections from the Writings of Nicholas Cardinal Wiseman* (London, 1898).

————, *Reapers for the Harvest* (London, no date).

Buckley, D. *The Miraculous Picture of the Mother of Perpetual Succour* (Cork, 1948).

Buggenoms, Louis de, C.SS.R., *Peace of the Soul or Path of Paradise* (Dublin, 1855).

————, *The Contemplative Life* (Dublin, 1859).

Burke, T., *Catholic History of Liverpool* (Liverpool, 1910).

Butler, Cuthbert, *The Life and Times of Bishop Ullathorne*, 2 vols (London, 1926).

Byrne, J.F., C.SS.R., *The Redemptorist Centenaries* (Philadelphia, 1932).

Cacciatore, Giuseppe, *S. Alfonso de' Liguori ed il Giansenismo* (Florence, 1944).

Callahan, W.J. and Higgs, D. (editors), *Church and Society in Catholic Europe of the Eighteenth Century* (Cambridge, 1979).

Camm, Bede (editor), *Sister Mary of St Francis, S.N.D.* (London, 1913).

Cannon, S., C.SS.R., *Irish Episcopal Meetings, 1788-1882: a juridico-historical study* (Rome, 1979).

Carr, John C.SS.R., *St Clement, C.SS.R.* (London, 1946).

Carwardine, Richard, *Transatlantic Revivalism: Popular Evangelicalism in Britain and America, 1790-1865* (Westport and London, 1978).

Casartelli, L.C., *A Forgotten Chapter of the Second Spring* (London, 1895).

C.B., *The Confessional Unmasked ... being extracts from the theological works of Saint Alphonsus M. De Liguori, Peter Dens, Bailly, Delahogue and Cabassutius* (London, 1851).

Chadwick, W.O., *The Victorian Church*, 2 vols (London, 1966 & 1970).

————, *The Popes and European Revolution* (Oxford, 1981).

Chapman, Ronald, *Father Faber* (London, 1961).

Claessens, P., C.SS.R., *The Life of Father Bernard, C.SS.R.: The Apostolate of a Redemptorist* (London, 1875).

Cleary, J.A., C.SS.R., *Confraternity Work and its Problems* (Dublin, 1932).

Coffin, R.A., C.SS.R., *The Oratory of the Faithful Soul,* a translation of L. Blosius, 'Sacellum animae fidelis' (London, 1848).

_____, *Devotions in honour of St Joseph* (London, 1860).

_____, *Prayers for the Church and Pope from St Alphonsus* (London, 1863).

_____, *Life of St Alphonsus* (Dublin, 1880).

Collette, C.H., *Romanism in England: The Redemptorist Fathers in St Mary's Convent, Park Road, Clapham* (London, 1850).

Collingwood, Cuthbert, *The Catholic Truth Society* (London, 1955).

Colton, Calvin, *History and Character of American Revivals of Religion* (London, 1832).

Congrégation de la Mission, *Répertoire Historique* (Paris, 1900).

Connolly, S.J., *Priests and People in Pre-Famine Ireland, 1780-1845* (Dublin and New York, 1982).

Corish, P.J. (editor), *A History of Irish Catholicism,* 6 vols (Dublin, 1967-71).

_____, *The Irish Catholic Experience: a Historical Survey* (Dublin, 1985).

Costello, N., *John McHale, Archbishop of Tuam* (Dublin and London, 1939).

Coveney, Peter, *Images of Childhood* (Harmondsworth, 1967).

Curly, M.J., C.SS.R., *The Provincial Story* (New York, 1963).

Currie, Robert, *Methodism Divided: A Study of the Sociology of Ecumenicalism* (London, 1968).

Currie, R., Gilbert, A. and Horsley, L., *Churches and Churchgoers: Patterns of Church Growth in the British Isles since 1700* (Oxford, 1977).

Cwiekowski, F.J., *The English Bishops and the First Vatican Council* (Louvain, 1971).

Daniels, W.H., *D.L. Moody and his Work* (London, 1875).

Decreta Quatuor Conciliorum Provincialium Westmonstariensium, 1852-1873 (London, no date).

Decreta Synodi Plenariae Episcoporum Hiberniae apud Thurles habitae, anno MDCCCL (Dublin, 1851).

Delft, M. van, C.SS.R., *La Mission Paroissiale: pratique et théorie* (Paris, 1963).

Delumeau, Jean, *Catholicism between Luther and Voltaire: a new view of the Counter-Reformation* (London, 1977).

293

Denvir, John, *Life Story of an Old Rebel* (Dublin, 1901).

Dieter, M.E., *The Holiness Revival of the Nineteenth Century* (London, 1980).

Dilgskron, F., C.SS.R., *P. Rudolf von Smetana: Ein Beitrag zur Geschichte der Kongregation des allerheiligsten Erlösers* (Vienna, 1902).

_____, *P. Friedrich von Held: Ein Beitrag zur Geschichte der Kongregation des allerheiligsten Erlösers* (Vienna, 1909).

Dolan, J.P., *Catholic Revivalism: The American Experience, 1830-1900* (Notre Dame, 1978).

Douglas, Edward, C.SS.R., *St Alphonsus Maria de Liguori* (London, 1887).

_____, *The Divine Redeemer and His Church* (London, 1896).

Drew, G.F., C.SS.R., *Bishop Eton and its Shrine* (St Helen's, 1951).

Duffy, Eamon (editor), *Challoner and his Church: A Catholic Bishop in Georgian England* (London, 1981).

Dumortier, F., C.SS.R., *Le Révérendissime Père Nicolas Mauron* (Paris, 1901).

Dyos, H.J. and Wolff, M. (editors), *The Victorian City*, 2 vols (London, 1973).

Edgell, A.T.T.W., *The Present State of the Church in England* (London, 1884).

Elliott, W., *The Life of Father Hecker* (New York, 1891).

Emery, C.J., *The Rosminians* (London, 1960).

Evans, T.E., *The Glories of Jesus or the Glories of Mary?* (London, 1865).

Evinson, Denis, *Pope's Corner* (Fulham and Hammersmith Historical Society, 1980).

Faber, F.W., *On Beatification, Canonization and the Processes of the Congregation of the Rites* (London, 1848).

_____, *An Essay on Catholic Home Missions* (London, 1851).

_____, *All for Jesus*, fourth edition (London, 1854).

_____, *The Blessed Sacrament* (London, 1855).

_____, *Devotion to the Pope* (London, 1860).

_____, *Hymns* (London, 1862).

_____, *Growth in Holiness*, Orchard Book edition (London, 1960).

_____, *The Creator and His Creatures*, Orchard Book edition (London, 1961).

Farina, John, *An American Experience of God: The Spirituality of Isaac Hecker* (New York, 1981).

Farrar, F.W., *Eternal Hope* (London, 1878).

Fennell, D. (editor), *The Changing Face of Catholic Ireland* (London, 1968).

Fitzsimmons, John (editor), *Manning: Anglican and Catholic* (London, 1951).

Fothergill, Brian, *Nicholas Wiseman* (London, 1963).

Foy, Anthony, C.SS.R., *Saint Alphonsus, Founder of the Redemptorists* (London, 1962).

Furniss, John, C.SS.R., *The Sunday School* (Dublin, no date).

———, *Books for Children* (Dublin, no date).

———, *How to teach at Catechism* (Dublin, no date).

———, *What every Christian must know and do* (Dublin, 1856).

———, *A defence of 'What every Christian must know and do' in reply to the 'Saturday Review'* (Dublin, 1857).

Girouille, Henri, C.SS.R., *Life of the Venerable Father Joseph Passerat*, translated by J. Carr (London, 1928).

Gray, Robert, *Cardinal Manning: A Biography* (London, 1985).

Guibert, J., *Le Réveil du Catholicisme en Angleterre au xixe siècle* (Paris, 1907).

Guy, R.E., *The Synods in English* (Stratford-on-Avon, 1886).

Gwynn, David, *The Second Spring, 1818-1852: A Study of the Catholic Revival in England* (London, 1942).

———, *Father Dominic Barberi* (London, 1947).

———, *Father Luigi Gentili and his Mission* (Dublin, 1951).

Haile, M. and Bonney, E., *Life and Letters of John Lingard, 1771-1851* (London, 1911).

Halévy, E., *A History of the English People in the Nineteenth Century*, 6 vols (London, 1947-52).

Hammond, E.P., *The Conversion of Children* (London, 1878).

Hammond, J.L. and B., *The Age of the Chartists* (London, 1930).

Handley, J.E., *The Irish in Scotland, 1798-1845* (Cork, 1945).

———, *The Irish in Modern Scotland* (Cork, 1947).

———, *The Navvy in Scotland* (Cork 1979).

Harrison, Brian, *Drink and Victorians* (London, 1971).

Headley, P.C., *The Reaper and the Harvest: Scenes and Incidents in connection with ... E. Poyser Hammond, M.A.* (London, 1885).

Herbert, Father, *The Preachers of the Passion* (London, 1924).

Heyer, F., *The Catholic Church from 1648 to 1870* (London, 1969).

Hickey, John, *Urban Catholics: Urban Catholicism in England and Wales from 1829 to the present day* (London, 1967).

Hill, M.M. (editor), *Sociological Yearbook of Religion in Britain*, vol. 6 (London, 1973).

Hoegerl, C., C.SS.R., *Heart calls to Heart: An Alphonsian Anthology* (Rome, 1981).

Holden, V.F., *The Yankee Paul: Isaac Thomas Hecker* (Milwaukee, 1958).

Holmes, C., (editor), *Immigrants and Minorities in British Society* (London, 1978).

Holmes, Derek, *More Roman than Rome* (London and Shepherdstown, 1978).

———, *The Triumph of the Holy See* (London and Shepherdstown, 1978).

Hosp, E., C.SS.R., *Weltweite Erlösung* (Innsbruck, 1961).

Hostie, R., *Vie et Mort des Ordres Religieux* (Paris, 1972).

Hull, Lawrence, C.SS.R., *The Redemptorist Centenary: A Hundred Years in England* (London, 1943).

Inglis, K.S., *Churches and the Working Classes in Victorian England* (London, 1963).

Irish in Britain Group, The, *The History of the Irish in Britain: a Bibliography* (London, 1986).

Jackson, J.A., *The Irish in Britain* (London, 1963).

Jackson, S.W., *Nicholas Cardinal Wiseman* (London, 1977).

Joyce, P.J., *John Healy, Archbishop of Tuam* (Dublin, 1931).

Keenan, D.J., *The Catholic Church in Nineteenth-Century Ireland: a Sociological Study* (Dublin, 1983).

Kelly, B.W., *Historical Notes on English Catholic Missions* (London, 1907).

Kent, John, *Holding the Fort: Studies in Victorian Revivalism* (London, 1978).

Kowalsky, N. and Metzler, J., *Inventory of the Historical Archives of the Sacred Congregation for the Evangelization of Peoples or 'De Propaganda Fide'*, new, enlarged edition (Rome, 1983).

Kirk, F.J., O.S.C., *Reminiscences of an Oblate of St Charles* (London, 1905).

Krebs, A., C.SS.R., *Zwei würdige Söhne des heil. Alphonsus Maria von Liguori aus neuester Zeit* (Dülmen, 1899).

Kuntz, F., C.SS.R., *De Vita Edwardi Douglas* (Rome, 1909).

Lans, M., C.SS.R., *Pater Joannes Baptista Lans* (Hertogenbosch, 1911).

Lacqueur, T.W., *Religion and Respectability: Sunday Schools and Working-Class Culture, 1780-1850* (New Haven, 1976).

Larkin, Emmet, *The Roman Catholic Church and the Creation of the Modern Irish State, 1878-1886* (Philadelphia, 1975).

———, *The Roman Catholic Church in Ireland and the Plan of Campaign, 1886-1888* (Chapel Hill, 1975).

———, *The Roman Catholic Church in Ireland and the Fall of Parnell, 1888-1891* (Chapel Hill, 1979).

_____, *Origines de la Congrégation du Très Saint-Rédempteur*, 2 vols (Louvain, 1953 & 1957).

_____, *Outline History of the Redemptorists*, translated by J.J. Gredler, C.SS.R. (Louvain, 1956).

Meyrick, F., *Moral and Devotional Theology of the Church of Rome according to the authoritative teaching of S. Alfonso de' Liguori* (London, 1857).

_____, *On Dr Newman's Rejection of Liguori's Doctrine of Equivocation* (London, 1864).

Milburn, D., *A History of Ushaw College* (Durham, 1964).

[Murphy, Thomas], *The Position of the Catholic Church in England and Wales during the last two centuries* (London, 1892).

Napier, Michael and Laing, Alistair (editors), *The London Oratory Centenary, 1884-1984* (London, 1984).

Nédoncelle, M. et al., *L'écclesiologie du xixe siècle* (Paris, 1960).

Newman, J.H., *The Letters and Diaries of John Henry Newman*, edited by Charles Dessain and others, 31 vols (London and Oxford, 1961-).

_____, *Lectures on [the Present Position of] Catholicism in England* (Birmingham, 1851).

Noel, Horace, *Extracts from 'The Glories of Mary' compared with Holy Scripture* (London, 1865).

Norman, E.R., *The Catholic Church in Ireland in the Age of Rebellion, 1859-73* (London, 1965).

_____, *The Catholic Church and Irish Politics in the Eighteen-Sixties* (Dundalk, 1968).

_____, *Anti-Catholicism in Victorian England* (London, 1968).

_____, *The English Catholic Church in the Nineteenth Century* (Oxford, 1984).

_____, *Roman Catholicism in England from the Elizabethen Settlement to the Second Vatican Council* (Oxford, 1985).

O'Byrne, J.W., *History of the Wexford Men's Confraternity of the Holy Family* (Wexford, 1910).

O'Connor, Kevin, *The Irish in Britain* (London, 1972).

O'Donnell, Patrick, C.SS.R., *Clonard Church and Monastery* (Muckamore, no date).

Oliver, G., *Collections illustrating the History of the Catholic Religion in the Counties of Cornwall, Devon, Dorset, Somerset, Wiltshire and Gloucestershire* (London, 1857).

O'Meara, Kathleen [alias Grace Ramsey], *Thomas Grant, Bishop of Southwark*, second edition (London, 1886).

One of the Missioners, *Missions in Ireland* (Dublin, 1855).

Oppitz, J.W., *Alphonsian History and Spirituality* (Suffield, 1978).

O'Reilly, B., *John McHale, Archbishop of Tuam: His Life, Times and Correspondence*, 2 vols (New York and Cincinnati, 1890).

O'Riordan, M., *Catholicity and Progress in Ireland*, fourth edition (London, 1906).

Orr, J.E., *The Second Evangelical Awakening in Britain* (London, 1949).

———, *The Light of the Nations* (London, 1965).

O'Shea, James, *Priests, Politics and Society in post-famine Ireland: a study of County Tipperary, 1850-1891* (Dublin, 1983).

Pejska, J., C.SS.R., *Jus Sacrum Congregationis Sanctissimi Redemptoris* (Brunae, Moravia, 1910).

Père Rédemptoriste, Un, *La Congrégation du Très-Saint Rédempteur* (Tournai and Paris, 1912).

Préclin, E. and Jarry, E., *Les luttes politiques et doctrinales aux xviie et xviiie siècles*, 2 vols (Paris, 1955-6).

Protestant, A, *Popery Made Plain as shown in Furniss's Popish Directory* (Inverness, 1857).

Purcell, E.S., *Life of Cardinal Manning, Archbishop of Westminster*, 2 vols (London, 1896).

Raponi, Santino, C.SS.R., *I Redentoristi oggi e domani* (Rome, 1982).

Reuf, J.J., C.SS.R., *Redemptorist Parish Missions, 1945-76*, 3 vols (Rome, 1976).

Reynolds, E.E., *Three Cardinals* (London, 1958).

Robillard, E. and Milanta, F., *The Catholic Pulpit* (London, 1849).

Ronan, M.V., *An Apostle of Catholic Dublin: Father Henry Young* (Clonskeagh, 1944).

Roche, J.S., *A History of Prior Park College* (London, 1931).

Roltman, A., *London Catholic Churches* (London, 1926).

Rowell, Geoffrey, *Hell and the Victorians* (Oxford, 1974).

Ryder, Cyril, C.SS.R., *Life of T.E. Bridgett, C.SS.R.* (London, 1906).

St John, Edward, *Manning's Work for Children: A Second Chapter in Catholic Emancipation* (London, 1929).

Schepers, G., C.SS.R., *Der hochwürdige P. Bernard Hafkenscheid, der erste höllandische Redemptorist* (Regensburg, New York, Cincinnati, 1884).

Schiefen, R.J., *Nicholas Wiseman and the Transformation of English Catholicism* (Shepherdstown, 1984).

Scott, T., *Hell* (London, 1875).

Selleck, R.J., C.SS.R. and Byrne, R.W., C.SS.R., *The Redemptorist Fathers: a Bi-Centenary and a Jubilee* (Sydney, 1933).

Skinner, T.L., C.SS.R., *The Redemptorists in the West* (St Louis, 1932).

Snead-Cox, J.G., *The Life of Cardinal Vaughan*, 2 vols (London, 1910).

Stebbing, George, C.SS.R., *Father Edward Douglas, C.SS.R.* (London, 1917).

_____, *The Redemptorists* (London, 1924).

_____, *History of St Mary's, Clapham*, (London, 1935).

Swift, R. and Gilley, S.W. (editors), *The Irish in the Victorian City* (London, 1985).

Tannoia, A.M., *The Life of St Alphonso Maria de Liguori*, edited and translated by F.W. Faber, The Saints and Servants of God, 5 vols (London, 1848-9).

Thermstrom, S. and Sennett, R. (editors), *Nineteenth-Century Cities* (New Haven, 1969).

Thomas, T. (editor), *The British: Their Beliefs and Practices, 1800-1986* (London and New York, 1988).

Thompson, E.P., *The Making of the English Working Class* (London, 1963).

Tierney, M., *Croke of Cashel* (Dublin, 1976).

Todd, J., *Lectures for Children*, first series (London, 1834).

Todd, W.G., *The Irish in England* (London, 1857).

Trevor, Meriol, *Newman: The Pillar of the Cloud* (London, 1962).

_____, *Newman: Light in Winter* (London, 1962).

Various, *Catholic Emancipation, 1829-1929* (London, 1929).

Vassall-Phillips, O.R., C.SS.R., *Life of Blessed Clement Hofbauer* (Dublin, 1888).

_____, *After Fifty Years* (London, 1928).

Vere, G.L., *Random Selections of Old Soho* (London, 1908).

Walsh, P.J., *William J. Walsh, Archbishop of Dublin* (Dublin and Cork, 1928).

[Walter, A., C.SS.R.], *Villa Caserta* (Rome, 1905).

Ward, Bernard, *A History of St Edmund's College, Old Hall* (London, 1893).

_____, *The Eve of Catholic Emancipation, 1803-1829*, 3 vols (London, 1911).

_____, *The Sequel to Catholic Emancipation, 1830-1850*, 2 vols (London, 1915).

Ward, Wilfred, *The Life and Times of Cardinal Wiseman*, 2 vols (London, 1897).

_____, *The Life of John Henry Cardinal Newman*, 2 vols (London, 1912).

_____, *William George Ward and the Catholic Revival* (London, 1912).

Warren, C.J., C.SS.R., (editor), *Circular Letters of St Alphonsus* (Boston, Mass., 1912).

Watkin, E.J., *Roman Catholicism from the Reformation to 1950* (London, 1957).

Whyte, J.H., *Catholics in Western Democracies: a Study in Political Behaviour* (Dublin, 1981).

Wilson, A., *Blessed Dominic Barberi* (London, 1967).

[Wiseman, N.], *Lives of St Alphonsus Liguori, St Francis de Girolamo, St John Joseph of the Cross, St Pacificius of San Severino, and St Veronica Giuliani* (London, 1846).

Wissell, J.C., C.SS.R., *The Redemptorist on the American Missions*, first edition (New York, 1875), second edition, 3 vols (New York, 1886).

Wohl, A.S. (editor), *The Victorian Family* (London, 1978).

Woodham-Smith, Cecil, *The Great Hunger: Ireland, 1845-49* (London, 1962).

C. ARTICLES

Ahern, J., 'The Plenary Synod of Thurles', *Irish Ecclesiastical Record*, Fifth Series, 75 (1951), 385-403.

Amherst, W.J., 'Frederick Lucas', *Dublin Review*, Third Series, 16 (1886), 329-428.

Anonymous, 'Protestant ideas of the Confessional', *Dublin Review*, 31 (1851), 122-44.

_____, 'Father Bridgett, C.SS.R.: In Memoriam', *Irish Monthly*, 27 (1899), 205-13.

Aspinwall, B., 'Charles de Montalembert in England', *Downside Review*, 88 (1970), 132-49.

_____, 'The Second Spring in Scotland', *Clergy Review*, 66 (1981), 281-90 and 312-9.

_____, 'The Formation of the Catholic Community in the West of Scotland: Some Preliminary Outlines', *Innes Review*, 33 (1982), 44-57.

Barry, Albert, C.SS.R., 'St Patrick', *Irish Ecclesiastical Record*, Third Series, 14 (1893), 627-38 and 946-8.

_____, 'Birthplace of St Patrick', *Irish Ecclesiastical Record*, Third Series, 14 (1893), 1122-31.

_____, 'Veneration of Joan of Arc', *Irish Ecclesiastical Record*, Third Series, 15 (1894), 812-30.

_____, 'Chronology of St Patrick', *Irish Ecclesiastical Record*, Third Series, 16 (1895), 151-88.

Barry, P.C., 'The Legislation of the Synod of Thurles, 1850', *Irish Theological Quarterly*, 26 (1959), 131-66.

Boland, S.J., C.SS.R., 'Edmund Vaughan, C.SS.R., and the beginnings of the Congregation of the Most Holy Redeemer in Australia', *Spicilegium Historicum Congregationis Sanctissimi Redemptoris*, 25/1 (1977), 250-71.

_____, 'The Conversion of Father Robert Aston Coffin, C.SS.R.', *Spicilegium Historicum CSSR*, 27/2 (1979), 353-74.

_____, 'R.A. Coffin and the English Oratory', *Spicilegium Historicum CSSR*, 28/1 (1980), 147-74.

_____, 'R.A. Coffin's Departure from the Oratorians', *Spicilegium Historicum CSSR*, 28/2 (1980), 431-56.

_____, 'The Conversion of Edward Douglas, C.SS.R.', *Spicilegium Historicum CSSR*, 29/2 (1981), 291-322.

_____, 'The Missionary Methods of the Redemptorists', *Spicilegium Historicum CSSR*, 30/2 (1982), 401-47.

_____, 'Early Redemptorist Missions in England and Ireland (1848-1865)', *Spicilegium Historicum CSSR*, 33/2 (1985), 283-320.

Britten James, 'The Work of the Laity', *Dublin Review*, Third Series, 18 (1887), 151-67.

_____, 'The Loss of Our Boys', *Month* 59 (1887), 457-68.

Cantwell, James, 'Confraternities: their object and use', *Irish Ecclesiastical Record*, Third Series, 3 (1882), 560-3.

_____, 'The Confraternity of the Holy Family', *Irish Ecclesiastical Record*, Third Series, 3 (1882), 627-32.

C.G., 'The Leakage of the Catholic Church in England: Its Remedy', *Month*, 59 (1887), 176-89.

Charles, Conrad, C.P., 'The Origins of the Parish Mission in England and the Early Passionist Apostolate, 1840-1850', *Journal of Ecclesiastical History*, 15 (1964).

Connolly, Gerald, 'The Transubstantiation of Myth: Towards a New Popular History of Nineteenth-Century Catholicism in England', *Journal of Ecclesiastical History*, 35 (1984), 78-104.

Corish, P.J., 'Cardinal Cullen and Archbishop McHale', *Irish Ecclesiastical Record*, Fifth Series, 91 (1959), 393-408.

Costigan, R.F., 'Tradition and the Beginning of the Ultramontane Movement', *Irish Theological Quarterly*, 48 (1981), 27-46.

Curry, J., 'The Leakage from the Catholic Church in Great Britain', *Irish Ecclesiastical Record*, Third Series, 12 (1891), 914-27.

Doyle, B., 'Bishop Goss of Liverpool (1850-1872) and the Importance of Being English', *Studies in Church History*, 18 (1982), 433-47.

———, 'The Education and Training of Catholic Priests in Nineteenth-Century England', *Journal of Ecclesiastical History*, 35 (1984), 208-19.

Durey, M., 'The Survival of an Irish Culture in Britain, 1800-1845', *Historical Studies*, 28 (1982), 14-35.

E.R., 'A few words on the authority of St Alphonsus', *Dublin Review*, New Series, 21 (1873), 485-90.

Frank, V.S., 'A Displaced Person: The Strange Life of Fr Vladimir Petcherin', *Dublin Review*, 445 (1949), 139-53.

Gilley, S.W., 'The Roman Catholic Mission to the Irish in London', *Recusant History*, 10 (1969), 123-45.

———, 'Protestant London, No-Popery and the Irish Poor', *Recusant History*, 10 (1970), 210-30 and 11 (1971), 21-46.

———, 'Heretic London, Holy Poverty and the Irish Poor, 1830-1870', *Downside Review*, 89 (1971), 64-89.

———, 'Papists, Protestants and the Irish in London', *Studies in Church History*, 8 (1972), 259-66.

———, 'Supernaturalised Culture: Catholic Attitudes and Latin Lands, 1840-60', *Studies in Church History*, 11 (1975), 309-23.

———, 'The Roman Catholic Church and the Nineteenth-Century Irish Diaspora', *Journal of Ecclesiastical History*, 35 (1984), 188-207.

———, 'Battling Bishop: Baines of Bath', *South-Western Catholic History*, 3 (1985), 13-18.

Geoghegan, M., C.SS.R., 'Our Confraternities: How are they to be worked effectively?', *Irish Ecclesiastical Record*, Third Series, 14 (1893), 235-55.

Guerber, Jean, S.I., 'Le rôle de Pio Brunone Lanteri [OMV] dans l'introduction de la morale liguorienne en France', *Spicilegium Historicum Congregationis Sanctissimi Redemptoris*, 6 (1956), 343-76.

Gwynn, D., 'Irish Emigration and the Church Abroad: England', *Irish Ecclesiastical Record*, Fifth Series, 61 (1947), 896-910.

Handley, J.E., 'Irish Emigration and the Church Abroad: Scotland', *Irish Ecclesiastical Record*, Fifth Series, 61 (1947), 910-24.

Hempton, D.N., 'The Methodist Crusade in Ireland, 1795-1845', *Irish Historical Studies*, 85 (1980), 33-48.

Hosp, E., C.SS.R., 'First Redemptorist Missions in Ireland according to Father Joseph Prost's diaries', *Spicilegium Historicum Congregationis Sanctissimi Redemptoris*, 8/2 (1960), 453-85.

Jackson, J.A., 'The Irish in Britain', *Sociological Review,* New Series, 10 (1962), 5-16.

Kent, John, 'The Victorian Resistance: Comments on Religious Life and Culture, 1840-80', *Victorian Studies,* 12 (1968), 145-54.

Larkin, E., 'The Devotional Revolution in Ireland, 1850-1875, *American Historical Review,* 77 (1972), 625-52.

Lennon, J., 'The Origin, Purpose and Necessity of Missions', *Irish Ecclesiastical Record,* Third Series, 17 (1896), 417-26.

Livius, Thomas, C.SS.R., 'The Order of Corporate Reunion', *Irish Ecclesiastical Record,* Third Series, 3 (1882), 479-91 and 545-60.

_____, 'Anglican Orders', *Irish Ecclesiastical Record,* Third Series, 16 (1895), 137-45.

_____, 'God and Another World', *Irish Ecclesiastical Record,* Third Series, 16 (1895), 453-68.

Lobban, R.D., 'The Irish Community in Greenock in the Nineteenth Century', *Irish Geography,* 6 (1971), 270-281.

Lowe, W.J., 'The Lancashire Irish and the Catholic Church, 1846-1871: the social dimension', *Irish Historical Studies,* 20 (1976), 126-55.

_____, 'Lancashire Fenianism, 1864-71', *Transactions of the Historical Society of Lancashire and Cheshire,* 126 (1977), 156-85.

Lumley, W.G., 'The Statistics of Roman Catholics in England and Wales', *Journal of the Statistical Society of London,* 27 (1864), 303-23.

McLaughlin, P.J., 'Dr Callan of Maynooth', *Studies,* 25 (1936), 253-65.

MacWhite, E., 'Vladimir Pecherin, 1807-1885, First Chaplain of the Mater Hospital, Dublin, and the first Russian Political Emigré', *Studies,* 60 (1971), 295-310.

_____, 'Towards a biography of Father Vladimir S. Pecherin (1807-1885): a progress report and bibliography', *Proceedings of the Royal Irish Academy,* 80, Section C, Number 7 (1980), 109-58.

Magnier, J., C.SS.R., 'Parochial Missions', *Irish Ecclesiastical Record,* Third Series, 16 (1895), 577-92.

_____, 'After a Mission', *Irish Ecclesiastical Record,* Third Series, 16 (1895), 894-904.

_____, 'St Alphonsus as Preacher', *Irish Ecclesiastical Record,* Third Series, 16 (1895), 1057-70.

_____, 'Meditation and Preaching', *Irish Ecclesiastical Record,* Third Series, 17 (1896), 714-25.

_____, 'The Rev. Thomas Edward Bridgett, C.SS.R.' *Irish Ecclesiastical Record,* Fourth Series, 5 (1899), 305-18.

———, 'Bibliotheca Alphonsiana', *Irish Ecclesiastical Record*, Fourth Series, 14 (1904), 419-35.

Manning, H.E., 'St Alphonsus and the Christian Remembrancer', *Dublin Review*, 37 (1854), 326-403.

Milvart, St G., 'The Conversion of England', *Dublin Review*, Third Series, 12 (1884), 65-86.

Mulcahy, W.J., 'Books and Reading', *Irish Ecclesiastical Record*, Fourth Series, 2 (1897), 16-43.

Neville, H.F., 'Theology, Past and Present, at Maynooth', *Dublin Review*, Third Series, 18 (1879), 449-64.

Newsinger, John, 'Revolution and Catholicism in Ireland, 1848-1923', *European Studies Review*, 9 (1979), 457-80.

Oates, A., 'The Lost, Strayed and Stolen of our Catholic Poor Children', *Dublin Review*, Third Series, 17 (1887), 157-77.

O'Donnell, Patrick, C.SS.R., 'The Formation of the Irish Province', *Search*, 1 (1977), 74-9.

———, 'Foundation of Limerick', *Search*, 2 (1978), 9-18.

———, 'Foundation of Dundalk', *Search*, 4 (1978), 44-50.

———, 'Missions in Irish', *Search*, 8 (1980), 64-71.

———, 'Holy Family Confraternity: Beginnings', *Search*, 9 (1980), 54-8.

———, 'The C.SS.R. comes to Belfast', *Search*, 10 (1980), 12-17.

———, 'Fathers of Mercy', *Search*, 11 (1981), 30-3.

———, 'Before the Redemptorists', *Search*, 12 (1981), 28-38.

O'Reilly, M., 'The Renewal of the Church in Great Britain and Ireland after Emancipation', *Sacrae Congregationis de Propaganda Memoria Rerum*, 3/2 (1976) 192-250.

O'Riordan, S., C.SS.R., 'Our Cultural Tradition', *Search*, 4 (1978), 65-6.

Ó Tuathaigh, M.A.G., 'The Irish in Nineteenth-Century Britain: Problems of Integration', *Transactions of the Royal Historical Society*, Fifth Series, 31 (1981), 149-73.

Rienzo, Maria Gabriella, 'Il processo di cristianizzazione e le missioni popolari nel Mezzogiorno: Aspetti istituzionali e socio-religiosi' in *Per la storia sociale e religiosa del Mezzogiorno d'Italia*, edited by G. Galasso and C. Russo, I (Naples, 1980), 439-81.

Rush, A.C., C.SS.R., 'Oxford Convert: Bishop Coffin, C.SS.R.', *American Ecclesiastical Review*, 113 (1945), 401-12.

Sampers, Andreas, C.SS.R., 'Documente de erectione Prov. Hollandicae et Anglicae (1854, 1855, 1865) cum quibusdam notis de fundatione domorum', *Spicilegium Historicum Congregationis Sanctissimi Redemptoris*, 3 (1955), 498-507.

_____, 'Bibliographia catalogorum CSSR tam generalium quam provincialium', *Spicilegium Historicum CSSR*, 4 (1956), 204-13.

_____, 'Autour de la publication de la premiere biographie française de St Alphonse', *Spicilegium Historicum CSSR*, 7 (1959), 471-77.

_____, 'Bibliographia scriptorum de systemate morali S. Alfonsi et de probabilismo, 1787-1922', *Spicilegium Historicum CSSR*, 8 (1960), 138-72.

_____, 'Congregatio SS.mi. Redemptoris et Concilium Vaticanum I, 1869-1870', *Spicilegium Historicum CSSR*, 10 (1962), 424-49.

_____, 'Bibliographia editionum Regulae et Constitutionum CSSR', *Spicilegium Historicum CSSR*, 11 (1963), 468-94.

_____, 'Bibliographia manualium ad usum sacerdotum CSSR', *Spicilegium Historicum CSSR*, 12 (1984) 421-4.

_____, 'Bibliographia librorum privilegiorum CSSR', *Spicilegium Historicum CSSR*, 12 (1964), 425-8.

_____, 'Circa traditionem Imaginis B.M.V. de perpetuo Succursu Patribus CSSR eiusque instaurationem cultus in Urbe quaedam notitiae et documenta, 1865-1866', *Spicilegium Historicum CSSR*, 14 (1966), 208-18.

_____, 'Index articulorum et notitiarum in "Spicilegio" vulgatorum ann. 1953-1972', *Spicilegium Historicum CSSR*, 20/2 (1972), 425-53.

_____, 'Wladimir Sergejewitsch Pecherin (1807-1885): Sein Austritt aus der Kongregation des allerheiligsten Erlösers, 1861', *Spicilegium Historicum CSSR*, 21/1 (1973), 165-97.

_____, 'Wladimir Sergejewitsch Pecherin (1807-1885): Dokumente in Generalarchiv der Redentoristen aus den Jahren 1855-1859', *Spicilegium Historicum CSSR*, 21/2 (1973), 329-63.

_____, 'Wladimir Sergejewitsch Pecherin (1807-1885): Dokumente in Generalarchiv der Redentoristen aus den Jahren 1840-1854'. *Spicilegium Historicum CSSR*, 22/1 (1974), 3-51.

_____, 'Two Recent Publications concerning Father Vladimir Pecherin', *Spicilegium Historicum CSSR*, 28/1 (1980), 237-41.

Schiefen, R.J., 'Anglo-Gallicanism in Nineteenth-Century England', *Catholic Historical Review*, 63 (1977), 14-44.

Sharp, John, 'The Redemptorists in the United Kingdom: The Early Years', *Clergy Review*, 67 (1982), 383-92.

_____, 'The Influence of St Alphonsus Liguori in Nineteenth-Century Britain', *Downside Review*, 101 (1983), 60-76.

_____, 'Juvenile Holiness: Catholic Revivalism among Children in

Victorian Britain', *Journal of Ecclesiastical History,* 35 (1984), 220-38.

———, 'The Apostolate of the Pen in the English Province in the Nineteenth Century', *Spicilegium Historicum Congregationis Sanctissimi Redemptoris,* 35/1 (1987), 83-95.

Shepherd, C., C.SS.R., 'A Forgotten Apostle: John Furniss, C.SS.R. (1809-65)', *Clergy Review,* 63 (1978), 99-104.

Silk, J.J., 'The Roman Catholic Church in Ireland, 1800-1922: a Survey of Recent Historiography', *Studia Hibernica,* 15 (1975), 61-104.

Simpson, Richard, 'The Catholic Church in England in 1859', *Downside Review,* 84 (1966), 171-192.

Steele, E.D., 'The Irish Presence in the North of England, 1850-1914', *Northern History,* 12 (1976), 220-241.

Stuart, E.B., 'Bishop Baines and his 1840 Lenten Pastoral', *Downside Review,* 105 (1987), 40-59.

Supple, J.F., 'Ultramontanism in Yorkshire, 1850-1900', *Recusant History,* 17 (1985), 274-86.

———, 'Robert Cornthwaite: a neglected nineteenth-century Bishop', *Recusant History,* 17 (1985), 399-412.

Thrane, J.R., 'Joyce's Sermon on Hell', *Modern Philology,* 57 (1960), 172-98.

Tierney, M., 'Dr Croke, the Irish Bishops and the Parnell Crisis, 18 November 1890—21 April 1891', *Collectanea Hibernica,* 11 (1968), 111-48.

———, 'A short-title catalogue of the papers of Archbishop Thomas William Croke in Archbishop's House, Thurles: Part I, 1841-1885', *Collectanea Hibernica,* 13 (1970), 100-38.

———, 'A short-title catalogue of the papers of Archbishop Thomas William Croke in Archbishop's House, Thurles: Part II, 1886-1890', *Collectanea Hibernica,* 16 (1973), 97-124.

———, 'A short-title catalogue of the papers of Archbishop Thomas William Croke in Archbishop's House, Thurles: Part III, 1891-1902', *Collectanea Hibernica,* 17 (1974/5), 110-44.

Tynan, J., 'The Conversion of England', *Irish Ecclesiastical Record,* Third Series, 12 (1891), 642-653.

Walker, R.B., 'Religious Changes in Liverpool in the Nineteenth Century', *Journal of Ecclesiastical History,* 19 (1968), 195-211.

Walker, W.M., 'Irish Immigrants in Scotland: Their Priests, Politics and Parochial Life', *Historical Journal,* 15 (1972), 649-72.

Walsh, W.J., 'The Alleged Gallicanism of Maynooth and of the Irish Clergy', *Dublin Review,* Third Series, 5 (1880), 210-53.

Walworth, C.A., 'Reminiscences of a Catholic Crisis in England Fifty Years Ago', *Catholic World*, 69 (1899), 396-406, 549-559, 662-673, 812-23 and 70 (1890/1900), 59-69, 239-252, 412-419, 506-513.

Werly, J., 'The Irish in Manchester, 1832-49', *Irish Historical Studies*, 18 (1973), 345-58.

Theses

Doyle, P.H., 'The Episcopate of Alexander Goss of Liverpool, 1856-1872: Diocesan Organization and Control after the Restoration of the Roman Catholic Hierarchy' (dissertation, University of London, 1981).

Gilley, S.W., 'Evangelical and Roman Catholic Missions to the Irish in London, 1830-1870' (dissertation, University of Cambridge, 1971).

Lesourd, J.A., 'Les Catholiques dans la Société anglaise, 1765-1865' (dissertation, 6 vols, University of Strasbourg, 1974).

O'Donnell, Roderick, 'Roman Catholic Church Architecture in Great Britain and Ireland, 1829-1878', (dissertation, University of Cambridge, 1983).

Index